PRAISE FOR

THE FIRST AMENDMENT LIVES ON

"A timely must-read for all who are committed to preserving our nation's cherished constitutional protections."
—Fabio Bertoni, General Counsel, *The New Yorker*

"Anyone who cares about the First Amendment should read this book, and anyone who doesn't should read it twice. It's definitive, scholarly, gossipy and fun!"
—Victor S. Navasky, National Book Award–winning author of *Naming Names*

"An inspirational and informative book that is a joy to read! Whether it is a breathless moment like the fate of the Pentagon Papers or a hard look at the current attitudes of university students or the power of social media, readers will be absolutely intrigued."
—Rikki Klieman, CBS News Legal Analyst

"A vitally important book to read as our nation continues the process of debate and dissent that forms the foundation of our ongoing great experiment in democracy."
—Anthony D. Romero, Executive Director, ACLU

"How do we know if the First Amendment is working? If it makes us uncomfortable—and more importantly, if it makes us think. This extraordinary book makes us realize why the founders of our country put this one at the top of the Bill of Rights."
—Karen Tumulty, Deputy Editorial Page Editor and Columnist, *The Washington Post*

"No one really knows where America's ongoing Free Speech crisis will take us, but *The First Amendment Lives On* provides us with many wise words from clear thinkers on the issue."
—Sanford J. Ungar, Director, The Free Speech Project, Georgetown University

"For over forty years, the Hugh M. Hefner Foundation has honored more than 150 unsung American heroes with its First Amendment Awards. So it is long past time to pay tribute to the Foundation's contribution to the fight for freedom of speech and freedom of the press. In *The First Amendment Lives On*, eight of our most prominent scholars and activists do just that—in eloquent conversations that explore the enduring importance of these bedrock democratic values."
—Christopher Finan, Executive Director, National Coalition Against Censorship

"Free speech and a free press are more fragile today than at any time since the drafting of the First Amendment. The book's conversations are an urgent reminder if we want to protect American democracy. Read them to celebrate the people who have been in the trenches to preserve our freedom to say what we want."
—Kyle Pope, Editor and Publisher, *The Columbia Journalism Review*

"At a time when the American press is facing unprecedented and existential threats, *The First Amendment Lives On* provides an invaluable resource, reminding us of what Hugh M. Hefner, a champion of press freedom, knew—that American democracy cannot function without aggressive journalism that holds the powerful to account."
—James Risen, two-time Pulitzer Prize winning investigative reporter and Director, First Look Press Freedom Defense Fund

"The First Amendment nurtures our creative spirit, and *The First Amendment Lives On* provides a rich understanding of why free speech and free press are so essential to our American way of life."
—Ruth Vitale, Founder of Paramount Classics and CEO, CreativeFuture

"Hopefully this book will help confer the importance of free expression to a new generation and generations yet to come."
—Greg Lukianoff, President and CEO, Foundation for Individual Rights in Education (FIRE)

"This is a book like no other—straight from the heads and hearts of the 'greatest generation' of First Amendment advocates. At a time when free speech and free press are threatened as never before, the skillful and incisive conversations give fresh perspective and cause for hope."

—Richard T. Kaplar, President, The Media Institute

"Pivotal First Amendment and free speech advocates illuminate fascinating past developments and timely questions about new social media challenges."

—Martha Minow, author, *Saving the News: Why the Constitution Calls for Government Action to Preserve Freedom of Speech*; 300th Anniversary University Professor, Harvard University

"A compelling collection of conversations with prominent leading defenders of freedom of speech and freedom of the press. While men may not have purchased *Playboy* solely for the interviews and creative writing, Hugh Hefner's magazine indisputably provided a platform for iconoclastic voices, a quality in all too short supply in today's polarized American society."

—Allison Stanger, Leng Professor of International Politics and Economics, Middlebury College

"These conversations with legendary advocates for First Amendment freedoms are lively and fascinating. This wonderful book is a fitting tribute to Hugh M. Hefner's legacy of fighting for and fostering the flourishing of these freedoms in our country."

—Theodore J. Boutrous Jr., Partner, Gibson, Dunn & Crutcher LLP and Steering Committee Member, Reporters Committee for Freedom of the Press

"This wonderful collection of conversations with the top experts on the First Amendment is a terrific exploration of some of the hardest and most important legal issues of our day."

—Erwin Chemerinsky, co-author, *Free Speech on Campus*; Dean, Berkeley Law

"The First Amendment is as alive and relevant today as ever, and this thoughtful book illuminates the real-world implications of what is at stake."

—Adonis Hoffman, Chairman, American Social Impact Foundation

THE FIRST AMENDMENT LIVES ON

THE FIRST AMENDMENT LIVES ON

CONVERSATIONS COMMEMORATING
HUGH M. HEFNER'S LEGACY OF ENDURING
FREE SPEECH AND FREE PRESS VALUES

STUART N. BROTMAN

UNIVERSITY OF MISSOURI PRESS
Columbia

Copyright © 2022 by Stuart N. Brotman
University of Missouri Press, Columbia, Missouri 65211
Printed and bound in the United States of America
All rights reserved. First printing, 2022.

Library of Congress Catalog-in-Publication Data

Names: Brotman, Stuart N., interviewer.
Title: The First Amendment lives on : conversations in commemoration of
    Hugh M. Hefner's legacy of enduring free speech and free press values /
    by Stuart N. Brotman.
Description: Columbia, Missouri : University of Missouri Press, 2022.
Identifiers: LCCN 2021048513 (print) | LCCN 2021048514 (ebook) | ISBN
    9780826222558 (hardcover) | ISBN 9780826222602 (paperback) | ISBN
    9780826274724 (ebook)
Subjects: LCSH: Freedom of expression--United States. | Hefner, Hugh M.
    (Hugh Marston), 1926-2017. | LCGFT: Interviews.
Classification: LCC KF4770 .B76 2022 (print) | LCC KF4770 (ebook) | DDC
    342.7308/53--dc23/eng/20211223
LC record available at https://lccn.loc.gov/2021048513
LC ebook record available at https://lccn.loc.gov/2021048514

♾™ This paper meets the requirements of the
American National Standard for Permanence of Paper
for Printed Library Materials, Z39.48, 1984.

Typefaces: Iowan Old Style and Minion Pro

*For all Americans who celebrate the glories of freedom of speech
and freedom of the press and remain dedicated to protecting these
cherished constitutional values*

Contents

Foreword by Christie Hefner	ix
. . . .	
Introduction	3
The Conversations	
Geoffrey R. Stone	11
Floyd Abrams	59
Nadine Strossen	81
Burt Neuborne	107
David D. Cole	127
Lucy A. Dalglish	145
Bob Corn-Revere	161
Rick Jewell	191
. . . .	
The Hugh M. Hefner First Amendment Awards, 1980–2020	215
Acknowledgments	241
About the Author	245

Foreword by
Christie Hefner

The First Amendment guarantees freedom of speech and freedom of the press. And you cannot have a free society if you do not have both.

—Hugh M. Hefner

MY FATHER, HUGH HEFNER, SAID he wanted to "live in a society where people can voice unpopular opinions" because, as a result, "our country grows and matures." It's a sentiment especially important today as we continue to combat efforts to curtail our constitutional rights to free speech and expression.

Hugh M. Hefner was a highly successful publisher, editor, and businessman, but he also was one of the first social entrepreneurs. Soon after he created *Playboy* magazine, he drafted the Playboy Philosophy to articulate the social goals for his new company. In eighteen installments, Hef described the guiding principles of his editorial and personal points of view.

Today, the Playboy Philosophy serves as the basis for the Hugh M. Hefner Foundation's philanthropic efforts. While times have changed since the philosophy was originally published, the sentiment described in the credo about our society, its morals, and our desire to see progressive values triumph are as relevant as ever.

As Hef stated in an early installment:

Progress necessarily requires the exchange of outdated ideas for new and better ones. By keeping open all lines of communication in our culture, every new idea—no matter how seemingly perverse, improper, or peculiar—has its opportunity to be considered, to be challenged, and ultimately to be accepted or rejected by society as a whole or by some small part of it. This is the important advantage that a free society has over a totalitarian, for in a free exchange of ideas, the best will ultimately win out.

Those who founded our nation understood that a citizen's ability to speak freely, without fear, is critical to the success of our democracy, and they granted us this right in the U.S. Constitution. Americans continue to navigate the shifting and sometimes uncertain terrain of this guaranteed right.

Challenges to free speech still exist. We see the voices of unpopular speakers being censored on campus, newsrooms and journalists under threat of physical assault, and the meaning and value of truth and facts disputed. It is no wonder that more Americans are concerned about their First Amendment rights than at any time in the past twenty-five years. Now more than ever, we must celebrate those who stand up for freely expressing ourselves and accessing all avenues of truth.

The Hugh M. Hefner Foundation was established in 1964 to protect individual rights in our democratic society. The primary purpose of the foundation is to support organizations that advocate for and defend civil rights and civil liberties. When *Playboy* celebrated its twenty-fifth anniversary, I arranged for the foundation to sponsor a national touring "Freedom of the Press" public exhibit. It featured fifteen historical papers, including four from the eighteenth-century trial of John Peter Zenger, which the foundation purchased at auction for donation to the Chicago Public Library. Zenger was the printer of the *New York Weekly Journal*, and his famous acquittal in a libel suit predated the American Revolution by forty-one years. The case established the first important victory for freedom of the press in the English colonies of North America.

In conjunction with the exhibit, the foundation also held an essay contest for students regarding what the First Amendment meant to them. As these year-long activities came to a close, the foundation then created the First Amendment Awards in my father's name, to honor individuals each year for their courage to protect the First Amendment.

Established in 1979, the Hugh M. Hefner First Amendment Awards have recognized individuals whose efforts help to protect and enhance

First Amendment rights for all Americans and to raise awareness of modern-day challenges to freedom of speech and expression.

Since the inception of the awards, more than 150 individuals, including high school students, lawyers, librarians, journalists, and educators, have been honored. They have made significant contributions in the vital effort to protect and enhance First Amendment rights for all Americans. We are grateful for these everyday heroes—both for their courage to stand up for the First Amendment and for the grace with which they have conducted themselves in their willingness to stand up not only for their own rights but for the rights of others.

Free speech and a free press are cornerstone values of our democracy. But those who exercise these rights increasingly find themselves under threat. These attacks reaffirm why it is critical to recognize and honor some of these brave defenders. I am proud that the Hugh M. Hefner Foundation continues to celebrate my father's free speech and free press legacy by recognizing everyday Americans who refuse to be censored. They fight to ensure that threats to the First Amendment do not go unchallenged.

In these times of social justice protest and political polarization, Americans have a vital civic interest in exercising their First Amendment rights with passion and vigor. As Martin Luther King Jr. noted, "The greatness of America is the right to protest for rights." Liberty must lie not just in our founding documents but also in our hearts and minds.

Furthermore, we must recognize that, inevitably, it is the marginalized and members of at-risk communities whose speech is most in need of our defense. These people particularly understand that decisions about what we read and what we say are best left to the marketplace of ideas—not the government. Fundamentally, believing in the First Amendment is an act of faith, a faith in that marketplace of ideas.

Perhaps most importantly and most encouragingly, the path back toward civility starts with respect for others and other opinions. We continue on our never-ending journey toward a more perfect union.

Christie Hefner, Chairman
Hugh M. Hefner Foundation

THE FIRST AMENDMENT LIVES ON

Introduction

> The First Amendment's connection of freedom of speech and freedom of the press is significant. Free speech and free press together allow people to obtain information from a wide variety of sources that are not dictated or restricted by the government, so that they can make decisions, develop opinions, and communicate their views to the government (by voting, assembling, protesting, sharing ideas, etc.). Together, free speech and a free press are essential to the public's ability to become informed and to actively participate in a democracy.
>
> —Facing History and Ourselves

I HAVE BEEN IMMERSED IN free speech and free press issues since my teenage years, and as a First Amendment scholar, teacher, and advocate for all of my adult life. In 2019, the Hugh M. Hefner Foundation granted me unprecedented, unrestricted access to the complete private scrapbook collection of the late Hugh Hefner, who I never met nor had any personal contact with during his lifetime. I learned that "Hef" had been his nickname since childhood, and that as the founder of *Playboy* magazine he was a major figure in American business and cultural change, perhaps the leading public figure who combined these two driving forces throughout the second half of the twentieth century. He had legions of fans and detractors too.

Hef may be best known for launching an iconic global lifestyle brand based on sex and his mansion full of Playboy bunnies, but he also set an amazing record with his intense scrapbooking hobby before his death, in September 2017, at the age of ninety-one. He is listed in Guinness World Records for owning the largest scrapbook collection in the world.

With over 3,000 leather-bound books, and at least 300,000 pages, Hef kept a detailed account of everything that happened behind the doors of the Playboy mansion, including photos of its very famous visitors, and items chronicling the formative aspects of his life beginning in early childhood, including material from his student journalist days, covering elementary school through college. I sat for days pouring over the scrapbooks in the storage facility in Hollywood that houses them now, a bit overwhelmed yet always eager to see what was in the next volume.

The entries in the scrapbooks document what Hef was thinking about and doing for more than seventy-five years of his life. No other public figure has chronicled his personal and professional history as extensively. On Saturdays, he would work on putting the scrapbooks together and personally write captions for the various entries. Amazingly, all the captions were written with the same typewriter wheel so that the font would remain constant from beginning to end. A small staff then made sure that each scrapbook was assembled and carefully wrapped in a protective cover for placement in chronological order on massive bookshelves in the library of the Playboy mansion.

The first issue of *Playboy*, its pages carefully clipped and bound in one of the scrapbooks, hit newsstands in December 1953 and featured a nude calendar photo of Marilyn Monroe. It sold more than fifty thousand copies, enough to cover its paper and printing costs and finance the next issue. The rest is history, of course. Hef became a living, and often controversial, instigator of the sexual revolution of the 1960s and 1970s. I was enthralled by his detailed chronicling of *Playboy* as both a business and a lifestyle. There are thousands of scrapbook pages with pictures and captions that bring these images to life.

But in reviewing the scrapbooks, it also became readily apparent that *Playboy*'s influence extended well beyond its centerfolds. Very early on in the magazine's history, Hef designed it to provide a platform for the work of controversial writers of the day, publishing issues that included excerpts from Ray Bradbury's classic novel about book banning, *Fahrenheit 451*, and Charles Beaumont's *The Crooked Man*, which depicts a world in which homosexuality is the norm and heterosexuality the persecuted sexual behavior. In addition, *Playboy* went on to publish many of the most iconic writers of our time, including John Updike, Ian Fleming, Joseph Heller, Gabriel García Márquez, Margaret Atwood, and Jack Kerouac. All of their pieces are in the scrapbooks too.

Then there are the hundreds of entries detailing the development by Hef of the "*Playboy* Interview," which not only became the model of the artform but has remained so for over fifty years. Hef said that he started the interviews in the early 1960s after reading excerpts from a conversation between *Roots* author Alex Haley, a freelance journalist at the time, and Miles Davis.

Since 1962, the iconic *Playboy* Interview has profiled many of the most notable figures of our time. For Hef, the section was intended to expose readers to a wide diversity of ideas from an unprecedented range of political, cultural, and social figures, including many whose views did not align with his own beliefs or business interests. All of them were, however, consistent with his bedrock belief in promoting a First Amendment marketplace of ideas. The interviewees included future president Jimmy Carter, actor Clint Eastwood, comedian Bob Hope, free-market economist Milton Friedman, conservative author William F. Buckley, segregationist George Wallace, CIA director William Colby, labor leader Jimmy Hoffa, anti–gay rights activist Anita Bryant, American Nazi Party founder George Lincoln Rockwell, American Atheists president Madalyn Murray O'Hair, and feminists Betty Friedan, Germaine Greer, and Camille Paglia, among others. These long and searching conversations are remarkable not only for the people who spoke to the magazine but for what they said. They too are an essential part of the scrapbooks.

Another aspect of Hef's life that the scrapbooks highlight is his unshakable commitment to freedom of speech and freedom of the press, not only as a publisher and an editor but as someone who understood that the importance of upholding these values went far beyond his interest in expanding *Playboy*'s brand and revenues. In scrapbook after scrapbook, I saw how he cherished the First Amendment, both for *Playboy* and because he understood, intellectually and at a gut level, its essential place in American democracy.

It was his belief in the importance of the First Amendment that inspired him to create the Hugh M. Hefner Foundation in 1964 to recognize and support organizations that advocate for and defend civil liberties. The foundation has funded individuals such as Lenny Bruce, who literally fought the law on many occasions when restrictions were placed on what he could say in his comedy performances at nightclubs across the country. And when lawyer Ruth Bader Ginsburg needed support to finance groundbreaking U.S. Supreme Court litigation asserting equal rights under the law for women, the foundation stepped up too. Another interesting item of note the scrapbooks show is that for twenty straight years, with no fanfare or publicity, Hef dutifully showed up to teach in a class on film censorship at the University of Southern California (USC) School of Cinematic Arts.

In reviewing Hef's scrapbooks, I discerned several major First Amendment themes that clearly animated his thinking and actions, which continue to influence the American social fabric.

Hef cared deeply about the First Amendment's role in (1) enhancing political speech, (2) stimulating investigative reporting from independent journalists, (3) enabling movies to reach audiences without government censorship, (4) promoting free speech on college campuses, (5) protecting the rights of student reporters, and (6) allowing readers and viewers an unfettered range of printed material.

The foundation, in turn, has reinforced these principles through meaningful financial support to key organizations that magnify Hef's expansive and cohesive First Amendment philosophy—promoting and defending against the threat of greater government control over new information, entertainment, and political thought. Among these organizations are the Political Rights Defense Fund, the Media Coalition, the National Coalition against Censorship, the Reporters Committee for Freedom of the Press, the Center for Investigative Reporting, and the Student Press Law Center. Hef pursued his First Amendment passions in word and deed, sometimes loudly but mostly quietly. His scrapbooks were his own private way to chart the progress of how he influenced attitudes about free speech and free press. I regret that I never had an opportunity to discuss these ideas with him in person or through correspondence but am grateful that I was afforded a singular opportunity to review the complete set of scrapbooks, which represent an extraordinary "hard drive" of his life.

Through the vision of Hef's daughter Christie, who succeeded him as CEO of Playboy Enterprises, the foundation established what may well be Hef's most public and impactful contribution to freedom of speech and freedom of the press. The Hugh M. Hefner First Amendment Awards recognize those with the zeal, and often the courage, to convey First Amendment free speech and free press values on a more widespread and lasting basis. The scrapbooks chronicle these awards, as told through the incredible stories of hundreds of individuals who have been honored with them during the past forty years.

In reviewing a list of those who have been involved in these awards, including those who have served as nominators, judges, and recipients, I realized that it included the most prominent and influential free speech and free press scholars and advocates alive today—the First Amendment's "greatest generation" (now in their sixties, seventies, and eighties). They came of age during an extraordinary period of American political and social history, including the (Senator Joseph) McCarthy era and the anti-war, civil rights, and feminist movements. The connection to these times, as the conversations in this book reveal, animates their thinking and acting to support free speech and free press values in such a vigorous way.

With the foundation's support and cooperation, I sought out seven extraordinary individuals who have been part of the Hugh M. Hefner First Amendment Awards in one of these capacities, along with a noted film history scholar who had a sustained view of Hef's deep interest in freedom of expression, based on his personal experience of teaching with Hef at USC. They graciously agreed to sit for their own in-person conversations with me from June through October 2019, conducted in the *Playboy* Interview style that Hef pioneered.

In preparation for each conversation, I immersed myself in seminal court cases and judicial opinions, and in the voluminous published works of each interviewee. I wanted them to speak about free speech and free press from both the head and the heart and convey their personal stories and passions about these values, and how their thinking about them has evolved over the course of their long and illustrious careers. Equally important, in these conversations I prompted them also to address major First Amendment challenges of our times in order to connect history with contemporary thinking.

The First Amendment's enduring free speech and free press values remain under attack to be sure. Put simply, this is a critically important time to hear and learn from these extraordinary individuals. Each of the conversations can be read at leisure and savored as a standalone piece. But collectively, they also create another reality—namely, their viewpoints about the First Amendment reflect differing, often sharply divergent perspectives. In doing so, they mirror the marketplace of ideas that Hef always wanted to flourish in American life.

At its core, this book will help enable us to speak with one another again with a greater understanding of, and appreciation for, these cherished constitutional values. Hef would have loved to be part of that, assembling a small group for an engaged evening discussion in his beloved Playboy mansion. I have no doubt he would have chronicled these conversations in additional scrapbook entries too. For him, and for all of us, the First Amendment lives on.

THE CONVERSATIONS

Geoffrey R. Stone

Geoffrey R. Stone is the Edward H. Levi Distinguished Service Professor at the University of Chicago Law School. He previously served as dean of the Law School (1987–1994) and provost of the University of Chicago (1994–2002). Stone joined the faculty in 1973 after serving as a law clerk to U.S. Supreme Court Justice William J. Brennan Jr.

Stone is the author of many books on constitutional law, including National Security, Leaks and Freedom of the Press *(2020);* Democracy and Equality: The Enduring Constitutional Vision of the Warren Court *(2019);* The Free Speech Century *(2018);* Sex and the Constitution: Sex, Religion and Law from America's Origins to the Twenty-First Century *(2017);* Speaking Out: Reflections of Law, Liberty and Justice *(2010, 2016, 2018);* Top Secret: When Our Government Keeps Us in the Dark *(2007),* War and Liberty: An American Dilemma *(2007),* Perilous Times: Free Speech in Wartime *(2004), and* Eternally Vigilant: Free Speech in the Modern Era *(2002). He is also an editor of two leading casebooks,* Constitutional Law *(8th ed., 2017) and* The First Amendment *(5th ed., 2016). He is an editor of the* Supreme Court Review *and chief editor of the twenty-five-volume series* Inalienable Rights.

Stone was appointed by President Barack Obama to serve on the President's Review Group on Intelligence and Communications Technologies, which evaluated the government's foreign intelligence surveillance programs in the wake of Edward Snowden's leaks. Stone is a fellow of the American Academy of Arts and Sciences; a member of the American Law Institute, the National Advisory Council of the American Civil Liberties Union, and the American Philosophical Society; and has served as chair of the board of the American Constitution Society.

Stuart Brotman: On a personal level, what were your formative First Amendment experiences?

Geoffrey Stone: When I was in college it was at the height of the Vietnam War and protests against the war were common. I was suspended from the University of Pennsylvania because of my participation in an antiwar protest. For those reasons I was very cognizant of the importance of free speech and the First Amendment. And when I came to law school at the University of Chicago, the war and the civil rights movement were both very central in people's minds.

The commitment to free speech was pretty clear on the part of the vast majority of students. I had the good fortune of having Harry Kalven as my professor. Kalven was probably the leading First Amendment scholar of his generation. And he was a very inspiring person who gave me a clear sense of the importance of free speech. I then went on a couple of years later to clerk for Justice William J. Brennan Jr. on the Supreme Court.

Brennan also was someone who had a very deep commitment to freedom of speech. I got to work on cases involving speech issues during that year. This was a time when it was the very end of the [Earl] Warren Court and the beginning of the [Warren] Burger Court. Law students and young lawyers and law clerks of that generation had a very strong commitment to the importance of constitutional law in our nation. All of the seven or eight law clerks who went directly into law teaching wound up working in the field of constitutional law.

But in my case, when I started teaching at the University of Chicago in 1973, the first article I began working was on an issue involving equal protection. At that time, I can't say that I had a necessarily strong focus on free speech rather than on the Constitution generally.

But that article was not actually going very well. I went to speak with Harry Kalven, to get his advice about the article. He said to me after reading the draft, "You're right. I don't think this is really going anywhere." Then he suggested to me a First Amendment topic. I said that's interesting and went off and wrote an article about the First Amendment. I believe that serendipity has a lot to do with who we become in life. It was that moment, I think, that moved me in particular into the First Amendment as the center of my focus as a scholar.

Brotman: Were you involved in any memorable protests when you were a student at Penn?

Stone: I was part of an antiwar protest during which several students climbed up onto a fence made out of iron that had spikes on top. As they climbed up on it, the top half of the fence broke off. I wound up getting one of those prongs in my back. It was pretty severe.

The students hailed a car and got me in the backseat. The driver drove me to the emergency room at the University of Pennsylvania hospital. The doctors treated me that night. This was at the very end of the spring semester, right before exams. I got a phone call the next morning from the dean of students office telling me to show up there "at ten o'clock today." I asked why. The caller said, "Just be there."

So I went and there was a disciplinary panel in the room. They said I was suspended for the rest of the academic year for participating in the demonstration. I said that I didn't do anything wrong. They said, "You were part of this demonstration and the demonstration resulted in damage to property." I was not directly involved in that, but they didn't care. So I was suspended for the rest of the semester. They said, "You cannot take exams, you have to leave campus now." I went back to my dorm room and I said to myself, "Well screw them." And I said, "I'm just gonna take my exams and not waste this whole semester."

Indeed, I took my exams and nobody seemed to have noticed. Three years later, I applied to law school. I went to the dean of students. I don't remember if it was the same person. I explained what had happened and I said, "I'm applying to law school now. So it might not be advantageous for me to have the fact that I was suspended on my record. Is there any chance you would expunge it?" And they did.

Brotman: How many other demonstrations were you involved in after that?

Stone: That was really the only memorable one.

Brotman: Did you think twice about taking part in another demonstration?

Stone: No, it was not any lesson learned. It's just that I don't think there were any that were proximate to me during the rest of the time I was at Penn.

14   The Conversations

Brotman: You talked a little bit about Harry Kalven, a seminal academic figure in the First Amendment. He obviously was very influential. What was his personal influence on you?

Stone: Kalven was a very inspiring teacher. He had a wonderful manner in the classroom. He was thoughtful and open-minded and challenging. And he had a passion, obviously, for the First Amendment. He was deeply committed to the idea that free speech was essential to a democracy, and to a free society. He was someone who I think his students, his colleagues, and others who got to know him found to be extremely inspiring and influential, in terms of his views and his ability to express them. I certainly found him to be a role model in many ways. Unfortunately, he died of a heart attack a year after I joined the faculty. That was devastating.

Brotman: And then Justice Brennan, who I know you had a very close relationship with. Talk a little bit about that relationship and some of the things that went on during your Supreme Court clerkship with him.

Stone: Justice Brennan was a wonderful man, very warm, very caring. His clerks and his colleagues all admired and liked him. He was very open-minded, and the relationship he had with his clerks was extremely engaging. We used to meet every morning in his chambers for roughly an hour to talk about whatever cases were on the docket, whatever opinions each of the clerks was working on, what we were drafting in preparing him for oral arguments that were forthcoming. We talked about Watergate, which was going on, and about the Washington Redskins, and whatever else was happening at the time. He was a truly warm, smart, and decent person.

This was the year that *Roe v. Wade* was decided. Brennan was a Catholic but he worked very hard to put his personal and religious beliefs about abortion to one side, and to fulfill his responsibilities as a Supreme Court justice. He fully understood that he should not be influenced by either his political views or his religious views. Working with him on *Roe v. Wade* was really a fascinating experience, partly because of the importance of the case, partly because he played a significant role in helping Justice [Harry] Blackmun to shape the opinion, and partly because of his openness in talking about the religion issue, and his responsibilities as a justice.

The other case that I worked on that was especially interesting was a case called *Frontiero v. Richardson*, which involved the Fourteenth

Goeffrey R. Stone

Amendment equal protection clause and discrimination against women. For most of the Court's history, it rejected the proposition that laws which discriminated against women were in any way problematic under the Constitution. It had upheld laws which held, for example, that women could not be bartenders and women could not be lawyers on the ground that women are different from men.

In 1971, though, the Supreme Court for the first time invalidated a law that discriminated against women, and it did so on the ground that the law was irrational. But in fact, the law was not irrational under ordinary standards of rationality. The Court was being disingenuous in finding that it was invalid for that reason.

Two years later when I was a law clerk, *Frontiero v. Richardson* was argued at the Supreme Court. Ruth Bader Ginsburg was an attorney in that case, and she raised the question directly, whether laws that discriminated against women should be regarded as suspect under the equal protection clause, so that they should be presumptively unconstitutional. The Court voted in conference to strike down the law, which discriminated explicitly against women, but it voted to do so on the ground that the law was irrational, just like the earlier decision.

Justice Brennan was assigned to write the opinion, and it was my case among the three law clerks. He said I should draft an opinion that was based on the prior decision and argue that the law was irrational. I drafted such an opinion, but I found it to be intellectually unsatisfying and somewhat disingenuous. So I took it upon myself to draft a second opinion that took the position that Ruth Bader Ginsburg argued in her brief in the case, to the effect that laws that discriminate against women are presumptively unconstitutional, and that they are analogous to laws that discriminate against African Americans.

I presented both of those draft opinions to Brennan, with some trepidation. He read them both and after reflection decided that the first one, the one that the majority of the Court had instructed him to write, was intellectually dishonest. On reflection, he decided that the second one was the right way of approaching the question. To say that the law was irrational was simply intellectually dishonest. We should address the issue straight up.

The same day that we circulated the second opinion, Justices Thurgood Marshall, William Douglas, and Byron White all sent back notes that they agreed with that opinion. But this was only four votes. Justice Blackmun had reservations about going along with this more ambitious and more aggressive opinion, primarily, he said, because the Equal Rights Amendment was now pending.

It seemed at the time that the Equal Rights Amendment was likely to be enacted. So for the Court to say that laws that discriminate against women were suspect under the equal protection clause would effectively moot the Equal Rights Amendment. Brennan argued in response that the Court's responsibility was to interpret the Constitution as it exists now. This did not persuade Justice Blackmun, and we did not get a fifth vote for that opinion. The Court never went as far as we tried to go in that case, and the Equal Rights Amendment never passed.

Brotman: Let's talk a little bit about the values in the First Amendment, particularly free speech and free press values. Why is free speech such an important value?

Stone: In a democracy, it is essential that people have the opportunity to learn about the wisdom and lack of wisdom of the ideas that they hold. It's important that they learn the facts and the reality about the world around them in order to make informed, intelligent, and responsible judgments about who should be their representatives and what policies they want their representatives to uphold. Having a robust marketplace of ideas is essential to enable a democracy to function in the way it is meant to function.

If the government has the power to decide what ideas or what facts cannot be expressed and conveyed to the American people, then the people in power have the authority to manipulate what the citizens of the democracy are able to deliberate on, and to learn, and the facts they're able to invoke in their lives and in making their decisions.

In order to have a well-functioning democracy, it is essential to have both a high distrust of the government and to recognize the temptation that government officials will inevitably manipulate public discourse in order to shape the understanding and knowledge of the community, in order to get people to do what the government wants. That's the antithesis of a democracy. We need to enable individual citizens to have access to ideas and information, as well as reaffirm their beliefs, so that they can seek greater knowledge over time.

In our society we have seen changes in our attitudes about race, and about women, and about gays and lesbians. That would never have come about had we allowed the government to suppress views that challenged the accepted wisdom. Those are just a few examples of many situations in which one can see that not giving the government the power to suppress the speech, but instead giving individuals the freedom to hear and to learn, is essential to what a democracy is meant to be all about. I think this is the central goal of free speech under the First Amendment.

Beyond that, there are goals about individuals making decisions for themselves about matters that are not necessarily directly related to democracy. Should I get married? Should I go to college? Should I buy a Ford as opposed to a Chevrolet? We in everyday life make decisions about matters that we care about and that matter to us on the basis of information that we have access to. It has nothing to do with politics, but it does have to do with how we choose to live our lives.

I think the second part of the protection of free speech, independent of the democracy component, which I think is the most central one, is that it gives individuals the freedom to make decisions about a whole range of matters that they care about. They shouldn't be constrained in their ability to decide how they want to lead their lives based on some judgment by public officials that says, "We don't want you to be able to hear about whether you should go to college or whether you should skip school or whether you should use drugs or whatever."

These are all things it's important for people to have the freedom to hear about. That includes sex. The freedom to have ideas and information about sexuality and about how to lead a healthy and satisfying sexual life is important. To have that suppressed because it's offensive to other people effectively interferes with a very central part of what many people see is at the core of their personal satisfaction and their lives.

The third element to this is this notion of self-fulfillment. The ability to say what you think, and to espouse what you believe, is itself essential to human dignity, and to individual autonomy. To tell someone you may not say what you think is to impair that person's dignity and autonomy in a way that is incompatible with the respect that we want to give to individuals in a free society. This is wholly apart from whatever benefit other people gain from hearing your views. The very ability to express

18   The Conversations

what you want to say is thought to be an important part of individual freedom and liberty that a free society should respect.

Brotman: Let's turn to freedom of the press. What are the values inherent in having a free press?

Stone: A free press serves many of the same values but in a somewhat different way. The central function of the press is to inform individuals of what the world is like so they can make decisions themselves, based on hopefully accurate and reliable information that informs their views, challenges their views. It enables them to make wise decisions about what they think the government should be doing, who should be their leaders, who should be their elected representatives, and what decisions they themselves should make in their lives.

We normally think that about the press primarily in the context of the political media. Maybe that is at the core of free press. We see it as an essential element in holding government officials to task, revealing mistakes that they make, revealing information that they would rather have people not be aware of, challenging the ideas and the attitudes and the values and the assertions of public officials, so that citizens are not bullied into having a certain set of beliefs. The press plays a critical role because it is able to be much more effective and efficient than individuals at gathering information. It gives people the time to devote their energies to understanding the reported information. The rest of us have jobs and have lives and don't have the time to gather that information on our own.

A professional press is essential to be able to do that for us. We then are able to hear the distilled knowledge and information and ideas that the members of the press are able to present. Without a press, we wouldn't really know very much, and we wouldn't be very informed. So the press enables us to be informed and to have more thoughtful views about society.

Beyond that, the press also serves the other function I mentioned, not limited only to government and to democracy. The press, defined broadly, also extends to entertainment, literature, theater, and therefore can convey all sorts of values and ideas and information. It's not about the government, necessarily, but it's about how to live one's life and how to think about the values that we choose to take into account. That includes

Goeffrey R. Stone   19

advertisements. The press is an essential mechanism to enable people to have access to the information that they need, in order to make informed and intelligent decisions whether about what their elected representatives should believe or what movie they should go see.

Brotman: What about the notion that it's hard to speak but it's easy to stay silent?

Stone: Obviously, the government has a role to play in enabling people to express themselves. Should the government play a positive role in supporting the marketplace of ideas? The answer is yes. The Supreme Court has recognized, for example, that the government has a constitutional obligation to allow speech in certain areas that are called public forums, which have been used by individual citizens for purposes of protest, meetings, debates, speeches, and so on. Classic examples are public parks and sidewalks and streets. Beyond that, I think that the government has a responsibility to facilitate the ability of the press and the media to fulfill its functions. It can do that in a variety of ways.

Brotman: How so?

Stone: In an ideal world, the government would facilitate the ability of the press to fulfill its functions in as effective a manner as possible. The risk there, however, is if the government gets involved in shaping the behavior of the press, it will then be tempted to manipulate the press to achieve the goals that it wants the public to believe.

The relationship between the government and the media is a complicated one. But there are ways in which the government can certainly help the press. It can make the press exempt from taxes for example, which is a good thing. It can give them resources in the form of the National Endowment for the Arts, for example, or the National Endowment for the Humanities, which are government entities that provide funding for expressive activity. But it's critically important that when the government does that, it does it in a way that is not manipulative and not designed to benefit one side relative to another in terms of the ideas being expressed. That's a very tricky business. The broadcasting fairness doctrine was a great example of government attempting to regulate the press in a way that would further its ability to meet its aspirations of serving the goals of a democracy.

Brotman: That deserves a fuller explanation.

Stone: When radio came into existence in the 1930s, the government became uneasy about the fact that it was now possible for a small number of very wealthy people to buy up a small number of frequencies that exist in any given area, and to then dominate them in a way that would give them enormously undue power and influence over what people in that city believed. The Communications Act, initially called the Radio Act, was passed to basically declare that the airwaves are owned by the public. Therefore, radio stations, and later TV stations, could have access to those frequencies only if the government licensed them. They could not own the frequencies themselves. Therefore, a rich person couldn't come along and buy a radio or TV frequency. The government had stewardship of the airwaves and licensed them only to those people who agreed to act in the public interest.

One of the ways in which that was defined by the Federal Communications Commission (FCC) was that radio and television stations had to act in conformity with the fairness doctrine, which required them to devote significant time and attention to public affairs. They had to do so in a way that was fair and balanced. If they presented one side of a position, they then had to present the other side as well. This actually worked quite well. But the Reagan administration got rid of the fairness doctrine, so it's been gone now for quite a while.

Brotman: But there still is largely a sense of a fairness requirement even after the fairness doctrine is long gone.

Stone: What's interesting is that if you look at most of over-the-air network television, they still pretty much function in the institutional mindset of the fairness doctrine. If you watch ABC, NBC, CBS, or PBS news shows, they tend to be fair and balanced, relatively mainstream and thoughtful. But cable news, which was never subject to the fairness doctrine, and the internet, are completely different. One of the problems that we face today in our democracy is that citizens are getting huge amounts of their information from much less thoughtful and reliable sources within the media. Back in the 1960s and 1970s, much of the information they got came from a relative handful of radio and television stations that were subject to the fairness doctrine.

Back then, for the most part, relatively mainstream newspapers and magazines, including even what we then thought to be the liberal and conservative ones, like the *New Republic* on the liberal side, or the *National Review* on the conservative side, were responsible, thoughtful organizations that had political and ideological views, but they were generally pretty responsible and analytically thoughtful.

Brotman: And today?

Stone: Now, with social media and with cable news, citizens are getting much less reliable information. One of the challenges going forward is the extent to which government should intervene in any of that and try to regulate it in a way that would be "fair and responsible."

The problem is, do we trust the government to do that? I think the government can play, has played in the past, a positive role in reinforcing the right values of the media in a democratic society. But I think now we're in a situation where we're way beyond that. The absence of government regulation, ironically, has created a situation in which there is a lot of chaos in the knowledge and beliefs and understandings of the people. Here, I think, education has failed us completely.

Brotman: I assume you are talking about our educational system writ large.

Stone: I don't think education is focused nearly enough on things like civics or American history to prepare people for their responsibilities as citizens, to make them skeptical and curious and eager to figure out the truth, rather than eager to find things that reaffirm their preconceived beliefs. We are in a dangerous moment now, in no small part because of the government's lack of participation in promoting fundamental democratic and free speech values.

Brotman: Is this passivity also making it easier to stay silent?

Stone: One of the great concerns in free speech is the possibility of a chilling effect. The notion is basically this: the average individual can have virtually no impact on public opinion. Whether I march in a demonstration, or sign a petition, or hand out a leaflet, or stand in a park and give a speech, or post a message on Facebook, I'm not going to have any appreciable impact on anything that happens in society. So for me as an individual to choose to do that, I may think it's the right thing to do, but I also know that whether I do it or not is not going to make any real difference in society.

Brotman: So does this lead to less speech in our society?

Stone: If there's a significant risk or even a slight risk that I will pay a price for exercising my First Amendment rights, then it's very easy for me to say, "Is it really worth it for me to go hand out this petition if I might wind up going to jail for a year, or to participate in a demonstration if I might wind up getting suspended from college?"

One of the things that I have come to understand over time is that this chilling-effect problem is a great challenge to a robust freedom of speech. Because as much as individuals may believe in free speech in the abstract, in principle it's not clear that they will exercise their freedom of speech if they know that their decision to do so is likely to have no meaningful impact on what the society as a whole ultimately decides to do. It might well wind up putting them in jail or having them be fined or fired or disdained or whatever.

We have to be cognizant of that risk, because you can't have a robust freedom of speech if people are inhibited in their willingness to say what they think. The Supreme Court, in general, has tried to take that into account in framing its principles and doctrines under the First Amendment.

Brotman: Let's focus on the evolution of the Supreme Court's thinking about these First Amendment principles and doctrines.

Stone: The First Amendment to the Constitution was applicable only to the federal government. But the vast majority of laws that regulate free speech were state and local laws, so the federal government did not have all that much impact on free speech. The most dramatic laws they had were at times of crisis. Congress enacted the Sedition Act of 1798, which effectively made it a crime for any person to criticize the government of the United States, the president of the United States, or the Congress of the United States.

Since statements of opinion could not be proved to be true, this law had a devastating effect on criticism of the [John] Adams administration at a time when there was great division in the United States about the direction the nation should take about our nation's relations with England and France.

The Adams administration attempted to silence any criticism of its policies or the directions in which it was leading the nation. There was opposition to that led by people like Thomas Jefferson and James Madison. But the Sedition Act of 1798 was a real demonstration of how even in a democracy, government officials can be tempted to abuse their authority and to use that authority in an effort to manipulate the political process.

The idea was to invoke a chilling effect, to basically tell people that if you criticize us, you may go to jail. During the Civil War, the government jailed many people who were critical of its actions, including a former congressman who was famously arrested and prosecuted by military authorities for his criticism of Lincoln. Many newspapers were shut down because of the criticism of the Lincoln administration.

Brotman: How were the federal courts responding to these actions?
Stone: Even as the federal government was doing this, the courts did not play an active or aggressive role in interpreting the First Amendment. They basically took the First Amendment to mean that if the government has a reasonable justification for restricting speech, it was free to do so. Building upon that tradition, the Wilson administration in World War I enacted the Espionage Act in 1917, and later the Sedition Act of 1918. The Sedition Act essentially made it a crime to criticize the war, the draft, or the government in any matters relating to the war.

These laws were vigorously enforced by federal court judges, with a few notable exceptions. When challenged at the Supreme Court, the Court upheld all the government's actions because the speaker should have known that speech critical of the government in wartime might have bad effects. Some two thousand people were put in jail during World War I because of their criticism of the war and the draft. The Supreme Court did not overturn any of those convictions. It basically interpreted the First Amendment as saying that if the government has a reasonable justification for restricting speech, it was free to do so.

Brotman: But the Supreme Court was not unanimous in this view.
Stone: It was in this period that Justices Oliver Wendell Holmes and Louis Brandeis began filing dissenting opinions that, for the first time, argued

24   The Conversations

speech could be restricted only if it caused a clear and present danger
of serious harm. They explained why free speech is important in a free
society, why it's important in a democratic society, and why it's important
to the individual. They wrote a series of eloquent decisions, all in dissent,
that maintained that the majority of the justices had missed the point
of the First Amendment. This was precisely the kind of situation where
it was essential for individuals to be able to criticize their government
and its policies. Their dissenting opinions laid the foundation for what
over the next fifty years came to be the core understanding of the First
Amendment.

Brotman: Other influential judicial voices of that era?
Stone: Learned Hand was not a Supreme Court justice but he was a very
influential thinker in this field. Hand was one of the most distinguished
federal district court judges in the country at this time. He was a federal
district judge in the famous *Masses* case. *Masses* magazine was a very left
wing—but quite fancy—magazine. Many distinguished authors wrote for
it. *Masses* strongly opposed the United States' entry into World War I and
the draft. In a particular issue of *Masses*, there were some cartoons that
mocked the war and the draft. There was a poem that praised the courage
of draft resisters.

The postmaster general, under the Espionage Act of 1917, refused to
permit that issue of the magazine to be in the mail. *Masses* sued the postmaster general, claiming that his action violated the First Amendment.
Learned Hand was the federal district court judge who heard this case.
He ruled that the Espionage Act should be interpreted so as to apply only
to speech that expressly advocates law violation.

Brotman: Examples?
Stone: If someone expressly advocates refusal of induction into the military or expressly advocates being insubordinate if one was in the military,
the actions would be outside what Judge Hand saw as the protections of
the First Amendment, because they were not advocacy for changing the
law by legal means but instead expressly advocated violations of the law
itself. But Hand reasoned that as long as the speech remains within the
boundaries of challenging the law, by claiming that it was illegitimate
or unfounded or thoughtless or inappropriate, that individuals had to

be absolutely protected. He therefore interpreted the Espionage Act as prohibiting only speech that expressly advocated law violation.

Nothing in the *Masses* magazine did that. Judge Hand therefore said that the *Masses* magazine could not be excluded from the mail. In doing this, he was being very courageous in writing this opinion because at this time it was already clear that the vast majority of the American people were going to be extremely hostile to such an opinion. They had been rallied very aggressively by the Wilson administration to support the war. Anything that was seen as undermining the ability of the government to fight the war successfully was thought to be disloyal and treasonous.

But not surprisingly, his opinion was reversed on appeal by the court of appeals. The *Masses* editors were then criminally prosecuted, and the magazine ceased publication.

Brotman: Learned Hand turned out in the long run to be a profile in courage.

Stone: Learned Hand in the early years of World War I really stood fast and took a courageous position in defending the principle of free speech. And I have to say that even Justices Oliver Wendell Holmes and Louis Brandeis, when they first heard cases involving the Espionage Act of 1917 two years later, did not do the same. It was only several months later that they turned around and started writing their powerful dissenting opinions. But in their first encounters with these issues, they upheld the convictions of individuals under standards very similar to the ones that Learned Hand had rejected.

Brotman: Where was public opinion then?

Stone: A lot of the restrictions at the beginning would have been supported by public opinion. A lot of it was based on exaggerated claims of national security and potential dangers to the war effort that whipped up public opposition to war critics. But a central reason for having judicial review, a central reason for giving courts the power to enforce rights guaranteed in the Constitution, is the recognition that Madison and Jefferson had that in a democracy, one of the dangers is that the majority will often be tempted to abuse its authority by silencing those who disagree.

Brotman: How so?

Stone: In two ways. One is to disadvantage those individuals who are members of groups that the majority sees as the "other" and as different, as not being worthy of equal or fair treatment. The second is that those in positions of authority will be tempted to use their authority to perpetuate their power. They can do that in many ways. They can do that by gerrymandering, they can do that by regulating speech, they can do that by regulating or not regulating money in the political process. They will surely be tempted to do that, human nature being what it is. The framers of the Constitution understood that we cannot trust majorities to do the right thing when they have a strong self-interest in abusing their power, and a vital area of concern had to do with speech. The central reason why you need judicial review, in general but in particular in the First Amendment area, is because we don't trust those people in positions of authority, even if they are supported by the majority.

Part of what you need courts for is to stand up in those circumstances where majorities are acting in ways that are seen as inconsistent with the aspirations of the Constitution. This is the First Amendment concept that Justices Holmes and Brandeis championed. The fact that the majority wants to do something doesn't mean it's permissible or acceptable, particularly when it comes to regulating politics.

Brotman: As Reverend Dr. Martin Luther King Jr. observed, the arc of history bends toward justice, right?

Stone: In this context, it took half a century for that to happen. Justices Holmes and Brandeis first started writing dissenting opinions in 1919. They continued to do so while they remained on the Court. They wrote some very eloquent opinions in the 1920s in dissent from what the majority was then doing. But they continued to write dissenting opinions, which in itself was an unusual thing to do in those days. Normally, when a justice loses, the justice says, "Okay I lost, now my job is to apply the law." Holmes and Brandeis refused to do that. They thought the stakes were too high. They insisted on continuing to advocate their position with respect to free speech in order to keep this debate alive. They understood how important it was for them not to give in, not to surrender to what they felt was a dangerously erroneous view with respect to the freedom of speech. They were not alone in this view.

Goeffrey R. Stone

There were scholars who took this view and who wrote eloquently about the matter.

Gradually, Holmes and Brandeis and their arguments began to hold sway. By the 1940s, in some relatively modest cases, the Supreme Court began to invoke the language of Holmes and Brandeis. It began with references to clear and present danger. But it was still a relatively tepid commitment to that view. And when we got to the Senator Joseph McCarthy era, the justices for the most part upheld the convictions of individuals who were seen as communists, currently or in the past. And they did so in ways that were often disingenuous.

It wasn't until the Warren Court, in a case called *Brandenburg v. Ohio*, decided in 1969, that the Supreme Court fully embraced the Holmes and Brandeis approach. The Court held that even express advocacy of law violation could not be punished unless it created a clear and present danger of grave harm. And that has been basically the stance the Court has taken in the half-century since, at least with respect to this particular type of free speech—speech in the public arena that challenges government policies.

Brotman: What caused the Warren Court to make such a dramatic shift in the Supreme Court's thinking about the First Amendment?

Stone: Part of it was the power of the Holmes and Brandeis argument. Looking back on the past, the Warren Court justices recognized that every time we had allowed speech to be repressed, we had made a serious mistake. It had seemed like the right thing to do in the moment, but with hindsight it was clear that it was wrong—and especially wrong for our democracy.

The Court gradually learned that lesson. As tempting as it was to yield to the pressures of the moment, learning from the mistakes of the past is an important way of understanding what's best for our democracy. And I think the justices came to the view that, "We may think that this speech is terrible, and that it should be suppressed, but every time we've done this, it's been a mistake. We should now step up and do the right thing." And they did. So I think that was central—the experience of repeated mistakes. The justices of the Warren Court came to understand why Holmes and Brandeis were right, not only in theory but as a matter of reality.

28   The Conversations

The Warren Court recognized that in the past the Court had reached the wrong results, even though in the moment those results felt right.

Brotman: What about applying these principles to speech that was deemed to be obscene?
Stone: There used to be no laws against obscenity. I mean, one thing that people today don't have any idea about is that there were no laws against obscenity in the history of Western society. There were all sorts of extremely sexually explicit material, whether statues or poetry or plays or books.

There was no law against any of them. Sexual expression was fine. Some people may not have liked it, but the law didn't intervene at all. That didn't begin to happen in the United States until the Second Great Awakening. In the first half of the nineteenth century, when religious forces began to play an important role in American politics, they began to demand the suppression of sexually expressive material. But even then, criminal prosecutions were very few and far between.

In the late nineteenth century, largely under the leadership of anti-obscenity activist Anthony Comstock, the challenge to sexual expression became a huge movement because of religious views that obscenity corrupted the mind and the soul and was incompatible with true Christian values. It was necessary to prevent people from being tempted. Laws against obscenity then were enacted across the nation. And this was the first time in American history that we had laws against obscenity. Those laws went so far as to ban anything that related in any way to sex or sexuality.

Brotman: For instance?
Stone: My favorite example of this was in the late nineteenth century. A local newspaper editor published a letter to the editor that revealed the following story. The letter said that this woman gave birth, and the childbirth was not successful, and she suffered serious physical injury. Her doctor told her she should not have intercourse for the next year because it would be dangerous to her health. Her husband was not willing to wait. The woman died. The letter to the editor argued that the husband should have been prosecuted for murder. After all, the letter reasoned, if you knowingly kill your wife with a gun, you would be prosecuted for

murder. If you knowingly kill her with your penis, you should be prosecuted as well.

The editor of the newspaper was prosecuted and put in jail for publishing that letter to the editor, because it described sex and used the word *penis*. So that was enough. Even though the story was a powerful and important story about human relations, the publisher was put in jail for publishing that letter. In short, any public discussion of sex was unlawful. Period.

Brotman: Wow. But this seems like such an odd case.

Stone: It was not out of the ordinary. I mean, in the late nineteenth century you could not talk about contraception. You could not talk about sex at all. You could not use words that were sexual in nature. We forget how extreme it was, but even in the movies made in the 1950s, you could not show a married couple in the same bed. That was regarded as obscene. There were court decisions that would not allow anyone to see anything related to sex in any way, shape, or form that would be potentially corrupting of the morals of a child.

The assumption was that something called obscenity was not protected by the First Amendment. Obscenity was understood to be very broadly defined. A movie that showed a young boy urinating, facing in the opposite direction, into a pond and at a distance, was found to be obscene.

This began to change in the first half of the twentieth century. Judges began to interpret anti-obscenity laws a bit more narrowly, but the idea that sexual expression might be protected by the First Amendment was not taken seriously.

Brotman: When did the Supreme Court begin to focus on obscenity under the First Amendment?

Stone: The Supreme Court first heard an obscenity case involving the First Amendment in a case called *Roth v. United States*. The Court, led by Justice Brennan, wrote that obscenity was not protected by the First Amendment, but he said that obscene material had to be sexually explicit. It had to appeal primarily to the prurient interest in sex. And it had to offend contemporary community standards in the presentation of sexuality. The Court's view in *Roth* was much more speech protective than the view of courts in the nineteenth century and in most of the early twentieth century, but it still left broad room for the suppression of sexually oriented material.

Brotman: And then?

Stone: Gradually, over time, the Supreme Court tried to figure out how to give a better definition to obscenity. That led to a period of some chaos. So from 1957 until 1973, the Court basically had no majority definition of obscenity. The justices began fracturing into their own unique definitions. And during this period, whenever there was an obscenity prosecution, particularly movies in those days, the justices would watch the movies in the Supreme Court movie theater. They were applying their own tests, having to decide whether they thought the movie satisfied or didn't satisfy their personal test for obscenity.

Brotman: The law was not blind in a literal sense.

Stone: This led to a lot of interesting moments. For example, Justice [Hugo] Black took the view that there was no such thing under the First Amendment as obscenity. It should be protected the same way any other speech was protected. Therefore, he felt no need to go see these movies. The crack he made was, "If I want to see a dirty movie, I'll pay for it." At one time, in frustration, Justice Potter Stewart said, "I don't know how to define obscenity but I know it when I see it." And in later years, the law clerks would sit in the Court's movie theater to watch the movies and shout out, "There it is. I know when I see it." That was sort of a standing joke.

Brotman: But Justice Harlan literally was blind.

Stone: Yes, Justice John Marshall Harlan, who lost his eyesight late in his career, could not see the movie screen. His clerks tended to sit next to him and had to whisper to him exactly what was on the screen. This no doubt made a Harlan clerkship less attractive for most potential law clerks.

But during this period, it was chaos and the justices could not agree on a single definition. That meant the lower courts could not handle obscenity cases in any intelligent, consistent way because there was no single standard they could articulate to a jury. It was a real mess during that period.

Brotman: So the Warren Court fell short here. But the Burger Court then began to develop a different approach to obscenity.

Stone: When Warren Burger was appointed chief justice in 1969, one of the things he most wanted to take care of was obscenity. In his view, as a result of the 1960s, with the sexual revolution, the amount of sexual expression had gone way beyond the point where he thought appropriate for a decent society. Burger was determined to rein this in and to get agreement on a specific definition that would allow much greater suppression of obscenity.

And in 1973, the same year I was a law clerk, the Court was sharply divided in terms of how to resolve this question. Justice Brennan had now come to the view, after all his years of experience, that the state could still protect nonconsenting adults and children from sexual material. But consistent with the First Amendment, he concluded that adults who wished to see obscenity willingly had the right to do so. Justices William Douglas, Potter Stewart, and Thurgood Marshall now shared that view. So the key question then was what Justice Lewis Powell, the swing vote, would do. Powell was a southern gentleman, someone who had never seen anything remotely sexual in his life. He initially took the view, in a conversation with Brennan, that, "well, I don't see why people shouldn't be able to see what they want," and he liked the idea of consenting adults being able to have access to whatever speech they wanted to see. But he never had seen anything like real sexual expression. His idea of obscenity was a dirty book written in the late nineteenth century. And then he went to the Court's movie theater and saw the movies that were at issue in the two cases under review. He was completely shocked. He had no idea that this was what was at issue. As he left the movie theater, looking stunned, he said to Brennan, "you lost."

So the Court at that time expanded the definition of obscenity. Burger held that to not be treated as obscene, sexual material had to have a *serious* artistic or literary side. If it lacked serious value, it would be deemed obscene if it was offensive to contemporary community standards and appealed primarily to the prurient interest in sex. Burger thought that with his opinion in 1973, there would be much greater restrictions on sexually oriented material than in the years of the sexual revolution. But it was not to be.

Brotman: That world was over.

Stone: Basically, what happened was that technology changed. First with the advent of the VCR, and then more fundamentally with the creation of the internet, the law simply could not as a practical matter control what people wanted to see online. There were so many platforms and so many places that one could go to see sexual material, much of which was produced out of the country, that it became increasingly difficult to control what people could see.

In practical effect, it became impossible for courts to enforce laws against obscenity in any meaningful way. So we've now reached a point, fifty years later, in which prosecutions against obscenity are essentially nonexistent. Extremely sexual material on the internet, wildly beyond anything anyone would have imagined in 1973, is now readily available to basically anyone who wants to see it. That even includes minors. Whether this has a good or bad effect on society is debatable. But the practical reality is that this is an example of a situation in which the advent of changing technology simply overwhelmed the ability of the law to control it.

Brotman: The Burger Court began to focus not just on obscenity but also on an even more amorphous notion of "indecency."

Stone: Yes, we have indecency, a whole new category, that is not obscene but is sexually offensive. On broadcast radio and TV, which require government licenses, the FCC adopted a rule that provided that indecent material was not permitted on radio and television.

That came to the Supreme Court in a case involving George Carlin's famous seven filthy words monologue, in which he identified seven words which he said were not permitted on radio or television. His comic monologue contained all seven of the words repeatedly. The FCC held that the radio station could not broadcast such material on the airwaves. The case came to the Supreme Court in the late 1970s, and the Court, in a sharply divided opinion, held that it was constitutional for the FCC to do this because radio and television are licensed by the federal government, unlike newspapers and magazines and movie theaters. And for that reason, the Court said that the FCC could prohibit indecency on radio and television, at least in the hours in which children are likely to be in the audience. So to this very day, you will not see on ABC or NBC or CBS anything that is remotely sexually explicit.

Brotman: But that is limited to over-the-air broadcasting.

Stone: Right. On cable and on the internet, you can see whatever you want, because cable and the internet cannot be regulated by the government in the same way. They are not using public property—the broadcast spectrum—that is licensed by the government. But cable television is like newspapers, and so is the internet. The Court therefore has held that even though the government is still allowed to regulate radio and TV, it's not allowed to regulate cable or the internet.

As a consequence, there's literally nothing that you can't see if you just type a sexually explicit search term in Google. You'll get infinite numbers of videos, all of which would have been prohibited fifty years ago.

Basically, the government has given up. There's just no way as a practical matter to control it. It's true that even today on broadcast radio and TV you cannot have the same access to that kind of sexual material. This may not be that bad a solution, frankly, because as long as people have access to cable and the internet, then broadcast radio and television tend to serve as a kind of safe space for people who don't want to confront this sort of material. And if they don't want their kids to see such images, they know they can turn off the TV and stop their kids from watching. I'm not sure this is a good legal idea, but it does have a kind of sensible outcome to it. It enables people to know that there is a certain place you can go, and your kids can go, where they won't see things that they don't want their kids to see.

Brotman: Was the Burger Court as conservative in its First Amendment thinking as it sounds?

Stone: The Burger Court was, by contemporary standards, pretty moderate. The conservative justices then were Warren Burger, Lewis Powell, Harry Blackmun, and William Rehnquist. By today's standards, they were quite moderate. We sometimes forget that three of the four Nixon appointees [Blackmun, Burger, and Powell] joined *Roe v. Wade*, for example, whereas none of the current conservative justices would ever have agreed with that decision.

Back to the First Amendment issues: as I said, the obscenity issue was very important to the Burger Court. Another issue that was important to the Burger Court dealt with commercial advertising. The historical approach was that commercial advertising was not protected by the First

Amendment. The First Amendment was all about political speech to support a democracy. It also was about artistic speech. But commercial advertising simply was economic behavior. It wasn't speech in the way in which the First Amendment was traditionally understood. But in the *Virginia Pharmacy* decision, the Burger Court took a different view and held that commercial advertising is speech within the protection of the First Amendment. But the Court also held that it was not entitled to the same degree of protection as political or other fully protected speech. The Court said that individuals rely upon commercial advertising to make important decisions about what car to buy or what clothes to buy or what drugs to take. They have an important interest in receiving information about those choices, and commercial advertisers thus play an important role in informing such decisions.

Now, you could say, of course, that you don't need commercial advertising. You have *Consumer Reports*. And the advertisers themselves have incentives that are highly likely to be distorted. But that's true for politicians as well. Anyway, the Court took a middle approach there. It gave a significant degree of protection to commercial advertising. Basically, it said that as long as it's not false and deceptive, if it's accurate, it cannot constitutionally be restricted unless the government can show that the regulation serves a substantial government interest. Over time, this standard has come to mean that, for all practical purposes, the government cannot regulate commercial advertising that's not false or misleading.

Brotman: Then the Rehnquist Court comes in, and the evolutionary path continues.

Stone: The Rehnquist Court both expanded and contracted the meaning of the First Amendment. On the contraction side, the Rehnquist Court dealt with a doctrine that was not clear. As early as 1938, the Court had held that individuals have a right to use public streets and parks for speech purposes, subject to only reasonable regulation.

The Court had held that these public facilities, called public forums, had historically been dedicated to allowing people to give speeches, hand out leaflets, engage in demonstrations, and so on. The government could reasonably regulate such activity but not prohibit it. But that raised the question, "What about other types of public property?" To what extent do individuals have a right to go into a welfare office to hand out leaflets to inform people about welfare policies? To what extent do they have a right to post signs on government buildings?

The more liberal justices tended to take the view that individuals should have access to public property when they are engaged in speech, unless the government has a reasonable justification for restricting it. The more conservative justices took the view that unless it is property that has historically been dedicated to speech purposes, government can for all practical purposes forbid such speech.

Brotman: For example?
Stone: An example of these cases was Fort Dix in New Jersey, which was a military base completely open to the public. It had stores. People could go there. But the military base prohibited anyone from giving a speech in the public areas of the base. The Court held that this was constitutional, because it was not a traditional public forum.

Another case involved state fairs, where people wanted to walk to a state fair and hand out leaflets to people about their religious and political views. The state fair operators said they could only hand out leaflets from a rented booth on the grounds of the fair. The Supreme Court held that this restriction was constitutional. In another case, people wanted to put signs on trees and lamp posts in a public park during a political campaign. The city said no one could do that. The Court said that was constitutional.

So during the Rehnquist Court, we saw a conservative approach taken to the asserted right of individuals to have access to public property for speech purposes, other than what were defined as traditional public forums. The liberal justices wanted to take a more flexible approach, to say that individuals should have a right to use public property generally for speech purposes unless there was a significant government justification for prohibiting it. This was one category of First Amendment controversy during this era.

Another set of First Amendment disagreements began to arise during that period with respect to campaign finance. During the early Burger Court years, the Court had a case, *Buckley v. Valeo*, in which Congress, after Watergate, enacted legislation that limited the amount that individuals could contribute to political candidates for federal office and the amount they could spend independently to support the election of such candidates. The Federal Campaign Finance Act, which was a bipartisan law, was created out of concern that money could have a distorting effect on the democratic process. It was thought to be problematic for wealthy individuals to have an undue impact both on the electoral process and on the decisions of the candidates they supported. The candidates, after all, knew what their donors wanted from them. And if someone was giving a substantial amount of money, then the candidate, if elected, would be tempted to support the policies that the individual wanted in order to get the money in the future. This was seen as a distorting effect on the behavior of elected officials.

There was also a concern that candidates who spent huge amounts of money, or individuals who spent huge amounts of money to elect candidates, would completely distort the electoral process. The idea was not to have candidates elected because of the cash that they had at their disposal, or because a handful of wealthy donors were willing to spend huge amounts of money to overwhelm their opponents. The idea was that elections should be decided on the merits of the candidates, not because of huge disparities of spending in the election process. The idea behind that law was to basically create what might be called a fair and balanced political process.

Imagine, for example, if in a presidential debate, time was allocated to the candidates based upon how much money they (or their supporters) were willing to spend for the time. That would not be the kind of fair debate that enables us to make decisions in an appropriate manner. We want everyone to have the same amount of time. Intuitively, we all get that. That's what the legislation was designed to do in the larger political process.

Brotman: The Court disagreed with this rationale.
Stone: In part. The Court held this law to be constitutional with respect to limiting the amount of contributions. It said that government can limit how much individuals can contribute directly to a candidate. The goal was to limit the potential undue influence that a donor might have. On the other hand, the Court held that the expenditure limitation was

unconstitutional. It said that the contribution limit is a modest restriction on the donor's use of her money. If I want to spend $50,000 to help elect candidate X, the contribution limit says, for example, that I can only give candidate X $1,000. But if I'm still free to spend the other $49,000 to support the candidate without giving it to him directly, then the contribution limit is not a big deal.

On the other hand, the Court said that prohibiting me from spending the other $49,000 to help elect the candidate of my choice was unconstitutional because I have a right to speak as much as I want. To tell somebody, "Okay you can give a speech for one hour in the public park to advocate the election of a candidate and then no more speeches by you," would be completely inappropriate. My right to speak is fundamental. The majority said that's true for money as well. To tell somebody you can only spend so much is inappropriate. And the Court said that the state interest in seeking equality in the amount that could be spent is illegitimate. It's not appropriate. And it's inconsistent with our First Amendment values.

The people who supported that view were the ones arguing for free speech. They said they were arguing for a robust freedom of speech on the part of the individuals who wanted to spend their money. Those who wanted to regulate the total amount individuals can spend independently, they argued, restricted free speech, even though the goal of doing so was to improve democracy.

Brotman: You seem to disagree with this premise. Why?
Stone: One of the purposes of free speech is to have a well-functioning democracy. So, there is a conflict of values here between how you achieve a good democracy—either by allowing unlimited free speech or by limiting the amount of free speech in order to have a better democratic process. Interestingly, even under the Rehnquist Court, the majority held that the amount corporations could spend could be limited consistent with the First Amendment.

These issues came back to the Supreme Court under the [John] Roberts Court when Congress enacted the McCain-Feingold Campaign Finance Act. This law limited the amount that corporations could contribute or could spend on behalf of candidates. Congress also limited the amount

38   The Conversations

that political parties could spend to get their candidates elected. Initially, the Court, in a five-to-four decision, held that the law was constitutional.

The Court basically took the view that the amount of money that had entered the political process was so far beyond anything that the Court could have imagined when it decided *Buckley* that the distorting effect of money had now gotten out of hand. Thus, the Court held that restrictions of this sort are constitutional. The government can limit the amount that can be spent and can be contributed, including contributions to the political parties.

Brotman: But that was short-lived, right?

Stone: Yes. Seven years later, when Justice Samuel Alito replaced Justice Sandra Day O'Connor, in another five-to-four decision, the Court flipped its position. It overruled the prior decision and held that the government could not constitutionally regulate even corporate contributions and expenditures, and could not restrict the amount of money that super PACs [political action committees] could spend.

So we're now back to this world where effectively there are no constraints on the amount that individuals and corporations can spend in the political process in order to influence both the outcome of elections and the actions of our elected officials (as long as there is no direct bribery). The amount that individuals, corporations, and other organizations can spend to shape the outcome of the electoral process is now unlimited. Citing this decision, among others, Chief Justice John Roberts celebrated his enthusiastic protection of the right to free speech.

Many liberals think this to be a terrible decision because of its potential distorting impact on our democracy. So we arguably have an interesting conflict here between an aggressive protection of the right to free speech on the one hand and the well-being of our democracy on the other. One of the core purposes of free speech is to facilitate and enable a well-functioning democracy. But there are differing views about what's the best way to have a well-functioning democracy—by allowing limitless free speech with the unrestricted flow of money, or by constraining it in order to improve the quality of democracy. It's a truly ironic conflict between the values of democracy and the aggressive protection of free speech.

Brotman: You have expressed the idea that electoral exceptionalism would justify greater free speech restrictions in this area under the First Amendment.

Stone: The notion of electoral exceptionalism is that there are certain contexts in which the government has a special need to regulate speech. An example might be in the military. A soldier in combat who urges his fellow soldiers not to obey orders can be punished, even though in society as a whole now, you can't punish someone unless they create a clear and present danger of great harm. In the context of the military, the government can punish the soldier who advocates disobedience of a commander's orders without such a showing of grave harm.

Or in prisons, the speech that prisoners have access to from the outside can be limited in order to create an environment that is not unduly disruptive in the prison setting. In schools, the Court has allowed the regulation of speech in ways that could not be regulated in general public discourse, because of the notion that, to function properly, schools need to control the distractions and the disorder that we are willing to tolerate in ordinary public settings. The argument is that there are certain contexts in which there is a legitimate need for government regulation of speech in order to enable those contexts to operate appropriately.

Brotman: So would you argue that elections are another category that would justify more speech regulation?

Stone: We would not allow candidates to buy time from the questioners, to pay the questioners to ask them the questions they want to be asked, or to pay to buy more time than their opponents.

We would agree, I think, that this such conduct would be completely inappropriate in a well-functioning political debate. We would insist upon following certain rules that are very different from the rules of normal discourse in society. So the question would be, what should we do in our political campaigns, a setting in which there's arguably a need for a certain degree of regulation to ensure that the campaigns ultimately fulfill the aspirations of the political system? We allow, for example, prohibitions on electioneering near voting booths. We don't want people handing out leaflets right as people go into the voting booth. Government can prohibit that.

40   The Conversations

Brotman: Should we regulate speech in the election process itself, a setting in which regulation should be appropriate because of its centrality to the functioning of democracy?

Stone: There is the election exceptionalism argument that some of the justices have made in their opinions in favor of upholding some regulations in the election process. The primary concern in restricting speech is when the government attempts to restrict particular points of view.

Take the point of view that the president is incompetent, that people should oppose the war, or that they should favor the right to abortion. The primary concern of the First Amendment is with government intervention designed for the purpose of silencing people who espouse particular points of view. These are the kinds of restrictions of speech that are regarded as most profoundly incompatible with the First Amendment.

On the other hand, many restrictions of speech are not like that. They are neutral with respect to the points of view being expressed. A law that says no one may use a loudspeaker in a residential neighborhood after nine o'clock at night is very different from a law saying no one will use a loudspeaker in a residential neighborhood after nine o'clock at night to criticize the mayor. A lot of neutral rules with respect to content are designed to regulate the means of expression. Such restrictions are generally seen as less threatening to core First Amendment values, because they can be applied neutrally. They're not about manipulating the marketplace of ideas in favor of some points of view and against other points of view. Those types of restrictions are generally permissible under the First Amendment, as long as they are reasonable.

One way to think about campaign finance regulations is that they are like laws regulating loudspeakers in residential neighborhoods after nine o'clock at night. That is, you're not regulating Republicans versus Democrats. You are regulating speech generally, regardless of what point of view is being expressed, not for the purpose of benefiting or harming any particular point of view but for the purpose of having public discourse that achieves the goals of democracy. The state interest, arguably, in regulating money in the political process is not to regulate one idea versus another idea but to have a well-functioning democratic process. That's more like regulating speech after nine o'clock at night with a loudspeaker in a residential neighborhood.

Goeffrey R. Stone 41

So those laws should be seen as permissible as long as they serve a sufficiently important government interest. The argument here is that we would never want to have a political system in which the amount of money being spent by one side relative to the other side dictates the outcome, especially when it's given by wealthy corporations and billionaires. It's not like everybody gets a hundred dollars and they can spend it in the political process as they want, so that the amount of money being spent is reflective of the views of the citizens generally. The argument in favor of upholding these regulations is that government should be able to restrict these expenditures because this is not a form of viewpoint-based regulation. The same rules apply to Democrats and Republicans. I think the justices who have invalidated these laws have distorted the First Amendment in a serious way that has done real harm to the central principles of our democracy—all in the name of "protecting" the freedom of speech.

Brotman: Let's talk about free speech in schools, including universities. I know you have been central in shaping thinking in this area obviously, chairing the committee at the University of Chicago, building upon the work of one of your influencers, Harry Kalven, who had authored a major report in this area a few decades earlier. What is your thinking about how the First Amendment does or doesn't apply in the university context?
Stone: First of all, it's important to understand that the First Amendment applies only to public institutions. The First Amendment applies to the University of California or the University of Illinois, which are public institutions, but it does not apply to the University of Chicago or Harvard or Stanford, which are private institutions. The First Amendment has no impact on the decision-making or autonomy of a private institution. So it's important to draw that distinction at the outset. On the other hand, even private universities should aspire to promoting free and open discourse and the questioning and challenging of ideas. This is accepted wisdom for the intellectual life of universities, in much the same way as the values embodied in the First Amendment have come to be understood over time.

That's not true, by the way, for all entities. Private corporations, for example, don't have the same values and aspirations as a university. But

42 The Conversations

at the core of a university is the search for truth. At the core of the university is the mission of seeking knowledge, seeking wisdom, seeking insights that give us a better understanding of our society, of science, and of culture.

In the same way that Justices Holmes and Brandeis argued that virtually unfettered speech helps to achieve truth in the political arena, the best way to achieve truth in the academic arena is not to have censorship but to have a broad and robust freedom of debate and discussion and disagreement. So even in private universities, there should be a commitment to free expression that is very similar to what the First Amendment itself imposes on government entities.

What that means is that the institution should not suppress the opportunity for students and faculty and other members of the university community to explore ideas in ways that enable them to advocate for what they see as wisdom, and to challenge what others may believe to be wisdom and truth and facts in order to seek greater knowledge. That's the absolute core of the mission of a university, and it's very much at the core of the mission of the University of Chicago in particular, which from its very founding has been a leader in the pursuit of those values.

Brotman: Let's begin with the Kalven Report.
Stone: In 1967, the president of the University of Chicago, Edward Levi, appointed Harry Kalven to chair a committee to look at the extent to which a university should itself adopt positions on matters of public policy. This was during the height of the Vietnam War, and a large part of the issue was whether universities should weigh in on whether the Vietnam War being a good or bad thing. I must say, at roughly that time, I was arguing as a student in college, and later as a student at the University of Chicago law school, that colleges and universities should take positions opposing the Vietnam War. I was wrong about that but I believed that was true. I was within my rights to advocate for it but it was the wrong position.

Brotman: And now?
Stone: I came to understand the Kalven Report, which was written at that time, took the position that the University of Chicago should not

weigh in on matters of public policy, unless those issues directly affect the university itself. But on matters of general public policy, if the university takes positions, it would have a serious chilling effect on the willingness of faculty and students to take positions that are in opposition to what the university has declared to be "the right position." Therefore, the university should be extremely cautious about taking formal positions on matters of public policy.

I chaired the University of Chicago committee on free speech fifty years later. It had to do with the fact that at that time, at colleges and universities across the nation, it was increasingly the case that students and faculty members were demanding that universities disinvite speakers, or that speakers who had been invited should be silenced because the views that they would express would be opposed by the students or faculty as wrongheaded, inappropriate, and offensive. The challenge for universities was (and still is) to figure out whether certain speakers should or should not be invited, or invited and then silenced because members of the community oppose their views.

Brotman: What were the Stone Report's conclusions?

Stone: The University of Chicago adopted a statement that is three pages long. The first half of it discussed the history of the University of Chicago and gave examples of its own commitment to a robust protection of free speech. Then the second part of it articulated an approach to free speech that basically says that free and open discourse is essential to the values and aspirations of a university and that a university therefore should not prohibit members of the community from inviting speakers who express views that others may find offensive.

Indeed, the report explained, it is the responsibility of the university affirmatively to protect the rights of students and faculty and other community members to speak themselves, or to invite speakers who would express views that others might find offensive. It should encourage students to listen to those views and to respond to the merits, to debate and to challenge those views if they disagree with them, but not to try to silence them, not to try to disrupt them or to prevent them from having their say.

Brotman: How has this been received?

Stone: Interestingly, we wrote that report specifically for the University of Chicago. But several universities, beginning with Princeton, recognized that they could lop off the first half of the report, which talked about the history of the University of Chicago, and then adopt the second half of the report, which discussed about the central principles. There now are some eighty colleges and universities across the country that have adopted what has come to be called the Chicago Principles. This is the standard that many institutions of higher education now embrace.

Brotman: And public universities?

Stone: Public universities have a different situation, because they are governed by the First Amendment. They do not have the freedom that a private university has, in theory, to reject those principles. So public universities have to conform strictly to what the First Amendment demands of them.

For the most part, that's what the Chicago Principles articulate: a public university, under the First Amendment, is responsible for allowing the expression by students, by faculty, and by visitors who are invited of views that may be disturbing or offensive to other members of the community, because they are subject to the basic principles of the First Amendment.

Brotman: How might this be limited in practice?

Stone: The commitment to free expression doesn't mean that in the classroom in, say, a mathematics course, a student can start giving a speech about politics. There are constraints on the time, place, and manner of speech, which are permissible even, as illustrated by my example, on the content of speech in narrow circumstances, like the classroom. Similarly, a commitment to free expression doesn't mean that professors cannot grade student papers or exams, based upon what the professor views as the wisdom or the excellence of the ideas that are being expressed.

The academic mission has within it a responsibility to teach and to evaluate scholarship. In so doing, one tries not to be ideological or political, but obviously the university and its faculty have to make judgments about who to hire, who to promote, which students get A's and which students get B's, and so on.

But in the realm of public discourse in the university, the notion that the university, or its students or faculty, should have the authority to silence others because they don't like the views being expressed is incompatible with the First Amendment in a public university and incompatible with the core values and aspirations of a private university as well.

Brotman: California treats public and private universities the same, right?
Stone: The state of California has apparently said there's no real distinction between a public university and a private university in this respect. Private universities have to act in accordance with the same standards that would apply in a public university.

Now this raises an interesting problem, because the private university has First Amendment rights to decide for itself what speech it wants or doesn't want to allow. A private university that seeks to achieve the goals and aspirations that I believe are essential to a true, well-functioning academic institution would itself choose to aspire to the same values that the First Amendment would apply to it. But they don't have to do that. They have a First Amendment right to decide for themselves who they are. So I think government laws that try to impose on private institutions obligations to comport with what the First Amendment would impose upon public institutions are making very difficult and delicate judgments about the academic freedom of a private institution.

Brotman: You seem firmly committed to the principle that universities should be silent when necessary.
Stone: Yes, I think the Kalven Report notion that universities themselves should not take official positions on political or other debates on public issues that do not directly affect the university is the proper stance. Because once a university goes down that road, it's very hard to say when to stop. Universities that declare certain ideas to be right or wrong will deter students and faculty members from challenging those ideas in a way that they should be free to do. It is simply not the business of a university to declare that abortion is wrong or that Trump was a bad president or that the war in Vietnam was a mistake. It is simply not the role of the university to take such positions except when such issues are directly related to the core functioning of the university itself.

It's not that I don't think there are right or wrong positions. But I don't think universities should take them, because they produce a chilling effect on the willingness of their students and their faculty to take counter

46 The Conversations

positions. That's a dangerous thing in terms of the larger aspirations of a university community.

Brotman: What about religiously affiliated universities?

Stone: In my view, a religious institution that insists upon its religious values as being the right values is not a "university" in the proper sense of the term because the university, by definition, should be committed to a free and open discourse. An institution that rejects the right of students and faculty to say, "there should be a right to abortion," for example, or "gays should be allowed to marry" is not a "university." It is essentially putting off-limits ideas that are, and should be, free and openly discussed and debated. It's their right to do that, but I just don't think that's really a university.

Brotman: Let's turn to how government controls the dissemination of its own information.

Stone: The basic question is, first of all, when can a government employee leak information that the government has decided should be kept confidential, or more formally as classified? To what extent does the First Amendment give the government employee a right to disclose publicly information that the government is determined to keep secret? Second, to what extent can reporters attempt to obtain information that the government wishes to keep secret, either by encouraging a government employee to leak or by intruding into government files directly, for example by breaking into government offices to steal government documents. Should the First Amendment protect a reporter who does that? And that raises a question as to what extent a news outlet, defined broadly, has a First Amendment right to publish information that has been obtained illegally from government sources?

At the time of the Pentagon Papers case, the first question was whether a government employee who agreed not to disclose classified information could be held legally accountable for doing so. Certainly, there are limits on what constraints government can put on a government employee in terms of their exercise of constitutional rights. For example, the government could not, as a condition of being employed as a secretary in a police department, require the employee to sign an agreement that she would not vote for a Democrat or read dirty books or support Black

Lives Matter. But when the asserted right is directly tied to the job, an individual can be required to give up what otherwise would be a right. Certainly in the context of being given access to classified information, it is reasonable for the government to say, "We will give you access to this information but you have to agree not to disclose it publicly as long as it's classified."

In the Pentagon Papers case, the Supreme Court based its decisions on several assumptions. First, that Daniel Ellsberg, the government contract employee who leaked the Pentagon Papers, could be criminally punished for leaking the information. That case never came to fruition because after the government brought charges against Ellsberg, the federal judge dismissed the charges against him because of government misconduct. The Nixon administration had ordered a break-in of Ellsberg's psychiatrist's office to get information about Ellsberg. The judge held that in so doing the government had acted unlawfully and therefore dismissed the charges against him. But the assumption was that if a government employee leaked classified information, in the absence of such government misconduct, he could be criminally prosecuted for doing so.

The Pentagon Papers consisted of a 77,000-page study commissioned by Robert McNamara when he was secretary of defense to review the history of how the United States got involved in the Vietnam War. McNamara meant it to serve as a historical document. Ellsberg, who had once been a strong supporter of the Vietnam War as a government contract employee in the Defense Department, eventually soured on the war and decided to leak the document because it revealed clear misconduct on the part of the government.

Ellsberg decided that it was important for the American people to understand the reality of the war and the truth about some of the things they had been deceived about. After going through the extensive document and excising those portions of it that he thought would be more harmful to national security than beneficial to disclose, he then started smuggling the pages out of the Pentagon. He and a colleague of his Xeroxed them, then smuggled the pages back in, so it wouldn't be discovered. Then more papers were smuggled out. This took place over a long period of time.

They then turned the pages over to the *New York Times*. The *Times* spent several months going through the pages and excised those portions of it that they thought should not be made public. Then they started publishing portions of the Pentagon Papers. When the Nixon administration learned about this, President Nixon's initial response was that this is only revealing information that is harmful to the prior Johnson and Kennedy administrations, and "that's fine with me." But Henry Kissinger persuaded Nixon that this was not a good idea because the disclosures would harm our ability to continue to fight the war effectively.

The Nixon administration then sought an injunction against the *New York Times* to prohibit it from continuing the publication. The federal district court issued the injunction. The *New York Times* and Ellsberg then turned the Pentagon Papers over to the *Washington Post*, which then began publishing them. The government officials then sought an injunction against the *Washington Post*, which was issued. Very quickly, the case came to the Supreme Court because an injunction is a prior restraint and the courts will act very quickly in ruling on whether a prior restraint is permissible.

Within a matter of days from the time the leaks began, the Supreme Court decided the Pentagon Papers case and held that an injunction against the newspaper was not permissible. The government had not demonstrated a clear and present danger of grave harm that was necessary to justify the injunction. What was quite stunning about the Court's action was that one of the government's arguments was that it had not even had time to read the entire 77,000 pages. The government wanted the injunction to remain in effect at least long enough for it to read the papers carefully to determine what harm might actually flow from the publication. But the Court held that unless the government could actually prove that the publication would create a clear and present danger, it could not prohibit publication.

Brotman: Another milestone in the arc of history bending toward justice.
Stone: This case demonstrated how far we'd come in the years since World War I when the Court upheld convictions that put people in jail simply for criticizing the government. Here you have the newspapers publishing classified information, where the Court itself was not in a position to even evaluate what harm might or might not flow from the publication of the information, because the government itself hadn't had time to look through the papers and make the case for what harm might flow. It shows how far we had come as a nation.

Goeffrey R. Stone 49

The Court there adopted basically an approach that was extreme in two respects. The "ideal" approach, one might say, in deciding when classified information can be leaked and published would be to restrain publication if the government could show that the harm caused by the publication outweighs the benefit of publication.

Brotman: But the Court did not decide this case on that basis.
Stone: The Court rejected this test because it's very difficult to make that judgment. We know from experience that government will often exaggerate the harm that flows from speech it dislikes and it's therefore often impossible to figure out whether the cost outweighs the benefit on a fact-by-fact basis. Therefore, the Court concluded that we have to have rules that overprotect speech.

On the other hand, the government employee can be punished for leaking the information to the press, thus seriously preventing the press from gaining access to the information in the first place. In effect, the Court embraced an odd compromise that said the government can overprotect its interests when it comes to government employees, but that courts will underprotect the government's interest when it comes to prohibiting the press from publishing information if it gets into the hands of the press.

The hope is that applying these two extreme, opposite views will somehow get us to be in the right place. Basically, what it means is that government employees will be extremely reluctant to leak classified information, but if they do, the press can publish it.

This was kind of a weird compromise, but it was designed to avoid the need for the courts to be in the position of trying to figure out on a case-by-case basis whether the harm caused by the publication outweighed the benefit of its publication.

Brotman: Then Edward Snowden came along in 2013 and leaked massive classified NSA [National Security Agency] information to the *Guardian*.
Stone: You have Edward Snowden leaking information, and two things have changed since the 1970s. First, when Daniel Ellsberg leaked the information he was a largely responsible, thoughtful, careful person who was quite knowledgeable about the nature of the information he was disclosing. He had read it all himself. He was a long-term, high-level

government contract employee who understood the possible consequences in a reasonable way.

Then you had the *New York Times* and the *Washington Post*, mainstream, responsible publishers who did not want to harm the national security but did want to get out the information that they determined was valuable for the public to know, which they were reasonably confident would not in fact harm national security.

Now we are in a world where a low-level, inexperienced private contractor, because of changes in technology, has access to a huge amount of government information about which he has no thoughtful understanding or comprehension of its potential harm if it's published. But he's able to leak enormous amounts of information because the technology—a thumb drive—enables him to turn over massive amounts of information to entities that are not terribly sophisticated or professional. The question is whether the Pentagon Papers ruling makes sense in the modern world.

Brotman: That's the Chelsea Manning WikiLeaks situation.

Stone: Exactly. So now you have a situation where the potential harm to the nation is likely to be far greater because here you don't have a government employee who's going to be careful and thoughtful and knowledgeable about what they leak. And the publisher now is not going to be careful and thoughtful and responsible for what it publishes. Instead, it recklessly prepares and publishes vast amounts of information about which it has no understanding about the risks to the nation.

So we've gone from a time which the risks were reasonably manageable, even though it's not what the government wants, to one in which the risks are much more likely to be reckless. And the question is what do you do with it?

I think we're now in a situation of having to try to figure out how to cope with that. A court will certainly say that a government employee who leaks classified information is committing a crime and can be punished. Just as Daniel Ellsberg, in theory, could have been punished. Chelsea Manning was convicted and put in jail. Snowden certainly could be convicted and put in jail for leaking enormous amounts of classified information.

Goeffrey R. Stone 51

Brotman: What about Julian Assange and WikiLeaks?

Stone: If WikiLeaks is basically being treated as if it was the *New York Times* or the *Washington Post*, the reason for giving it that degree of protection is not nearly as obvious or as logical as it was when you were talking about mainstream American sources that are pretty trustworthy.

So one of the things that's going to have to get sorted out as we go forward is how to deal with these two dramatic changes. One is the capacity of a government employee who is much lower down than Ellsberg to leak vast amounts of information that they don't begin to understand and aren't in a position to comprehend its potential harm. Combine this with the ability to leak it to entities that will publish it without nearly the responsibility of the *Times* or the *Post*, which were the entities involved in the Pentagon Papers case. So the question that the courts are going to have to figure out as we go forward is how do we cope with this new state of affairs?

The other side of the equation after the Snowden leaks is the public outcry about the NSA and the fact that a lot of information may have not been out there in the public. During the Obama administration, President Obama said, "Let's take a closer look at this."

Brotman: You became part of a small group that President Obama asked to advise him on this.

Stone: After the Snowden leaks, President Obama appointed a five-person committee, called the NSA Review Group, that consisted of Richard Clarke, who had had extensive experience in cybersecurity—in the Department of Defense, the White House, and the State Department in several administrations but was now out of government—Michael Morell, who had had a career in the CIA, including as both deputy director of the CIA and also acting director of the CIA; Cass Sunstein of Harvard Law School, one of the great legal scholars of our time, who had spent several years in the Obama administration in the Office of Management and Budget; Peter Swire, who had worked for several administrations on issues of privacy and information technology. Peter was a professor at Georgia Tech; and me. I knew Obama when I was dean at the University of Chicago Law School and he taught here. He asked me as a First Amendment scholar to be part of this review group.

Brotman: What was the scope of your collective mission?

Stone: We were charged with the task of making recommendations about how the federal government should deal with the issues of national security and leaks, triggered in particular by the Snowden disclosures. We worked for several months. It was a remarkable and fascinating experience. The five of us came from very different backgrounds, very different perspectives. Some of us, like myself, had a civil liberties perspective, and others came from the national security arena.

It seemed to us when we first got together at our secure facility in Washington before going to the White House to meet with Obama in the Situation Room, "This is crazy. We won't agree on anything." We spent the next four months working in the secure facility and dealing with the CIA, the FBI, the NSA, the Department of Homeland Security; with various organizations like the ACLU and the press organizations; with the Senate and House Judiciary and National Intelligence Committees; and with Google and similar tech companies.

We ultimately wrote a report with forty-six recommendations that tried to address these tensions. First, remarkably, the report was unanimous, not because we traded off with one another—we didn't. Rather, because over this intense experience, we came to trust each other and to recognize our comparative advantages. We wrote a report that all five of us agreed on completely. It was amazing.

Brotman: What preconceptions did you have as you began your work there?

Stone: Before I got involved in this, my assumption was that the NSA had run amok and that the programs that Snowden had disclosed were reckless and irresponsible, largely because the NSA had done these things in secret, without any review or approval. That turned out, I learned, to be completely wrong. The NSA, to my surprise, was a thoughtful, careful, responsible agency that took great pride in being lawful and careful. All the programs that Snowden leaked had been reviewed and approved, not only by officials within the NSA but by officials in the White House, House and Senate Intelligence and Judiciary Committees, approved by the Foreign Intelligence Surveillance Court, by the Executive Branch, and so on. The programs were pretty carefully monitored by the various entities to ensure that they performed appropriately.

So one lesson we came away from in all of this was that the motivations of the NSA in particular were good motivations. They were determined to protect the national security and to do so vigorously, but they also were not cops. They were military and tech people, and their determination was to do this in a way that was technologically sophisticated, consistent with and obedient to the rules of law that had been put in place. The real problem was insufficient review on a regular, ongoing basis of the various programs that were put in place.

Within the national security world, there was a strong desire to act within the law and to enforce and implement the programs in a way that was consistent with legal restraints. But what was lacking was a kind of constant oversight, of asking, "Can we do this better? Are there ways that we can revise these programs that will be even more responsive to the concerns that people would have, and should have, about the possibilities of misuse and abuse of information?"

Brotman: And the outcome?

Stone: The vast majority of our forty-six recommendations were adopted, which amazed me. What I came away with was a sense that there needs to be a range of different perspectives that challenge those who are inside the national security world, where it is so easy to get sucked into the often genuinely dire risks that they are addressing. There's a need for fresh perspectives on a constant basis to look at these programs and challenges in a way that will constantly reinvigorate and reinforce ways to make them better.

Brotman: Do the courts help or hurt this process?

Stone: Until the late 1970s, when it came to foreign intelligence surveillance, we were dealing with classified national security information without courts having access to that information. Regular courts do not have top-secret clearances, the judges don't have the clearances, the law clerks don't have clearances, and so on. This means you can't deal with these issues in regular courts. The assumption was simply that the president had complete autonomy in dealing with foreign intelligence surveillance, and the courts had nothing to do with it.

In the 1970s, when the Senate Select Committee to Study Governmental Operations with Respect to Intelligence Activities, chaired by Senator

54   The Conversations

Frank Church, came into being, it was determined that J. Edgar Hoover and Lyndon Johnson and Richard Nixon had engaged in such extensive abuses of their supposed national security authority that there was a need for judicial oversight. The Foreign Intelligence Surveillance Court then was created, which is a court with top-secret clearance capacity.

All the judges have top-secret clearances, all the secretaries have it, all the clerks have it, and so on. The court is located in Washington, D.C. The Foreign Intelligence Surveillance Court—the FISC—became capable of reviewing the policies and behavior of national security organizations in the same way that an ordinary court can oversee government action more generally. The judges who sit on the FISC are ordinary federal court judges who have gone through the process of getting top-secret clearances. They are then able to sit on this court.

Brotman: Did any of your group's recommendations affect how the Foreign Surveillance Court operates?
Stone: One of the things we recommended that has been adopted is that when the FISC was created, the assumption was that its primary function would be to make sure that when the government engaged in particular foreign surveillance activities directed against particular individuals, that there was sufficient justification for engaging in the investigation. This is similar to the way that a search warrant has to be issued by a judge.

As time went on, though, the judges on the FISC increasingly decided not only whether to issue a warrant but also how to interpret the statutes that authorized our national security programs. But those interpretive questions raised much more complicated legal issues. The way they were functioning is that the only legal arguments that they were hearing were from the representatives of the government, who were arguing in favor of their positions and interpreting sections in ways that gave the surveillance programs greater authority.

So we recommended that the government should create privacy and civil liberties advocates, who would be private lawyers with classified security clearances able to argue the civil liberties position to the FISC. President Obama embraced this and there are a number of lawyers who serve as civil liberties advocates against the government lawyers. This is just one example of the kind of changes over time that can improve the process.

Brotman: That still leaves open how leaks will be handled.

Stone: The danger here is that most of the programs—and we got to look at some of the most aggressive programs—will involve leaks. If you try to protect the nation and other nations around the world against terrorist attacks, then you need to be able to gather all sorts of information. You need to engage in investigative techniques that will be effective at preventing attacks before they occur. You need to connect the dots, you need to do what America didn't do before 9/11.

Doing that requires very intensive, complex investigations, gathering lots of information and figuring out how this piece of evidence and that piece of evidence connect. That is an immensely sophisticated and complex task. The problem is that once you gather the information, you have a vast amount of material that can be abused. The fear is not only in the gathering of information but in the risk of abuse once the government has it. If the government has a vast amount of information, say, about the phone calls of Americans, that's fine in theory as long as nobody looks at it, except for proper purposes under clear restraints.

But imagine if you have another J. Edgar Hoover who decides he wants to get dirt on his opponents. Information gathered by the FBI was not supposed to be used this way. The law prohibits using it that way. But as we've seen in the past, that may not turn out to be the case. So how do you prevent that information from being abused by officials who are willing to disobey the law?

Here's one example of this: the NSA program gathered metadata from phone calls made by American citizens. Metadata means not the content of any phone calls but just the phone numbers. Everyone you've called and everyone who has called you was in a huge database that only the NSA had access to. Under the metadata program, the NSA could query the database if it had reasonable grounds to believe that there was a possible connection to a particular individual engaged in terrorist activity. One thing we were concerned about is if the NSA held the database, then a J. Edgar Hoover or a Richard Nixon could simply direct somebody to go into that database and get information about their political opponents. We recommended that the data should not be held by the NSA but rather should remain in the hands of the phone companies. The government could only access it by getting a warrant from the FISC where there would be an independent opposing counsel. The FISC could give an

56	The Conversations

order that the phone company must turn over the needed information, but the government would not have direct access to the database itself. And that was another thing that was adopted. In the years since then, the metadata program has been terminated.

Brotman: Let's move to another area. Is there something else that should be done to promote more counter speech? Are we at a point in time where counter speech no longer is a problem because everyone has access to receive unlimited counter speech and to convey counter speech?

Stone: Counter speech is more possible today in some general sense, maybe more than ever before. The problem we have now is not with access to counter speech. The bigger problem is that we have too much. We have fake speech, false speech, and foreign intervention. This is dangerous to the democracy that the First Amendment is designed to protect. Now, counter speech in the current technological world we're living in has the distorting effect of false and misleading speech that individuals have become much more susceptible to than they were in the past.

The product of technology is that you have this vast array of sites that individuals can gravitate toward, and that give them misleading and false information, and they don't hear anything else. That's a huge problem in a democracy. In some sense, it always existed. People had their clubs and they would go to the clubs and so on. But the mainstream media was the dominant source of information for most people. The mainstream media in general was reasonably responsible, even if there were lots of instances when they were careless. But then there could be counter speech. We now have this world where Americans are far less capable of identifying true facts than they have been in the past. And you can't have a democracy where people are being misled and are believing in falsehoods, where public officials are manipulating them intentionally, and foreign entities are manipulating them intentionally too.

So I think we face a crisis in terms of the future of democracy right now. And part of it is figuring out how to cope with the inability of many of our fellow citizens to recognize that they are being fed false information and that they're being manipulated. How do we get past that point? That's a huge challenge, and I don't think anybody quite knows the answer to that. To have the government be able to intervene to outlaw false speech and misleading speech is extremely dangerous, because that gives the government the power to determine which speech to go after. We've never given government the power to do that. We don't let the government prosecute allegedly false statements except in the commercial speech area and in situations like fraud and perjury. To give the government that power more broadly scares the hell out of me because it can so easily be abused. On the other hand, though, if we don't do something, then free speech can become the death of us. It's a real dilemma.

Brotman: It sounds like you would like something like the fairness doctrine now for the internet.

Stone: I've talked about the notion of maybe a fairness doctrine for algorithms if you're online. One possibility might be to require all internet platforms to provide contrasting viewpoints to a certain type of information. They would be automatically set. The opposing information could just pop up on the screen. Of course, this doesn't mean you're going to read it. So it may not work because people just don't read it. But it should be tested at least.

Brotman: So that brings us back to better civic education.

Stone: Americans have to be informed. I think what this is fundamentally about is education. We have to find some way to educate the American people to understand the dangers of our current social media reality. This would be at all levels of education. Some would be formal and some would be informal. Certainly, kids should be educated about these things in a very sophisticated way from the time they're young, and this should continue throughout their education. But then we have all these older people who are not in school.

I think there needs to be some recognition that the best interest of the nation would be served by teaching people how to use this extraordinary facility that now exists. They don't know how to use it in an intelligent way. I think you need public officials who are prepared to say, "This is both a great asset and a danger." We have to educate people. We have to educate people about the dangers that are a part of our digital life.

I don't know that there's a simple solution to this. It's not that I want the government telling us what the truth is. But I would like the government to help educate people, getting them to the place where they understand the importance of knowing what the truth is and seeking it instead of taking the easy way out. That's hard. It's very difficult.

Brotman: Reforming the political system seems fundamental to your better world of free speech.

Stone: I don't think that any rational person would structure a political system like the one our country has today. Without knowing who would win or lose, I don't think any neutral person would want a political system that's functioning the way ours is today either. This is a grave danger.

Brotman: It sounds like you are sober about the free speech challenges we are facing in current times.

Stone: I feel a degree of pessimism. The Supreme Court today is a major part of the problem. Instead of strengthening democracy, these justices manipulate it in ways that strike me as dangerous. This is illustrated by the Court's decision holding the Voting Rights Act unconstitutional, and by its decision refusing to put a check on gerrymandering. These are all related issues that go to the larger question of democracy and free speech. I think these are fundamental challenges to our democracy. The Supreme Court is failing to fulfill its core responsibility in these respects.

Brotman: I'm not sure you want to end here on an upbeat note, even though it might sound good as a concluding thought.

Stone: I'm pessimistic at the moment about our democracy. I don't think it's unalterable. I think we are at a particularly challenging moment. In terms of free speech, I like the fact that people have access to a broad range of information and ideas. But I am not comfortable with the fact that they have gotten polarized to the degree they have. The idea of free speech is that you're exposed to other ideas, that you're challenged with competing views, that you learn. It's not that you lock yourself into a box and you only hear the things that you'd like. So it gets back to the core values. We want people to have informed judgments, even if we disagree with them. At the moment, that is a challenge for the future.

Floyd Abrams

Floyd Abrams was described by the late Senator Daniel Patrick Moynihan as "the most significant First Amendment lawyer of our age." He is senior counsel in Cahill Gordon & Reindel LLP's litigation practice group in New York City. He is an expert on constitutional law, and many arguments in the briefs he has written before the U.S. Supreme Court have been adopted as constitutional interpretative law as it relates to the First Amendment and free speech. He is a visiting lecturer on law at Yale Law School and served as the William J. Brennan Jr. Visiting Professor at the Columbia University Graduate School of Journalism.

Abrams is author of The Soul of the First Amendment *(2017),* Friend of the Court: On the Front Lines with the First Amendment *(2013), and* Speaking Freely: Trials of the First Amendment *(2005).*

He was elected to the American Academy of Arts and Sciences and received Yale Law School's prestigious Award of Merit and the Walter Cronkite Freedom of Information Award presented by the Connecticut Foundation for Open Government.

Abrams also was awarded the CUNY Graduate School of Journalism's Lifetime Achievement Award. He is the recipient of the William J. Brennan, Jr. Award of the Libel Defense Resource Center; the Learned Hand Award of the American Jewish Committee; and the Thurgood Marshall Award of the Association of the Bar of the City of New York.

Abrams has also received awards from, among others, the American Jewish Congress, Catholic University, the New York and Philadelphia Chapters of the Society of Professional Journalists, Sigma Delta Chi, the New York Civil Liberties Union, the Association for Education in Journalism and Mass Communication, and the National Broadcast Editorial Association.

He served as chairman of the Committee on Freedom of Speech and of the Press of the Individual Rights Section of the American Bar Association and of the Committee on Freedom of Expression of the Litigation Section of the American Bar Association.

In 2011, Yale Law School announced the formation of the Floyd Abrams Institute for Freedom of Expression, whose mission is to promote free speech, scholarship, and law reform on emerging questions concerning traditional and new media. Developed in cooperation with Abrams, the institute includes a clinic for Yale Law students to engage in litigation, draft model legislation, and advise lawmakers and policymakers on issues of media freedom and informational access.

Stuart Brotman: Let's start with your earliest thoughts about the First Amendment. Did they start in college or earlier?

Floyd Abrams: It was in college at Cornell, when I was an undergraduate, that I first started thinking about addressing various First Amendment issues. But in those days, I was more on the other side. That is to say, I was very impressed with the English system. It made a lot of sense to me thnn that if a court can't accept or allow a jury to hear a coerced confession, then a newspaper shouldn't publish it. It made sense to me that publishers and editors ought to be held to pretty strict standards of accuracy. And I suppose one could say that by chance or not, by starting with the law of a free nation without a First Amendment has made me a better lawyer in this area.

Brotman: What about experiences with free speech?

Abrams: I did college debating. That was a formative matter for me, in part because I found I did it well. I would say it was probably the only area at college in which I sort of stood out. I was also a pretty young man; I was sixteen when I started. So I was unformed in all sorts of ways. And there was McCarthyism. That was something I did care about. I certainly was on the libertarian side of that.

Brotman: How did McCarthyism affect Cornell then?

Abrams: Just as one example, when I arrived at the campus as a young freshman, I received from the university an identification card, which I signed and carried. It said in effect that the university can get rid of you for any reason it wants. It was very clear that included speaking out. That was one of the things that was always at risk.

Floyd Abrams

Brotman: Did you ever see repercussions like that for speaking out?

Abrams: I must say no. At least for a campus like Cornell, the times were silent ones. There were fraternities and non-fraternities, there was no overt racial conflict, there was hardly a person of color on the campus. I don't recall seeing a male student of color who was not on the football team or some other team. It was a time of at least surface equanimity.

I came from a public school in Queens [New York]. I had to look around a lot to see how people behaved in this world. But I was glad I went, and everything was new. I met a poet once. That surely was new to me. He quoted Dylan Thomas, and I'd never heard of Dylan Thomas. I thought it was exciting. Yeah, it was. Absolutely. But it was a whole new world.

And what about being exposed? I know during that period there were things like [D. H. Lawrence's] *Lady Chatterley's Lover* and [Vladimir] Nabokov was teaching at Cornell during that period. One of the worst decisions I ever made was to drop his course. I did show up to one lecture at least. His wife was there, she always attended his classes. But I didn't know what he was talking about. He was talking at such a high level. Foolish, ignorant young man at seventeen.

Brotman: What type of issues were argued by your Cornell debate team?

Abrams: To give you an idea of the time, I did a debate against traveling law students at Cambridge, who were doing a national tour of the U.S. The topic was whether West Germany, as it was then called, should rearm. It was something I was quite prepared to take either side on. But I remember saying in a debate attended by a few hundred people, because of these Cambridge guys, something to the effect of, "Why should we now, ten years after the war, be more concerned about the Germans than the French?" And a professor let me know, in a very nice way, that I should read something about World War II before spouting off in a way that equated the risks of German rearmament just a few years after World War II with that of France.

But that's how I learned things in college. The debating part of it was very helpful for me. The notion that being assigned a topic and assigned a side, looking back on it, seemed sort of liberating. I didn't have to have a side. I didn't have to know about the subject. Walking into a new topic, I could learn it freshly, while simultaneously focusing on what arguments

62   The Conversations

were more persuasive for my assigned side. And I've often thought that for practicing lawyers, who sometimes take difficult public policy positions because of their clients' needs, that is sort of morally liberating, to be assigned as it were. Because that's what lawyers do, you know. But the starting point there is we have to win this thing. Right.

Brotman: Any influential professors?

Abrams: Professor Robert Cushman. A great constitutional scholar who believed deeply in the First Amendment. And a fine man. One day Professor Cushman invited a class in which I was a student to his home. For me it was like the movies. The snow was coming down. He had a dog. He had a fireplace. Tweed jacket. Oh yes, out of the movies. And there he told me, "After Cornell, then you go to Yale."

Brotman: He meant Yale Law School, right?

Abrams: Yes. Well, first of all, Yale Law School and Harvard Law School for years before and years after I was there had been adversaries in what had been characterized as in a thirty-year war. Yale was liberal, Harvard was conservative. It was as easy as that. Yale had a bankruptcy course called "Debtors' Remedies, Debtors' Rights," Harvard had a course called "Creditors' Rights."

That was for real. They both were talking about the same thing. The differences were obviously exaggerated. The Harvard faculty was much more interested in legal process. But it was true that Yale was more interested in results, social policy consequences of litigation, and the like. By chance, I came to be assigned to a first-year constitutional law course with Professor Alexander Bickel. Professor Bickel had been to Harvard Law School and clerked for Justice Felix Frankfurter. His first year of teaching was my first year as a student. I was assigned alphabetically, with other people whose names started with A, B, and C, to a seminar that Professor Bickel was teaching.

Brotman: Was this when you just started in the fall at Yale Law School?

Abrams: My first term and it was his first time teaching. This was constitutional law. He was very tough on all of us. We were all left of center in some way, however loosely. I had taken courses in constitutional law at college, and they were so different from the course I took that first

Floyd Abrams 63

term in constitutional law. Bickel was very process oriented. What should a court do? What is the role of the Supreme Court? What powers does the president have? Issues like that. I remember one day in class when a fellow student was called on, and he gave some very left, liberal answer. And Bickel said, "Where does that come from?" And my classmate said, "The Declaration of Independence." Everyone laughed.

So I learned a lot from Bickel at law school. It was also sort of like an undergraduate place for me, because I had been so young in college. Now at least I was going out. I had friends to go out with, men and women, and it was a different world.

Brotman: Other professors at law school that impressed you?

Abrams: I took courses with scholars whose views were far different than Bickel's. Fred Rodell, a far more liberal-oriented professor than Bickel, taught a wonderful course which I took in which he would assign each student, let's say eighteen students, nine justices on the court. So, two students per justice, and the assignment was to write an opinion in the way that that justice would. It was a wonderful teaching tool. So you would have to go back and find everything that justice had said before on a particular topic. Learn their writing style and thinking. It didn't matter what side they were on or anything, just the process of going through that was a great learning experience.

I graduated, having taken out six months in the army, in February 1960. And I'm still not a First Amendment devotee yet. But my views had changed in that direction since college, based on reading and being persuaded by a lot of the opinions that we were assigned or otherwise. I certainly found that the more liberal jurists were more persuasive.

Brotman: But you remained in academia after graduating law school rather than go into private practice.

Abrams: I went right from Yale to work with Alphious Mason, a professor at Princeton, who was doing a book about the office and powers of the chief justice. So that's where I went from law school.

He wrote a letter to the law school, which was posted, saying he was looking for a research assistant. It sounded really interesting. Another professor at Princeton had written a book about the office and powers of the president, and Professor Mason had an idea that he would do one on the chief justice. Unfortunately, there weren't many powers of the chief justice then. So I spent eight months at Princeton doing draft chapters about the chief justice. It never really worked. Mason never really wrote it. The book never came out. Professor Mason and I decided together that I should leave. But I learned a lot there because I had been spending full time now reading judicial biographies and opinions of chief justices.

Brotman: So you were on the road to be a budding professor.

Abrams: I had seen a letter on the wall at Yale about working at Princeton. What was I going to be doing after graduating? Maybe going into teaching? Or maybe going back to graduate school, notwithstanding the foreign language requirement. I had a movie vision of what life and academia would be.

But I observed that professors didn't get along as I had imagined. They were human, not the creation of movies. They seemed jealous of each other. I was surprised, far more than I should have been, that my idealized vision of college academic life was unworldly, even unreal.

Brotman: What next then?

Abrams: One of my friends in law school was clerking for a judge sitting in federal court in Wilmington, Delaware. He called me up to say that the judge was looking around for a new law clerk. So I went down; interviewed with Judge Paul Leahy, a fine jurist and great mentor; received an offer of his clerkship; and spent two happy years there. I was so content with that experience that I probably would have stayed for longer. He was nice enough to tell me it wasn't in my interest to stay more than two years. But I also got a very nice sense there of the practice of law. I got a little more self-confidence that I could do that.

When it was clear that I would be leaving, I asked the judge to recommend impressive New York law firms that appeared before him. He picked up a piece of paper and wrote five names down alphabetically. I made arrangements for interviews and came up to New York. Cahill was the first alphabetically. They made me an offer. It was terrific.

Brotman: When you came to Cahill, what did the firm tell you what you would be doing?

Floyd Abrams

Abrams: I don't think that conversation happened. I joined the litigation department. I'd be getting two years' credit for my clerkship. So that was coming in at $10,000 after two years. Our people make a little more now. I enjoyed doing the research and the like, occasionally getting to go to court with a partner.

The partners knew what they were doing. I started to do some First Amendment work because the firm represented NBC and had for many years. After I'd been there three years, a lot of work started coming in from NBC. Particularly after the Chicago Democratic Party National Convention in 1968, journalists were being called to testify often about events that everyone had seen.

Dr. [Benjamin] Spock [a famous American pediatrician whose books on parenting enjoyed wide circulation] was accused of some sort of crime relating to his opposition to the [Vietnam] war. The government called journalists to testify as to what Spock said in a public press conference. There was no law about things like that. I started doing briefs for NBC. I think in a year NBC had over one hundred subpoenas. So did CBS. So did ABC. We filed a brief, we would sometimes file together, asking for protection for the journalists. This was at the same time that journalists started to be subpoenaed to reveal their confidential sources. Those cases were in the courts, with more and more judges making essentially *ad hoc* decisions about how much the information was needed and how intrusive it was. But again, there was no law at the time dealing with this situation.

Brotman: What were you advising NBC to do?
Abrams: In the 1960s, journalists started to be subpoenaed in situations in which it was not just an enormous burden on time but a significant risk of being obliged to identify confidential sources.

Now, the media companies were ready to go to the mat to find a way to stop all these subpoenas from descending on them. At that time, libel law was just starting to be affected by the First Amendment. It took a while for the First Amendment to be relevant for the Supreme Court to federalize standards under the First Amendment for libel law.

There were still state libel suits being filed. Lots and lots of lawsuits. There was a whole civil rights movement at risk with these lawsuits against one after another national media company, heard by white, southern jurors who imposed enormous, staggering judgments in those days, even when the press was absolutely right. But it took a while for these cases to wither away after the Supreme Court finally said public figures could sue only when actual malice—knowing falsehood or a reckless disregard for distinguishing truth from falsity—could be proven, which was very rare.

Previously, certainly before the 1960s, lawyers that did libel defense work really worked for insurance companies. They would always have a detective on their staff. You get sued for libel, send the guy and find out what happened, what you can use to settle the case or at trial. But none of this glorified First Amendment stuff. It was police work, and it was a separate body of law. There were rules in libel law, still are, but so much of it now has been federalized because of the importation of the First Amendment into it. That changed everything. So firms like mine moved on to other First Amendment work.

Brotman: Sounds like you were making steady progress at Cahill up the career ladder.

Abrams: I became a partner in October 1970. By that time, there were a number of new First Amendment cases. The media lawyers were for the first time meeting each other. Unknown to me, the *New York Times* had been working for a few months on a blockbuster story about the war in Vietnam. Of course, the war there was going terribly. It was getting more and more controversial, as more young men were drafted and more of them were killed in the war.

Secretary of Defense [Robert] McNamara in the late 1960s ordered a study to be prepared about how we got into the war in Vietnam. I've often thought that one would have preferred if the study were made before the war. So the Pentagon Papers were created. That was called the McNamara Report—twenty-three volumes of Defense Department documents, all of them were highly classified, and some of them really secret by their nature.

At that time, there was a consolidated case in the Supreme Court about confidential sources dealing with three similar cases. I'd worked on the NBC side and in the lower courts, and the media lawyers for the other two cases had an idea. Why don't we do one brief for all of us? The question was who would we get to write such a brief.

Floyd Abrams 67

We scheduled a meeting to discuss the idea. My suggestion was Alex Bickel, my professor from Yale. It was clear by then, we thought, that we really had four votes in our favor—the four really liberal guys on the Supreme Court. But we didn't know about anyone else.

Hiring Bickel also would be strategic. He was viewed as a conservative and indeed was a conservative scholar about the Supreme Court, yet one who wrote for the *New Republic* and supported Robert F. Kennedy [in his 1968 presidential bid]. In any event, Bickel was highly respected by the justices on the right of the Court in those days. So Bickel was retained. I was the one that called him to do that. I remember the call very clearly.

Brotman: Bickel then came for the meeting with the media lawyers in New York, right?

Abrams: Yes, he came in to meet his clients. I don't think he ever had a client. In fact, I know he'd never had a client. There were all these media lawyers in the room. It was June 14, 1971. The Pentagon Papers started to be published on a Sunday. The lunch that I hosted was on a Monday, the next day. So everybody was talking about the *New York Times* and its publication over two days of articles based on this secret study.

Now what I didn't know, and what was unknown outside the *New York Times*, was that the government had threatened the *Times* if they published these articles. There were great internal debates, and this would have involved calls with Attorney General John Mitchell. A telegram was then sent by Mitchell, the night of our lunch at which Bickel and I mostly spoke about confidential sources. But we all agreed that the *Times* would be fine.

I've often said, lawyers without clients are the surest people in the world. Why would Nixon go to court? We didn't know. Secretary of State [Henry] Kissinger was telling Nixon about secret negotiations with China, for what later became an important and valuable meeting. Kissinger was saying, "There won't be any respect for the U.S. in China if we can't control our own secrets." The government wrote a telegram to the *New York Times* saying they were going to go to court if the *Times* didn't stop publishing. But Bickel had said at our lunch, "You know, there haven't been prior restraints on journalists publishing the news. And this is the news." Then the telegram arrived at the *Times* threatening litigation if the paper did not stop further publication.

68 The Conversations

So they called Alex at midnight, one in the morning. They agreed that he needed a law firm to work with.

Brotman: Wasn't this because the law firm representing the *New York Times* declined the case because of a conflict of interest?
Abrams: When the *Times* called, their outside law firm that had represented then for sixty years, that firm (headed by former U.S. Attorney General Herbert Brownell)—which had strenuously urged the *Times* not to publish the Pentagon Papers—refused to represent them. So the *Times* found itself without counsel in the most threatening case of its existence, one that their outside counsel had told them could well lead to criminal convictions of the newspaper and its publisher. And that was when, with our luncheon fresh in mind, they called Alex Bickel at midnight and asked him to lead their defense of the case. Bickel had never argued a case in court. But he was a constitutional expert of great distinction and was held in high regard by the Supreme Court, particularly its more conservative members.

With Bickel on board, James Goodale, the *Times*'s general counsel who had strongly urged the newspaper to publish articles based on the Pentagon Papers, called me to ask if I and my firm, Cahill Gordon and Reindel, would work with Bickel in defending the *Times*. I told him that I certainly wanted to do so but would need my firm's approval, which I obtained the next morning.

I picked up Bickel in a taxi about one in the morning from his mother's apartment and the two of us went to my office where we spent the night first locating and reviewing the Espionage Act, which the government was claiming the *Times* had violated, and then reviewing the most important Supreme Court cases that we thought might be central to the case. The next morning, we received a call from Goodale and proceeded to the *Times* for our first meeting with our client. As we traveled uptown, I wondered if anyone at the *Times* knew that Bickel had never tried any case before and that I, the youngest partner in my firm, had never even been in the Supreme Court before.

Brotman: This must have been before dawn.
Abrams: Absolutely. And we read it for the first time. We went to the *Times* the next morning for a meeting. Neither of us knew anyone on

Floyd Abrams 69

the *Times*, but I knew a good bit by then and started talking about what could happen. The *Washington Post* also was in the picture at that point. During the meeting, a telephone call was received from the lawyer who headed the Civil Division of the U.S. Attorney's Office in New York, saying that the government was going to court at noon. We went to court and appeared before a brand-new judge, Murray Gurfein, just appointed by President Nixon. We went there with Jim Goodale, the general counsel for the *Times*.

It was noteworthy to us that in World War II, Judge Gurfein had been in army intelligence and therefore had had access to classified material. We were sure (and we were right about this) that his military service would be highly relevant, since it could put him more at ease dealing with classified documents and claims of harm from their revelation.

I remember Judge Gurfein saying, "We're all Americans," which we feared (but could not know) was a barb aimed at the *Times* and its lawyers. The government urged him to enter a temporary restraining order. Bickel argued that no such order had ever been entered and that doing so could not be consistent with the First Amendment.

The government was using language about irreparable harm. Judge Gurfein said to us, in effect, "Why don't you give me a chance to study this? So why don't you agree not to publish until a few days later?" Goodale called the *Times*. He was the leader on this. But the answer, which Goodale had urged and we all agreed with, was that for a newspaper, the status quo was the right to print, not enforced silence. The *Times* would continue to publish.

Judge Gurfein then entered the order of prior restraint based on the government's representation of the highly classified nature of the documents, and that American POWs were being held. Publishing, the government argued, could interfere with getting them out.

We had a number of meetings at the *Times* during the unusually brief case (it lasted only fifteen days from start to finish) and the one I remember best was at the very beginning of it. It was a meeting chaired by Punch Sulzberger, the *Times* publisher, in which shortly after the meeting began he said that whatever the decision of the court was, that the *Times* would obey it.

Tom Wicker, their Washington correspondent and columnist said, "Punch, I thought that's why we were meeting, to discuss if we were going to obey the order. Let's talk about it." Bickel basically said this to them: "What this is all about, and what we are fighting for in this case, is obedience to law—in this case, the First Amendment. That means abiding by law even if you disagree with it."

I offered a more strategic response, urging on them that if we violated a court order in the case and wound up in the Supreme Court, that the Court would be furious with the *Times*—doing so would make it far more unlikely that we would persuade jurists who were not fond of the press generally, and the *Times* specifically, to rule in our favor.

So everyone at the meeting signed off to obey the order but mount an aggressive legal challenge to it. Thereafter, we had the litigation. Bickel argued just about everything himself. My partner Bill Hegarty came to work with him on the secret stuff—national security stuff—which was heard in a secret session of the court.

Brotman: Take me behind the scenes as the litigation began to be organized at your end.

Abrams: From the very beginning of the case, we realized we had one particularly high hurdle to overcome. The nation was at war, American soldiers were dying, with others held as prisoners of war, and the Executive Branch was representing to the Court that further publication of the Pentagon Papers would do irreparable harm to the nation. In that context, why should the Court intervene? I kept thinking as the case progressed that if we were in the midst of World War II and a similar issue had arisen, that while a court might have ruled for us, it would not have wanted to do so and might well not done so.

One way to address those fears was to try to persuade the Supreme Court that the government was exaggerating the potential for harm from the *Times*'s publication. Accordingly, we obtained affidavits from high-ranking former State Department and CIA officials stating that publication of the sort of material in the Pentagon Papers was not really harmful to the war effort, that what they revealed was not weapons technology, plans of military operations, or the like. We were helped, we thought, by the reality that what the Pentagon Papers themselves demonstrated was a pattern of government falsehoods through the years about the Vietnam conflict, a pattern that we did not quite say, but inevitably inferred, was continuing into the case.

Floyd Abrams

The cross-examination by my partner William Hegarty of a chief military witness for the government was extremely helpful in this respect, since it showed that the witness was upset about even the least revealing information about national defense.

At the same time, we sought to minimize any supposed harm from publication of the Pentagon Papers by the submission of a superb affidavit by Max Frankel, former executive editor of the *Times*, about well-established norms in Washington. Even classified information was commonly made available to journalists by government officials for a variety of motivations—personal and policy-related—which had the impact of significantly informing the public. The publication of portions of the Pentagon Papers, Frankel argued, was one example of that.

There were a number of hearings in the case, including a particularly threatening one that I argued. That was the government directing the *Times* to turn over the Pentagon Papers that they had, which we were immediately told would compromise the identity of the source because his fingerprints were all over it. At that point, Daniel Ellsberg was not visible and not known. His name was unknown to us too. But we were told that the source could be discovered, so I argued on that issue.

At that time, the *Times* had another case in the courts in California on the issue of confidential sources. One of their journalists, Earl Caldwell, had been subpoenaed and was protected by a court order that was on appeal. That was one of the cases that went to the Supreme Court later, the case I mentioned that Bickel had been called in to write a combined brief for media companies.

So my argument was not to make us have to turn over the documents. Bickel came up with the idea: "Well, why can't you tell them what documents you have, without actually giving them?" Which we did and which they promptly forgot. But it turned out to be really important. The *Times* would not have complied with that order, they would not have turned over the actual Pentagon Papers that they had, thinking that it would compromise the source. If that happened, then everything would have gotten off the tracks. The Supreme Court was not about to protect journalists who were violating court orders to judges. We would have a real problem when the case went to the Supreme Court.

72   The Conversations

Brotman: And you knew the Pentagon Papers case would be going to go to Supreme Court.
Abrams: We knew. But it was very fortuitous that we told the judges about what was in the documents without actually turning them over.

Brotman: It sounds like you all were on a 24/7 schedule.
Abrams: We were all working day and night. No one's sleeping, and no one knows anything anymore. You forget things. I don't mean now. I mean then.

Brotman: You had a relatively small legal team, right?
Abrams: Well, we had like eight people. But in terms of who knows this or that, it was very small. The government continued to maintain, throughout the case, that the *Times* had certain documents that were not on our list. But it's not because they thought we lied; they paid no attention to the list we gave them.

Brotman: And in lightning speed, the case reaches the Supreme Court.
Abrams: It took fifteen days, from beginning to end. Bickel's argument in the Supreme Court had one central moment. He thought, and I thought, that was when he was answering the question of Justice Potter Stewart, who asked in effect, "Suppose when we go back to our chambers and we read the Pentagon Papers, we find that publication of material at issue would result in the death of twenty American young men who simply had the misfortune to have a low number in terms of being drafted. Is your position then that we must allow you to publish?"

Bickel started, lawyers often do this, "That's not this case." That was true but it also was an answer that frequently irritates judges who know that and are posing hypothetical questions to explore the breadth of an argument. Finally, Bickel said that if this were the situation, then his dedication to the First Amendment would clash with his dedication to the security of the country. And yes, the *Times* would not publish that. That answer was viewed as such a sellout by the ACLU that they submitted a brief denouncing it. I thought they were wrong, terribly wrong, and that his answer was absolutely required for an advocate for the *Times* to make.

Floyd Abrams 73

Brotman: Were you aware they were going to file that?

Abrams: Not in advance. The case came and went, it was over on June 30. We won six to three. I have been struck by the fact that even the justices who voted for us had been persuaded by the government that publication would do some harm. They were wrong about that. But basically they said the government had failed to prove that the amount of harm that would be done outweighed the First Amendment, so the near-total ban on prior restraints carried the day and we prevailed.

Brotman: How important was it that the *Times* was the client?

Abrams: It was very important that the *Times* was the client during the case. A less-respected entity might well have lost the case. But even as to the *Times*, there remained the risk, as indicated by what some of the justices observed, that there could still be an Espionage Act prosecution of the *Times* after publication. In effect, the Supreme Court suggested if the *Times* wanted to take the chance that it was going to be indicted, you know, this remained a risk at that point.

Brotman: What advice were you providing about this potential criminal prosecution?

Abrams: We didn't really have a strong view as to what would have happened regarding a charge of breaching the Espionage Act. We had argued to Justice [Thurgood] Marshall, who agreed with us on this, that the Espionage Act didn't cover journalists reporting news in good faith. Marshall went along with that, but certainly Justice [Byron] White and Justice Stewart did not. That did not happen though. So the case really was over. And my life started to change.

Brotman: How so?

Abrams: That started a period of a few years in which I got to do a large number of the Supreme Court arguments on freedom of the press. And we did well. We had cases about the constitutionality of a Virginia statute, which made it a crime to reveal information that was provided in secret. It involved a judicial proceeding about whether a judge should stay on the bench. The way their system worked there, if someone filed a complaint against a judge, for misconduct of some sort, it went to

74   The Conversations

a secret panel that decided that there was enough information to go forward publicly.

Brotman: Your client had reported on this secret proceeding.
Abrams: Landmark, our newspaper client, found out about charges against a juvenile judge and published it. I represented them in the Supreme Court. We prevailed and then prevailed again in a case arising in West Virginia. That was a junior high school student who had killed one of his classmates and had fled. A helicopter caught him and brought him before the juvenile authorities. There was a state statute saying you couldn't publish anything about matters in front of the juvenile court without the permission of the judge. Our client didn't have the permission but they published it. We won that case too, citing the earlier *Landmark* decision. Then a significant amount of other cases came through in the 1970s into the 1980s. We lost some, but we won a number of others. Along the way, I also took on capital punishment cases, two cases with guys on death row.

Brotman: So you weren't at Cornell anymore. I mean it sounds like you had clearly gone over to the other side regarding protections for free press under the First Amendment.
Abrams: Yeah. I clearly found a side. Then in 2008, I got a call from Senator [Mitch] McConnell, saying that he'd heard that I was favorably inclined to his side with respect to the about-to-be adopted campaign finance law. Together with Ken Starr, I represented McConnell in the Supreme Court case that we mostly lost but which led to *Citizens United,* which was argued in 2010 and which we won.

Citizens United also was a campaign finance case in which the issue was basically again the constitutionality of the campaign finance law, in which it was illegal for a conservative political group to spend its corporate money in support of, or in opposition to, a candidate for public office. It arose after a documentary had been prepared by this conservative group blasting Hillary Clinton at a time when it looked as if she would be the Democratic nominee for president.

The whole thing was an attack on her, so it certainly fell within the statutory language. There were other statutory issues. In terms of the question of whether this was what the statute was about, it certainly was. My view was that the notion of making criminal the preparation and

Floyd Abrams 75

broadcast of a documentary, however one-sided, saying someone was unfit to be president had to violate the First Amendment.

Brotman: Did you expect the amount of blowback to that argument, which the Supreme Court adopted?

Abrams: I really didn't. I knew that the public generally, and my liberal friends particularly, including people I don't know, were deeply invested in the notion that campaign finance reform was one of the most important sorts of legislation that was sought for political reform of our election system. But I really had not imagined the ferocity of the reaction to the opinion.

Brotman: So in some sense, even after nearly a decade since that case is over, you continue to have to argue it in the public arena?

Abrams: Yes, that's right. I did become very much the guy they could call on to be the defender of the case, and I was glad to do that. I really haven't suffered as a result of this. But I really was surprised at the fury.

Brotman: It remains as a controversial opinion that liberals want to overturn through legislation.

Abrams: Yes, now it's a very hot issue. It was then and it will remain so.

Brotman: Here's my understanding of your position. You could have the *New York Times* as a corporation speaking to support or oppose a political candidate, and then you could have another entity, which would not be allowed to speak as a corporation. And why would that distinction be made?

Abrams: Well, I'd start with why. There was always a question of whether the *New York Times* itself could be affected by the statute, as a corporate entity. Essentially, the government lawyer was asked, "Well, how about if Congress passed a law making it a crime for a clever corporation to fund a book which endorsed a candidate? And the answer the lawyer gave, I thought, after trying to duck the question honorably, he said, 'Yes, they wouldn't be able to use their own money.'"

By all accounts, there was what is always referred to as gasps in the room. That had always been in a way the best argument against the law, which is if you're saying corporations, you're saying that you could

76 The Conversations

include them all. Now there was a media exemption in the statute, so the *Times* would not have been covered, but if not for that narrow exemption, it could have been covered.

Brotman: What if you had been asked the same question as a lawyer for the other side?

Abrams: There have been lawyers who have tried to come up with better answers. And some of them, I think, are more plausible but still weak. You might think the government should have said, "But there's never been a case about a book. There's no problem with that. We would never prosecute that." But it did say that and it lost.

Brotman: Now we also are in the WikiLeaks era. Your thoughts?

Abrams: We're all Americans here. I think that WikiLeaks could be fully entitled to try to take advantage of the governing rule of law set forth in the Pentagon Papers case. The government would argue that WikiLeaks is not journalism. I don't think that's going to be the issue as to whether it's really a journalistic organization. It was playing at least a sort of journalistic role.

That said, WikiLeaks has engaged in conduct that is deeply disturbing. It goes beyond publishing a little more of this or that. It released the names of human rights workers, whose lives have been imperiled. Presumably the *New York Times* never would have done that. Indeed, when the *Times* has worked with WikiLeaks, the *Times* wouldn't agree to release specific names that could put people in danger.

WikiLeaks has published social security numbers of anyone who works at some big company that is hacked. That's happened already. It's published names of people and confidential classified documents. All this came out in the recent indictment. It also worked with the Russians for the purpose of affecting American elections.

Brotman: Do you think those differences are enough to make it distinct from the *New York Times*? Or another institutional press organization?

Abrams: I hope WikiLeaks wins even that case, even though I find their behavior repeatedly deplorable. But I think they will have problems. Look, I thought we would lose the Pentagon Papers case. What if we hadn't been

Floyd Abrams

the *New York Times* but rather had been the *Village Voice*? I mean, people forget how close the vote was in that case—six to three. While the current Supreme Court is a very pro–First Amendment court, it is also a court that is respectful of government claims of harm to national security. So I think WikiLeaks is going to have real problems in the courts.

Brotman: The First Amendment talks about the press as an institutional entity, or group of entities. What is the press as an institution today?
Abrams: Let me start this way. First, I'm not sure the courts will think that is the question. I say that in the sense that the courts have been deciding more and more First Amendment cases on an across-the-board basis. No breaks for the press but no limitation on the press either, because of the breadth of our protection for free expression. But if there were a WikiLeaks case, I have no doubt. The government already has made it clear: they will be arguing it's not the press. WikiLeaks, of course, will be arguing that it is.

Brotman: What role should the institutional press take to benefit from the advantage of its First Amendment rights?
Abrams: The amount of protection that the American press receives is unknown in the history of the world, even our own history. It has more protection now than there has ever been. That said, one would certainly hope that care is taken by the press. If anything, care should be taken together with the freedom to publish almost anything. This comes up now more than anything in the social media era. With social media, Congress has a lot of power.

Brotman: Presumably, Congress may exercise some power over Facebook. But it seems that the First Amendment is a firewall against any real legal action.
Abrams: Now, it's one thing to say, "You better take that down. And we want you to take it down now. It's going on, it shouldn't go on a second more." But to talk about prior restraint of social media, that would violate the First Amendment.

So there are going to be a lot of hard issues, especially with social media. All but impossible to do anything in advance. It's also one of the very pro-democratic benefits of social media—people don't need permission from anyone. It's like the proverbial place for a public soapbox in London—Hyde Park. And it's Hyde Park plus one, since we give anonymity.

That makes the United States very distinct from other parts of the world. Look around the European Union. Look at New Zealand. They don't just ban guns, they ban speech. While we do allow punishment of speech, which is really incitement to criminal conduct, even there we do so with a heavy dose of First Amendment protection. That's generally a good thing.

When the Pentagon Papers case was over, my wife and I went to Europe. We were in England and Switzerland and Israel. I met with a lot of journalists in each place. They were all shocked at the result of the case because their countries would never allow publication of highly classified material—top secret at the highest level of government—with an assertion of potential harm. I make a point of not passing judgment on Germany for making it a crime to deny the Holocaust happened, of not passing judgment on India for taking steps to avoid communal violence when Hindus and Muslims say terrible things about each other's religion. I'm not saying those are good decisions either.

Brotman: Where would you draw the line?
Abrams: I'm not sure what the answer is. We have a situation where the Westboro Baptist Church shows up at funerals for American soldiers who died defending our country. They have signs wherever the police will allow them to stand denouncing the soldiers and saying this is God's will because the U.S. is too soft on homosexuals.

U.S. Supreme Court Chief Justice [John] Roberts then writes an opinion as if it was the easiest thing in the world, saying, "Don't you understand this sort of thing gets special protection? This is political speech. This is a speech about the role of gays in American life, the role of gays in the military, what could be more protected?"

The United States is alone in so much speech that we protect. First Amendment types like me celebrate it, but we celebrate it while understanding that there are other democratic countries—Canada is such a great example not so far from us—that also have a liberty-loving tradition but will put people in jail for saying the same thing.

Brotman: You might not even be friends with your younger First Amendment self as you began college.

Abrams: I'm pretty far over to the other side from my Cornell days. One of the reasons I'm pretty far over relates not to the First Amendment as such but to the reality that time and again, the dangers that are cited by the government don't happen. It is so rare that one can posit a situation where the speech has caused the terrible harm that the government is concerned about. I don't think it's crying wolf. I understand they genuinely believe it.

I'm not saying they would easily cross the road to the English system either. I guess I'd say that we all invest in competing social values. Some of those values are not the values of free speech. Some of those are values of privacy, national security, of personal security, of truth, of talent. The First Amendment doesn't mean that you can't put someone in jail for lying under oath. It's speech. But perjury is a crime, and we just live with that. We don't apologize for that.

Now most of the rest of the world treats as criminal so many more things like perjury than we do. They are able to distinguish what they think is good speech from bad speech. Censorship is contagious. Contagion doesn't have to kill you. It can make you sick, and it can limit your ability to get out and play. It really is an interesting issue abroad. So trying to be practical, as well as ideological, a lot of the proposed limits on speech wind up doing more harm than good. They sometimes limit very valuable speech for one reason or another, and at the same time often fail to serve the interests that they claim their statutes or lawsuits or jails are trying to do.

Brotman: Does that make our First Amendment a beacon for the world?

Abrams: Well, it is. It's not that there is no other way for a democratic nation to function. But the bet that we make is that avoiding the dangers of government control over speech is worth the risk that allowing more speech will do grave harm to the nation and its people.

Brotman: Is that your starting point? Is that where you begin?

Abrams: It just makes me more comfortable taking rather broad positions in favor of free speech. Grave consequences are unlikely, even when there's a plausible case to be made that this speech or that speech is really beyond the pale. The only way to do it as a matter of policy is to have, however one phrases it, a very strong, very consistent, very powerful pro-speech position.

Brotman: Are you optimistic about the future in this area? Or pessimistic? **Abrams:** I don't think the press, or people saying unpopular things generally, are going to be at risk in America in the foreseeable future. But these are dangerous times, so we had best take great care to assure that freedom prevails.

Nadine Strossen

Nadine Strossen is the John Marshall Harlan II Professor of Law Emerita at New York Law School. She has written, taught, and advocated extensively in the areas of constitutional law and civil liberties, including through frequent media interviews and congressional testimony. From 1991 through 2008, she served as president of the American Civil Liberties Union (ACLU), the first woman to head the nation's largest and oldest civil liberties organization. Professor Strossen is currently a member of the ACLU's National Advisory Council, as well as the advisory boards of FIRE (Foundation for Individual Rights in Education), Heterodox Academy, and the National Coalition Against Censorship. Strossen is a member of the Council on Foreign Relations.

In 2017, the American Bar Association presented Strossen with the prestigious Margaret Brent Women Lawyers of Achievement Award, which "celebrates the accomplishments of women lawyers who have excelled in their field and paved the way to success for other women lawyers." The National Law Journal *named Strossen one of "The 100 Most Influential Lawyers in America,"* Vanity Fair *included her in "America's 200 Most Influential Women," and* Ladies' Home Journal *named her among "America's 100 Most Important Women".*

Strossen's writings have been published in many scholarly and general-interest publications, and she is credited with more than three hundred published works. Her 2018 book, HATE: Why We Should Resist It with Free Speech, Not Censorship, *has been widely praised by ideologically diverse experts. Her earlier book* Defending Pornography: Free Speech, Sex, and the Fight for Women's Rights *was named by the* New York Times *as a "Notable Book" of 1995.*

She graduated Phi Beta Kappa from Harvard College and magna cum laude from Harvard Law School, where she was an editor of the Harvard

Law Review. *Before becoming a law professor, she practiced law for nine years in Minneapolis (her hometown) and New York City.*

In October 2001, she made her professional theater debut as the guest star in Eve Ensler's award-winning play The Vagina Monologues *during a weeklong run at the National Theatre in Washington, D.C.*

Stuart Brotman: How did the notion of free speech shape you in your early school years?

Nadine Strossen: I remember being concerned about free speech very far back in my personal history, starting in childhood, long before I had any concept or vocabulary to describe it. I felt frustrated when my parents intervened to stop me from saying things, when my schoolteachers, starting in kindergarten, intervened saying there are certain things not to be discussed.

I was a very good student in school, except I was regularly punished for being disruptive and noncooperative. I remember that very clearly. My first-grade teacher wrote on the blackboard, "Nadine is uncooperative." She put me out in the hall, which was the punishment for disciplinary infractions. All I had done was asked a question about something that was said.

It became more serious when I was fifteen years old. The Vietnam War was going on, in the fairly early phases, the very beginning of an antiwar protest movement. One of my teachers at my public high school in a Minneapolis suburb put together a slideshow of images from Vietnam, including the napalm violence against civilians, with no commentary at all. No words in the background, only folk songs. That was considered so incendiary and so subversive that a campaign began to oust him from his position.

The local newspaper ran editorials calling for him to be disciplined or fired. So I organized a petition drive among students. I wrote an explanation as to why it was so important that we were exposed to those ideas, and I published a letter in that newspaper. I actually went back and forth with the editorial board a couple of times.

A little bit earlier, when I was still in junior high school, I began to be a debater. I would travel around Minnesota and the surrounding states to engage in debates. By the time I was in high school, I was being sent around to various schools in the area to engage in public debates for a schoolwide audience on the Vietnam War, on civil rights, on other issues of the day. So I was very much a practitioner of free speech and debate and dissent. The minute I learned that there was a constitutional right that could be invoked, and an organization that was dedicated to protecting that right—the ACLU—it was like a match made in heaven. I had been waiting to discover it my entire life. There were actually people who spent their professional careers doing this.

Brotman: How did debate connect to an interest in studying law?
Strossen: One of the years when I was in high school, the debate topic was a legal one, so I would take the local bus and go to the University of Minnesota Law Library and do legal research. I absolutely fell in love with law. I was the only female on the debate team, I said to my male debate partners, "You should go to law school." It never occurred to me that I could do that. I needed a role model before it occurred to me that I could be a lawyer. That didn't happen until I went off to college and very quickly became involved in the women's rights movement and the reproductive freedom movement, and for the first time in my life met women lawyers. Then, of course, I realized I can do that.

I definitely wanted to be an advocate for civil liberties, including freedom of speech. When I was in college, it was a very similar time to what we're experiencing now in the sense that to be a classical liberal, who truly defends free speech and due process, it was pretty much as reviled then as it is now.

I remember having debates in my dormitory with others who were members of one group more to the left than the others. They were very much opposed to freedom of speech for speakers from the administration who were defending the war or defense contractors. While I was very involved in the antiwar movement myself and participated in all the demonstrations, I thought it was wrong to silence those who had a different perspective. I remember being denounced by one of the SDS [Students for a Democratic Society] members as a liberal bourgeois. Then we went through a period where to be liberal was considered to be an extreme left-winger. George Herbert Walker Bush attacked Michael Dukakis for being a card-carrying ACLU member and the "L-word" was considered a dirty word. [Bill] Clinton, of course, had to reinvent it.

So it's very interesting to see how the pendulum has swung. I believe that to the best of my ability, I'm open minded and constantly trying to reexamine first principles. But I keep coming back to this doggedly neutral position that we absolutely have to rigidly defend freedom of speech, including for the ideas we despise, precisely because the pendulum is constantly going to swing. You could never depend on having the power to impose your point of view, even assuming you would want to do that.

Brotman: Then you brought your passion to Cambridge, Massachusetts.
Strossen: I had a great education—seven years at Harvard College and Harvard Law School. It was despite an absence of any meaningful relationship with a faculty member at Harvard, both at the undergraduate and the law school levels. There were very large classes, very large ratios of students to teachers. The virtue of the education really came from your interaction with your fellow students, and whatever experiences you created for yourself.

I would say the closest I came to having a professor who was really inspiring to me in terms of neutral defense of civil liberties was Alan Dershowitz, who was just beginning his illustrious and controversial career of taking on cases. He taught a seminar about criminal justice issues. He talked a lot about his cases. He very much was living out the spirit of zealously advocating the rights of his client, even if a client has despised and unpopular ideas. One of his very first clients was somebody who was with the Jewish Defense League. Alan was not defending his ideas as such but just his right to express them. That made him very much of a role model for me.

Brotman: How did you then emerge into the larger legal world?
Strossen: I graduated from law school in 1975. The ACLU took on the village of Skokie, Illinois, regarding the Nazis' right to march in the heavily Jewish Chicago suburb in 1977. That was the first time I really got into a lot of debates about viewpoint neutrality. In the early 1980s, free speech was under attack from a combination of so-called radical feminists and the Moral Majority's pornography commission. They were strange bedfellows. This was an alliance from the extreme left to the extreme right, ganging up on sexually oriented expression in particular, but other kinds of controversial expression too.

Brotman: Talk a bit about the namesake of your chaired professorship at New York Law School, Justice John Harlan Marshall II.

Strossen: John Marshall Harlan II was the most distinguished graduate of New York Law School. He was a very interesting Supreme Court justice because he was a Republican, conservative Wall Street lawyer before he went to the Court and continued to be viewed as a conservative justice on the very liberal Warren Court.

Yet he wrote some opinions that continue to this day to be some of the most important pro–civil liberties decisions. Harlan was way ahead of his time. He was the first justice ever to read into the very broad, open-textured language of the due process clause a so-called implied right to privacy that extended to what we would now call reproductive freedom. He did it in a case where the majority of the Court just didn't even reach that issue at all. They arrived at that position a few years later. I love to point out to my students and to others that this ultimately became the right to abortion, the right to same-sex intimacy, the right to marriage equality.

People now see that as part of this left-wing judicial activism. But that it was none other than John Marshall Harlan II—Republican Wall Street lawyer, conservative lawyer—who was the first one to articulate what became a whole series of rights of personal autonomy and freedom of choice.

With respect to freedom of speech, if I had to pick just a handful of great Supreme Court opinions, I think many people would be surprised to learn that one of them was written by John Marshall Harlan II. It's not a case that is so well known, but it included support for so many principles that we now take for granted. He was way ahead of the times.

The case was called *Cohen v. California*. It was decided in 1971. The facts will sound familiar to most people. Cohen was a student in California during the Vietnam war protest era. He was wearing a jacket that said, "Fuck the Draft" in a courthouse in Los Angeles, and was actually arrested, prosecuted, and convicted for breach of the peace. The California courts upheld the conviction. That's what's so interesting. They were enforcing the First Amendment law at the time. The fact that the Supreme Court with an opinion by Justice Harlan overturned the conviction really shows that he was changing the law. The lower courts were following the law as it then existed, and he was the crucial deciding vote.

Brotman: Tell me more.

Strossen: Not only did the opinion have many holdings that are really significant even beyond the particular facts of the case, but it was written in extremely eloquent language. One of many important points that he made was how a lot of people said, "This is such a trivial case, how can you possibly even write an opinion that deals with this particular word. It's not detracting from his message to stop him from just using that particular word. You can have an antiwar message voiced in many, many other ways."

One of the points that he made was that denying somebody the choice of a particular word with its particular force and significance to the individual is denying freedom to convey that thought. People said, "Oh, but that word doesn't convey any ideas. It's just conveying anger and emotion." But Harlan said freedom of speech protects not only the right to convey fully articulated thoughts but also the right to self-expression, to convey emotions. That may be even more important to many people than rationally engaging in a debate about ideas.

Another point that I always make today when the F-word is constantly used is what an extremely shocking term it was at the time. To me, it is tantamount to the N-word today. Here's a way to illustrate it. Everybody used the euphemism. The F-word itself was considered absolutely shocking and repugnant. How dare you say that word?

It was not allowed, even in the Supreme Court. Chief Justice Warren Burger instructed the ACLU lawyer arguing the case not to use the word. I've read and interviewed people who were involved in preparing him for the argument. The ACLU lawyer, Mel Nimmer, himself didn't want to use the word. It was considered a shocking, vulgar, and horrible word, certainly in the halls of the Supreme Court. But those who were coaching him said, "You have to use that word. Because if you self-censor, that is supporting the idea that there's some danger in this word that warrants it being suppressed and punished."

So right after Chief Justice Burger gives his opening spiel, "We know the facts so you're not to go into them, counsel," Nimmer then says, "Okay, I'll just summarize in one sentence. This is a case about the right to say 'fuck the draft.'" And that was the only time he said the word.

Brotman: Saying it in the argument was absolutely essential.

Strossen: At that point, he won the case. He would have lost it if he had gone the other way. But I think it really shows the power of the Supreme Court's protection of that word. So after the vote was taken, and Harlan was assigned to write the opinion, Chief Justice Burger literally begged him not to use that word. He said, "John, you're not going to use that word, it would be the end of this court, if you did."

But Harlan did use the word in the opinion. I think that really underscores how far in the vanguard he was, despite the fact that he was this mainstream conservative. Another way of describing it is that staunch defense of free speech, even for terms and ideas that are considered the most unacceptable, and the most provocative and the most controversial, is a mainstream conservative value. It doesn't belong just to the liberal activists of the world. This part of the reasoning in that case is why the antiwar message was so controversial.

I have to explain that to those who didn't live through that era. People were getting killed in Vietnam. It wasn't only that you thought it was unpatriotic to denounce the war. We know that's controversial enough. But fathers and brothers and uncles were over there fighting and being killed. It was emotionally traumatizing. All the arguments that are being made for censorship today—that it could lead to violence, and that it emotionally traumatizes people—were involved in that case too. Again, we had a very ideologically diverse cross-section of the Court, including Justice Harlan, to thank for establishing a principle that the Supreme Court continues to enforce completely across the ideological spectrum today.

Brotman: That principle is based on the importance of political speech, right?

Strossen: The Supreme Court has consistently held that speech about public affairs is of special importance in our democratic republic. We the people hold sovereignty, and those we elect to represent us are accountable to us. How can we meaningfully hold them accountable unless we have the most robust freedom of speech to debate and discuss their ideas, their policies, their qualifications, and so forth? I certainly accept that speech about public affairs does have special importance. But I reject the notion that the entire Supreme Court had for many years—that we can make a meaningful distinction between speech about public affairs and other speech.

Take, for example, sexual speech, which pretty much has been at the opposite end of a hierarchy in terms of protection. Even such a great defender of free speech as Justice William Brennan would actually be the one to create, and I used the word *create* advisedly, the obscenity exception to the First Amendment's free speech clause.

Back then in 1956, speech about sex had always been somewhat frowned upon traditionally in our society. In 1973, Justice Brennan came to repudiate the exception that he himself had created.

The Supreme Court itself since then in many ways has treated expression about sexuality not as the freedom of speech stepchild that it had long treated as one. The obscenity exception still exists. There are still certain factual contexts where sexual expression is given somewhat different treatment, I should add.

Another major example of speech that was considered second-class was commercial speech. For many years, it was considered not to be protected at all. Yet the trend for this, as well as for sexual expression, is for a broader understanding of speech that relates to public affairs. After all, when you have so many public policy discussions about abortion and contraception and gender discrimination and gender identity and sexual orientation, these are issues of public policy that relate to sexuality.

Where is the distinction between speech about public affairs and speech about sexuality? Where's the distinction between speech about public affairs and speech about commercial matters when we live in a capitalist society? I think the vast majority of the Supreme Court has come to recognize that these distinctions can't be drawn.

Brotman: But sexual expression always seems to be a lightning rod.
Strossen: Sexual expression has been, and continues to this day, to be controversial. There's this consistent demonization of sexual expression. It has been seen as being inconsistent with "traditional family values." I'm putting that in quotes because that was a favorite phrase of the religious right. It's been seen as inconsistent with traditional religious values. I assume the reason is because within the construct of a so-called traditional family, sex occurs between a husband and wife, a male and a female, for purposes of procreation.

In the 1960s, under President [Lyndon Baines] Johnson, a commission was appointed to examine whether traditional anti-obscenity laws should be reconsidered. Johnson was the president right before Nixon, of course. People often get it mixed up, because the commission was appointed under Johnson but delivered its report to Nixon. This commission was headed up by the dean of the University of Minnesota Law School, William Lockhart. He had been very much in favor of the traditional censorship of obscenity. Interestingly enough, as a result of his work on the commission, he changed his viewpoint because he was convinced, as was the majority of the commission, that there is no danger from being exposed to sexually oriented expression.

The assumption was that it leads to violence. It leads to "juvenile delinquency," to quote a term at the time. Did it erode family stability and society? They concluded there was no such harm. The commission presented its report to President Nixon, calling for complete decriminalization of sexual expression, except with respect to minors—they didn't reach that issue—or to nonconsenting adults.

But for consenting adults, whatever they choose to see, they should be free to see. Nixon denounced this report in the strongest terms and basically said this is going to unleash anarchy. I think that was the fear that somehow freedom in the sexual realm was just going to unravel whatever order there is in society more generally, at a time when there was great concern about social upheavals in terms of the antiwar movement and the civil rights movement.

This became part of it—sexual expression is revolutionary and dangerous. Interestingly, that was actually a term that was used at the time, the sexual revolution. To me that had positive connotations about a revolutionary change in women's status and opportunities, individual freedom in terms of sexual conduct and contact and relationships.

But for those who had a more traditional view, it was very unnerving and threatening. We had a very different attack on sexuality and sexual expression coming from the other end of the political spectrum—the so-called radical feminists. Andrea Dworkin and Catharine MacKinnon were the most well-known leaders of that movement. They made a seemingly very different argument that free sexual expression, and sexual freedom more generally, including access to contraception and abortion, is just a way of perpetuating the male patriarchy that allows men to prey on women through sexual expression.

They were making an argument from the left that to advance women's equality and safety and dignity, we have to censor sexual expression. They used the term *pornography* because they did not support the traditional concept of obscenity. Obscenity was attempting to define a category of sexual expression that violated traditional, majority community morality. The harm of that sexual expression was to undermine traditional morals that are accepted by the majority of the community. Part of this thinking was based on the Puritan ethic in the country.

That was of no concern to the so-called radical feminists, the antipornography feminists. They wanted to target a supposedly different subset of sexual expression, which they labeled *pornography* and defined essentially as sexually explicit expression or sexually suggestive expression that is demeaning or degrading toward women. The reason why I say that it's a supposedly different definition is that both of them are so inescapably subjective. Basically they would license whoever is enforcing the law to outlaw and punish whatever sexual expression they consider to be offensive and objectionable.

All of us who were in the anticensorship feminist camp predicted that the work of MacKinnon to create a model law was so loosely worded that it would have enabled even their own antipornography diatribes to be censored. I took no satisfaction at all when that proved to be true. Our neighboring country of Canada did adopt this approach, a "MacDworkin" concept of illegal sexual expression (referring to the concept spearheaded by Catharine MacKinnon and Andrea Dworkin). Among the first casualties were books by Andrea Dworkin herself because in the process of denouncing pornography, she had the most vivid descriptions of what she considered to be the most outrageous examples of it.

Brotman: What did the Canadian law teach us?

Strossen: Books without pictures were among the first casualties in Canada. Not surprisingly, not only were feminist bookstores attacked but also LGBT bookstores—there weren't very many in Canada at the time—and to the best of my recollection, all or almost all of them were driven out of business.

The fact that lesbian sex is voluntary and consensual, as described in a story with no pictures, made it more demeaning to the government censors, more degrading, that somebody would voluntarily submit herself to this kind of sexual conduct. A lesbian magazine that contained that story was one of the first targets of censorship under this supposedly pro-feminist antipornography law. So the paradox in these kinds of laws is that I share the underlying premise that we live in societies where sexism and misogyny are deeply baked into many of our social and legal structures. But why would you want to add to those very structures this inherently subjective power? How can you possibly expect that it's going to be used in a way that is liberating and equalizing to those who have traditionally been subject to second-class status?

Brotman: Is that period an artifact of history or something of contemporary importance too?

Strossen: For a while, it seemed to me that the feminist pro-censorship position really had gone so deeply out of fashion. Their movement seemed to have not only faded but really been obliterated. There was a tidal wave not only of availability of pornography, but young women, including on college campuses, where the antipornography movement had been the strongest, were reveling in their sexuality and dressing in extremely sexually provocative ways. One of my friends who studies pornography talked about the "pornification" of fashion—kinds of attire that you used to see only in porn films much more similar to what we see women wearing now, even when they come to class or go to work.

There seems to have been a pendulum swing against sexual expression of late. Again, it's always a slightly different spin in a slightly different context. So now in the context of the #MeToo movement, the movement against sexual violence and sexual assault, there seems to be again much more of this sentiment. Of course, I condemn any kind of violence and any kind of coercion, any kind of harassment. That couldn't be more antithetical to my values as a feminist and as a civil libertarian.

But I get extremely nervous when the definition of sexual assault and sexual violence becomes so overly broad that it extends even to words that are seen as conveying a sexist or discriminatory idea. We've been moving very much in that direction as part of an overall culture on college campuses where people are opposing expression that makes them uncomfortable. Now they're equating that with violence, right? "I feel threatened, I am assaulted."

I'm very nervous about that. On this dimension of free speech, the Department of Education and the Department of Justice issued a letter in 2011 to colleges that basically said, "You are in danger of losing your federal funding unless you adopt this extremely overbroad definition of sexual harassment." This extended to expression that was seen as subjectively unwelcome messages about sex or gender.

I actually strongly support the recent proposed rollback of those federal guidelines to be much more protective of free speech and due process, along with other civil liberties values that were swamped by that overzealous attack on sexual assault. Sexuality is seen as being dangerous. We have to constantly be vigilant to defend the freedom to express controversial ideas about sex and sexuality and gender identity. I think that we should strongly encourage, as a matter of professional responsibility and just common courtesy, to use whatever gender pronoun somebody wants, but do I want the government or university enforcing that norm of courtesy and respect now?

Brotman: Then there is the freedom not to speak.
Strossen: Freedom of speech includes the right to choose not to say something. Freedom of speech includes the right to discourage somebody from saying something, to exert your peer pressure and whatever other persuasive techniques you have as an individual. I am channeling the Supreme Court going all the way back to the great defense by Justices Oliver Wendell Holmes and Louis Brandeis, when they said the answer to speech you dislike is not government suppression but counter speech, raising our own voices to try to silence the message. But the end result is the same, right? The message is being silenced.

So how do you draw the line between counter speech that is positive and counter speech that ends up having functionally the same repressive, coercive effect, perhaps even more so than outright government punishment? We are social creatures, and many of us care more about what our peers say or what our boss says or what our customers say. I recently was reminded of the fact that John Stuart Mill's classic essay "On Liberty," which continues to be one of the most powerful defenses of free speech, is addressed to social pressure. At the very beginning, he says, "I'm not talking here about government laws, I'm talking about social pressure, which for all practical purposes is even more coercive than government power." I think all of us have to be very careful how we exercise counter speech.

One of the best articulations is from Derek Bok when he was president of Harvard University. Some fraternity, some social club on campus had issued flyers that were deeply misogynistic. Bok issued a statement that to this day, decades later, is still on Harvard's website the last time I looked. It is such a wonderful model. He very strongly defends the free speech rights of the students to issue that statement. But he also explains why he considers it so important to explain the values that he and Harvard University cherish—the values of gender equality. He then says, "I understand, especially given my powerful position, my merely speaking out to criticize these ideas can have a suppressive effect. So let me reiterate that there will be no punishment at all." I thought that was a pretty good dance. You have to really bend over backward to say, "I'm trying to change your mind. I'm trying to express myself, but I really don't want to silence you."

Brotman: It sounds like you encourage this type of First Amendment dance.

Strossen: I'm not so much a free speech absolutist. I've wrestled with it a lot, because I really am concerned about self-censorship, which is a strong problem not only among students but also among faculty members. Surveys have shown that people are not only not voicing certain ideas, but not even broaching certain subjects, because of fear of the backlash.

We are "the land of the free and the home of the brave." You have to have the courage of your convictions to participate in a society. You should not demand to be shielded from criticism, but you should be shielded from punishment. I think a really strong deterrent effect on campus comes when professors are not allowed to teach certain courses anymore, or when they are not allowed to teach at all anymore, or when they are somehow actually treated differently in their stature within the university. That has happened much too often.

Or when a student group is denied funding or student group is denied the prerogative of having a certain speaker. So I would draw the distinction between actual denial of certain benefits and opportunities that has to be protected against versus we're not going to shield you, even from very strong, very hurtful, very unfair criticism. You ought to be free to express really controversial ideas, even if other people say, "Those ideas hurt me."

Brotman: I'm not sure your position would sit well with the famous Kalven Report adopted by the University of Chicago in 1967, in which the university pledged not to take positions on public issues.

Strossen: I understand there is a plausible argument where the university says very strongly, "We are not going to take a position as an institution, on the public policy issues of the day, precisely because we want to amplify and support the freedom of every single member of this community—professors and students and others—to voice their ideas without fear of being punished, without any chilling effect by the university."

But it seems to me that universities are constantly proclaiming adherence to certain values that are important to them. The University of Chicago is Exhibit A. If you ask most people, and I revere the University of Chicago, about what association they have with the University of Chicago, I think they say its free speech principles. Here is the university publicly proclaiming them in the most wonderful, eloquent, persuasive way. It supports freedom of speech and academic freedom.

Why is it inconsistent for the university to say then, "We also champion equality of opportunity, nondiscrimination on the basis of not only what you think and what you believe but also on the basis of who you are." It seems to me inconsistent to so strongly proclaim one set of values as a university and not be willing to also fervently endorse what seems to me to be an integrally intertwined set of values.

Many other universities are going the opposite direction, where they celebrate diversity of every sort—of race, gender, gender identity, complete diversity in terms of who you are—but not diversity in terms of what you think or what your ideas can be. I believe very strongly that university leadership should constantly reaffirm its commitment to equality of opportunity and inclusive diversity. How could it condemn each particular incident of hateful expression? I think if it's a swastika or some clear-cut racist or sexist expression, the university should condemn it and its leadership should condemn it. I would get a little bit nervous, though, if it's somebody who's coming in and voicing an unpopular position on immigration issues, or even transgender policy issues. I get nervous when an unpopular idea that happens to have an impact on certain people is equated with hateful, incendiary, dehumanizing attacks on people. It's a slippery slope, I know.

Brotman: Public opinion seems to be moving in the other direction.

Strossen: Going back to the data from Gallup, they found that 37 percent of students on campus found it acceptable to essentially shut down speakers. And then 10 percent said they thought that violent means can be used to do that. How do we begin to promote a culture of counter speech in an environment where the data is showing us something very different? I and others have always argued in the pornography context, as well as in the hate speech context, that freedom of speech and equality and safety and dignity, far from being inconsistent are mutually reinforcing. That's been my constant theme as an advocate on all of the issues of controversial speech that we've been talking about.

Clearly, we have not made that case with sufficient persuasiveness to the current generation of activists. I always see the glass half-full as an activist myself. After decades of passivity on college campuses and statistics showing that students weren't even interested in following the news at all, let alone having an active role in current events, it's just been absolutely thrilling to see this resurgence in the past several years—of student activism and commitment to social justice and racial justice and gender justice. That's wonderful.

The dispiriting aspect is that they clearly see robust freedom of speech as undermining their equality goals. I have been trying to the best of my ability to be open-minded. I do not exalt freedom of speech above all else. There are values of equality and safety and dignity that are of equal importance. But I have always seen these values as being ultimately mutually reinforcing, at least in the long run.

In particular instances, there might be tensions or even conflicts. We have many years of actual experience with European countries and Canada, Australia—all over the world—undertaking the censorship of so-called hate speech. We have experiences in the United States of

96 The Conversations

other approaches to dealing with problems of hatred, discrimination, and stereotyping.

Censoring broad swaths of hateful expression cannot currently be permitted under our First Amendment. Why? Because it's not the least restrictive alternative to promoting equality and countering discrimination or discriminatory violence. What I'm describing is the test that the Supreme Court uses, because even the most zealous advocate of free speech on and off the Court doesn't say it's absolutely protected. If government can show that the particular restriction is necessary, and the least restrictive alternative, is to promote some countervailing goal of great importance—which certainly would include safety and human dignity and equality—then the censorship is justified. But the evidence from around the world has convinced me more than ever not only of the ineffectiveness of punishing more people for speech but that actually it is counterproductive.

Disproportionately, in country after country, we see what happened without a strong protection of speech earlier in U.S. history, which is that precisely those who are in the minority politically, or disempowered or marginalized, are the ones whose speech is disproportionately suppressed under every hate speech law. It's well known that the antidrug laws are being enforced in ways that are completely discriminatory on the basis of race and gender. Why in the world would we think that a law that gives even more unfettered discretion to the enforcer over speech that's disparaging or demeaning would work?

You know, hate is an emotion. The concept is inherently subjective. What is really interesting to me, looking at the evidence and the writings of other countries, is how many human rights activists there are in other countries that very broadly suppress hate speech. How many of them are criticizing their laws and saying their countries ought to move more in the direction of the United States? Under their country's free speech systems, it's completely permissible to censor a wide swath of hate speech. How is that actually and meaningfully advancing equality and countering extremist violence?

Brotman: What about hate speech that takes place in a private company or a private university?

Strossen: Most people are shocked to learn that not only does the First Amendment not give you any rights against Facebook or the *New York Times*, but to the contrary, all of those entities have their own First Amendment rights, which include the right not to publish or the right to kick off somebody who had been given a platform in the past.

I strongly defend their free speech rights. I would oppose any government law that purported to tell, for example, a social media company, "You must censor certain speech, or you may not censor certain speech." That would violate their own free speech rights. But I do strongly encourage powerful private sector entities that, for all practical purposes, are a gateway to the rest of us voicing our ideas. I strongly urge them to please voluntarily exercise your power in a way that is consistent with First Amendment values.

Take our university campuses again. Many people will be shocked that the Harvards and the Princetons of the world, by virtue of being private-sector institutions, have no obligation to respect academic freedom, freedom of inquiry, freedom of research, freedom of speech, and yet the vast, vast majority of private-sector educational institutions voluntarily choose to honor those same principles that would be constitutionally mandated on a public campus. That's because they believe it is consistent with their mission.

Let's take social media as an example. It is no longer subject to debate that the most important platform is the internet, and in particular social media, for exchanging not only conversations and communications among all of us but between "We the People" and those we elect to represent us. So it is absolutely critical, not only to individual liberty but also to our democratic system of government, that we have the same robust freedom of speech on today's functional equivalent of the proverbial public square. But we have the worst of both worlds now, because power that only governments used to have in terms of either fostering or suppressing free speech now belongs to these huge social media giants. Yet as a legal matter, they are accountable only to their shareholders.

In the case of Facebook, that means only to one person, right? So on the one hand, they have even more power than government has had in the past. On the other hand, they are not subject to the First Amendment constraints that the government is subject to. They have the power to suppress our speech, including selectively suppressing our speech. They have no accountability.

In the past, as a civil libertarian, I used to say, "Well, it's a trade-off between whom do I distrust more, the government or the private sector. Now, I have to say, at least in theory and through the structure of our Constitution, the government is accountable to us." But we can't really hold the private-sector actors here accountable. I'm very concerned about how that power is being exercised.

I disagree with conservatives who say, "Oh, the social media companies are discriminating against conservatives." But the fact is, they could blatantly decide to do that. It would be completely constitutional and lawful, or they could decide we're going to censor the ACLU or civil libertarians, and there would be no legal mechanism to stop that. I consider this just an extremely serious problem for free speech.

Brotman: There is a growing perception that social media may be a free speech problem itself.

Strossen: I will be the first person to admit that my thoughts on this in terms of potential solutions are completely half-baked. I say that not apologetically, because it is such a complex issue. I'm thinking about it every day.

Today, I had a conversation with three people from Facebook who are working on content moderation standards. I can define the problem very strongly but I'm very nervous about the solutions. To me, the potential solutions are in the category of what is the lesser of all of the available evils. Is it going to be government regulation?

I remember the problems with the so-called fairness doctrine that used to be enforced against the broadcast media. Sounds very good. I know a lot of liberals supported it, but well-intentioned as it might have been, I think it did more harm than good and became a tool for a government to manipulate the media. I'm not happy having Facebook or Twitter exert all that power, but I don't want government exerting it either.

I'm not anti-capitalist. I defend the free market system. I think it's the best way we've come up with so far. I respect their First Amendment rights. If only we developed user empowerment tools to facilitate every end user of social media or websites or any communications outlet online, to develop and choose our own filters. One person could say, "I don't want any hate speech." Another could say, "I don't want any nudity or pornography," and another person could say, "I don't want any conservative speech," right? I know, people will say, "But that's just the echo chamber."

So what? We have a freedom to choose what we do not want to hear, as well as what we do want to hear. I think that third parties could be empowered technologically to offer filtering options. I could go for the ACLU program, or somebody else could go for the Christian Coalition program, or somebody else could go for the Andrea Dworkin program. That would not only facilitate individual freedom of choice but the businesses would be trying to create congenial environments for their users. If each user has the power to design his or her own menu of options, how much better tailored could it be?

Brotman: What about speech that undermines our way of life, our social order?

Strossen: That was the rationale in the McCarthy era, the Cold War era, for the Supreme Court. It actually allowed criminal punishment of leaders of the Communist Party and of others merely for teaching classic works of Marxism and Leninism. The Court reasoned that the danger was not very imminent, but it would be catastrophic if it led to a communist overthrow, no matter how far in the future that might be, no matter how remote.

More recently, the Supreme Court has used the emergency standard to limit when government may restrict speech. The overall concept is when speech directly causes specific, serious, imminent harm. Even those words allow some room for discretion. I think discretion cannot be eliminated completely, but demanding a tight and clear causal nexus between the speech and a specific, serious harm, and demanding that the government produce evidence of that imminence and likelihood, should sufficiently reduce the discretion.

The Supreme Court has more strongly in the past fifty years coalesced around that concept, abdicating what used to be called the bad tendency, or harmful tendency, concept, which is still something that is adhered to by many people, including on college campuses. To them, that speech

100 The Conversations

might lead people to have negative ideas and might lead them to engage in violence or discriminatory conduct. I think it's really important to explain when we had that looser, more permissive standard that is exactly what government used to punish any leftist ideas, any ideas of social justice or law reform.

It's hard for people today to imagine or to remember how dangerous and subversive and threatening and offensive and insulting speech in support of civil rights was considered to be, not to mention women's rights. There were speaker bans on college campuses. Not only left-of-center socialists and communists but also civil rights advocates were banned from speaking at many universities throughout the South.

Brotman: What about protection of artistic expression?
Strossen: I have to explain that artistic expression is protected by the First Amendment. That might sound very obvious, but it was something that had been seriously debated in this country. No less influential a lawyer and jurist than Robert Bork, who had been nominated for the United States Supreme Court, wrote a very celebrated article in which he argued that the First Amendment should not apply to artistic expression but should only apply to political expression. Bork had the narrowest view of protected speech as being speech that is directly related to the political process. That meant it had to be speech that was on an expressly political or public policy topic, which was communicated from one person to another.

One of the reasons why John Marshall Harlan's opinion for the majority in the *Cohen v. California* case was so important is that it so strongly and persuasively rejected both of those limiting concepts. It explicitly rejected the concept that you had to have acceptable mainstream political ideological discourse, a discussion of public policy ideas. He defended the right to use a very shocking word that would not have been considered part of mainstream political discourse.

He also very strongly said that an independent reason for protecting speech is self-expression. Even if you are not communicating an idea or anything to anybody else, the fact that you are expressing your own emotions, as well as your own ideas, is independently protected under the First Amendment. That idea, that very broad concept of protected expression,

Nadine Strossen 101

actually goes all the way back to a landmark opinion by Justice Louis Brandeis. He very famously said freedom of speech is protected, not only as a means to communication and self-government, but also as an end in and of itself.

A free individual should be able to freely express anything, including emotions as well as ideas. Art certainly satisfies all those definitions. Now the question about government funding is a little bit more tricky because that goes beyond the question whether art is protected expression to whether government denial of funding for art is an abridgement of speech? Congress could not pass a law denying Robert Mapplethorpe the right to display his photographs, or denying an art museum the right to display his photographs. But is Robert Mapplethorpe or the museum that's displaying his photographs entitled to government funding for that art?

Brotman: This issue has arisen in funding provided by the National Endowment for the Arts.

Strossen: The issue is a little bit more complicated, because on one hand, you have no right to a government subsidy for your expression. On the other hand, if the government creates a program where it voluntarily decides we want to promote the arts and therefore we are going to fund that, it must do so in a way that does not discriminate against particular works solely because of their viewpoint.

It would be completely lawful for the government to say, "We think that the artistic merit of these works is not worthy of government funding." That would be a logically neutral criterion. But the ACLU represented feminists and LGBT artists who were using their art to express ideas of sexual, gender, and sexual orientation equality. It was very clear from the evidence that was the reason that they were denied funding. And that should be unconstitutional.

Brotman: Money as speech is another thorny issue to confront.

Strossen: Campaign finance is the toughest issue to persuade liberals. I think most people seem to equate money and politics with danger and evil and the undermining of democracy. To me, it's part of the same category of regulations we've been talking about, where the regulation is advocated for a very worthy purpose that I completely support. The restrictions on pornography advocated by feminists in the pro-censorship faction are to promote equality for women and safety for women. I couldn't support that more enthusiastically. Restrictions on hate speech are proposed to advance equality and dignity and diversity and inclusiveness. I couldn't support those goals more, likewise.

With respect to so-called campaign finance reform, its goal is to open up equal access to the political process for all of us, to encourage a multiplicity of opportunities for candidates and for voters. Equal access not only to run for and be elected to office but also to influence those who are in office. I couldn't be more enthusiastic about all of these goals.

Yet, as well intended as all these measures are, they are not effective in promoting their asserted goals. Worse yet, they are actually counterproductive. When you look at how the campaign finance laws have actually operated in practice, they are incumbent protection laws. They make it harder for any new candidate, or they did make it harder before the age of social media, which raises another possible objection to these laws. In the old days, you really needed a lot of money to get your message out there, through advertising over the broadcast media. It's not a coincidence that these laws overlapped with increasing reelection of incumbents and decreasing opportunities either for insurgent candidates to challenge to get the nomination and run for office or for somebody who was not already in office to be elected.

Is there any chance that those who are in power are going to write a law that's going to make it harder for them to get reelected? I don't think so. The ACLU had a long history of bringing challenges to laws that were asserted to benefit those in the grassroots. Those in the grassroots were actually being silenced by how these laws operated.

Take Eugene McCarthy. Let me explain to those who don't know who he was. McCarthy was a Democratic senator from Minnesota, a leading opponent to the Vietnam War, and ran an amazing insurgent candidacy against President Lyndon Johnson based on the antiwar issue. He threw his hat in the ring on that issue and brought it to the forefront before Robert Kennedy did. I think history gives McCarthy an enormous amount of credit for energizing the antiwar movement, getting Johnson to decline to run for reelection.

McCarthy energized my generation to get involved in the political process. He had a wonderful progressive impact on an energized grassroots. I remember college students, even high school students, had a mantra, "Clean for Gene." They got involved in the political process as a kind of a precursor to what we've seen more recently with another new young generation. Gene used to say, "I don't understand how people can support these campaign finance laws; don't they understand that my candidacy could never have gotten off the ground if any of those restrictions had been in effect."

That's because by limiting the amount of money that you can raise from any one source, it means you have to have a much wider base of support. This was easy to do if you're an incumbent. But when you're unknown, and when you're challenging somebody who's the president of the United States, the only way to develop the momentum to get your message out there so that you can reach all those people is by having to start with a core base of supporters and they each are able to give you a huge amount of money. So the idea of campaign finance reform sounds good, but in practical reality it's been absolutely counterproductive.

Brotman: What's the alternative?

Strossen: The question is, what do we do instead? I think it's really important as a civil libertarian and as an advocate, and as an educator, to not just shoot down people's preferred speech suppressive method to achieve goals, especially when I support the goals wholeheartedly.

Here's where I would part company with a lot of conservatives, if not all conservatives. I think we need really complete, comprehensive government financing of campaigns for all ballot-qualified candidates. It's a pittance. The amount of money is shockingly small, you know, dwarfed by the advertising budgets and the support of major corporations. I think that would be the best investment that we could make in democracy. To some extent, what I've just said is even less pressing in the context of social media, where it doesn't take as much money. It certainly doesn't take the amount of money that it used to take to buy broadcast ads to get a message out there. And it's easier to raise. So the alleged justifications for limiting campaign finance are even less

104 The Conversations

persuasive in the age of social media. It's almost like, "Where's the problem?" See how many new faces are able to be elected now?

Brotman: Doesn't free speech rely on cultural support for legitimacy in the law?

Strossen: That's exactly the right question. I really do think that the culture is the driving force of the law. Learned Hand gave this famous Bill of Rights speech in 1944 called "The Spirit of Liberty." He said, "The spirit of liberty lives in the hearts of men and women. If it lives there, it needs no law, no court, no constitution to save it. If it does not live there, no court, no constitution can save it."

A similar idea was voiced by Zechariah Chafee, who was a pioneering free speech scholar at Harvard Law School. He wrote one of the first treatises on freedom of speech and was one of the founders and early board members of the ACLU. He said that in the long run, people will have as much freedom of speech as they want. I really think that that's true.

If there is not cultural support for free speech, we're not going to elect candidates who support free speech. We'll then have judges who don't support free speech, not to mention having new laws that don't support free speech.

We have to distinguish between an instinctive response and a more considered one. It just seems like everybody has an instinct about why you should not have the right to say something that's so horrible. I'm trying very hard to persuade people to examine this with a more considered perspective. I'm encouraged because I have encountered quite a few people who have told me that they were very skeptical of my position but now completely changed their views or strongly moved closer to my direction.

Brotman: It sounds like you could be called a free speech optimist.

Strossen: I'm a congenital optimist. I think it comes hand in hand with being an activist, but it also comes hand in hand with a review of history. I think the trajectory has been a constant increase of support for civil liberties, not only in the law but also in the culture.

As we've just discussed, you really can't have legal or political advances without cultural support. The pendulum always is swinging back and forth. I think there is even a silver lining to the cloud of the censorship that exists today, which is mostly self-censorship, and the more external censorship that is being exercised by those who are not constrained by the First Amendment, namely the social media companies.

So many activists are complaining about how they are being censored on Facebook, Twitter, and so forth. Black Lives Matter, for example, is complaining. When they are quoting hate speech for purposes of denouncing it, for purposes of calling out racism, for purposes of seeking support for people who are disparaged, and for other completely laudable purposes, that itself is treated as hate speech. Their accounts are taken down or their posts are blocked.

This is part of a continuing pattern ever since content moderation began, no matter how well-intentioned the guidelines are. I have no doubt that these companies are predominantly liberal. From what I can tell, they are supportive of racial and gender justice.

I hope to be able to convince people that censorship is not the way to go. The stronger message I really want to pound is about the value of counter speech. My research has convinced me that censorship is even less effective than I had thought before. I also am much more optimistic about the efficacy of counter speech than I had been before.

I've recently been steeping myself in all the different ways that we can use our voices to change people's hearts and minds. Some of it has to do with just building relationships. People will say, "Oh, but there's all this evidence that if somebody has this wrongheaded idea, or bad idea, that if you give them evidence that's not going to change their minds. It's just going to harden their positions."

That may seem very frustrating. When you probe deeper, it has to do with the fact that people often support hateful or discriminatory ideas not due to ideological reasons or analysis. Instead, they have emotional reasons, psychological reasons, sociological reasons. They have some family situation problems. They are alienated, isolated, or have bad school situations. Then they become recruited either online or offline and a bond forms. Then they will adopt an ideology to be part of the group.

The good news is we can work on dissolving those bonds and creating other bonds. There are all these narratives about people who are so generous, who build compassionate, empathetic relationships, even with leaders of hate-mongering organizations. It sounds a little bit religious. A lot of religious people are involved. They redeem these people, not by having ideological debates but just by building alternative human relationships, gradually developing trust, and then ultimately these people will do their own conversion away from hate.

That's why I think major support can be found in the growing movement toward criminal justice reform, all across the ideological spectrum. The notion of restorative justice is powerful. If we're going to forgive condemned murderers and those who commit other violent crimes and look for rehabilitation and restoration rather than punishment, why in the world can't we do that for somebody whose infraction is to say something that's hateful? So this approach to free speech really is consistent with an overall shift in emphasis away from punishment and retribution.

Burt Neuborne

Burt Neuborne is the Norman Dorsen Professor of Civil Liberties Emeritus and founding legal director of the Brennan Center for Justice at New York University Law School. For more than fifty years, he has been one of the nation's foremost civil liberties lawyers, serving as national legal director of the ACLU from 1981 to 1986, special counsel to the NOW [National Organization of Women] Legal Defense and Education Fund from 1990 to 1996, and as a member of the New York City Human Rights Commission from 1988 to 1992. He has argued numerous Supreme Court cases and litigated literally hundreds of important constitutional cases in the state and federal courts.

He challenged the constitutionality of the Vietnam War, pioneered the flag-burning cases, worked on the Pentagon Papers case, worked with the late Justice Ruth Bader Ginsburg when she headed the ACLU Women's Rights Project, anchored the ACLU's legal program during the Reagan years, and defended the nation's legal services program against unconstitutional attacks. From 1995 to 2007, he directed the legal program of the Brennan Center, focusing on efforts to reinforce American democracy and secure campaign finance reform.

Neuborne has forged a national reputation as a constitutional scholar and teacher. In 1990, he was the recipient of the university-wide Distinguished Teacher Award at New York University for excellence in classroom teaching. He is the author of four books and over eighty law review articles on diverse areas of constitutional law and procedure. In 2001, in recognition of his scholarship and his work in the courts, Neuborne was elected to membership in the American Academy of Arts and Sciences.

Stuart Brotman: Let's start with the beginning of your own First Amendment journey.

Burt Neuborne: I've been deeply aware of the First Amendment for much of my life. I don't know that I would have called it the First Amendment in those days, but I was deeply aware of issues of free speech, freedom of conscience, and freedom of political belief. I grew up during the [Senator Joseph] McCarthy era. My father was a very strong opponent of McCarthy. He was a deeply committed, left-wing radical, proud of his World War II service against fascism. He may even have been a member of the American Communist Party. I don't know, he never told me one way or the other.

But I watched my father and his friends live with real fear during this period. I closely followed the efforts of many of his friends to avoid having their lives ruined because of what they believed. It made an enormous impression on me.

I was born in 1941, so I came to political understanding in the late 1940s and early 1950s. That experience shaped my thinking about the First Amendment as a shield for people with unpopular, controversial beliefs. In the early 1960s, I watched as the First Amendment provided a shield, enabling groups like the civil rights movement, Dr. [Martin Luther] King's opposition to the war in Vietnam, and a host of social movements to demand greater justice. It seemed to me that robust protection of free speech provided the umbrella under which reformers could shelter while they spoke and organized, seeking to have an effect on the population at large. So, I came to view robust First Amendment protection as a precondition to serious reform. It would allow weak groups to organize and gain traction, eventually assembling enough mass support to really change things.

I've never believed that courts, standing alone, could change things. What I did believe is that courts could keep government off the back of people long enough so that they could organize and put themselves in a position to change things.

I've always viewed the courts as an instrumental mechanism that provided for breathing space between the weak and the government, allowing the weak to organize in an effort to change things structurally.

Brotman: Was any of this discussed at your family kitchen table?
Neuborne: I came from a very political family. My father and I talked about politics all the time. I went to law school in large part because I wanted to become a union organizer. I thought that the union movement,

which I viewed as the First Amendment right to free association in action, was the mechanism by which the poor could organize and become strong enough to effect real change.

When I was in college, it's no coincidence that I majored in Chinese history. The idea of China "turning over" and becoming this new, powerful workers' state fascinated and inspired me. I was sure that law school would empower me to work within the union movement for a worker-dominated society.

Then, I went to Harvard Law School. Within three years, I had abandoned my dream of working in the labor movement. Newly married, I wanted to impress my in-laws, who were lovely but quite conventional people. I did a 180-degree turn. Instead of working for a union, I went to Wall Street and practiced as a tax lawyer for the rich. The union movement had bitterly disappointed me. It was being used to block people of color and women from entering and thriving in the workforce. It was being run by white male shop stewards who were abusing their power in what seemed to me to be corrupt and unequal ways.

I lost faith in the union movement in those three years. How much of that was the intellectual influence of Harvard Law School, how much a desire to please my in-laws, and how much the failure of the union movement, I'll never know.

At the end of those three Harvard years, I took a job with a major Wall Street firm. Since I was very good at tax law, and very good at property law, I thought, "that's what God was telling me I was supposed to do." So, I took a Wall Steet job as a young associate with a specialty in estate taxation. Believe it or not, I helped plan the estates of several very prominent and wealthy families, so that they could move their vast assets from one generation to another with virtually no taxation. Those were the years when we had a really high estate tax topping out at 90 percent, but you could get around it if you were good. And I was good. So, I thrived on Wall Street for three years but became increasingly unhappy with my work.

Brotman: Let's talk a bit more about the source of your unhappiness.
Neuborne: This is the late 1960s. The world was going to hell in a handbasket, and I'm planning estates and tricking stupid, rich kids into signing agreements that tied up their money? Their rich parents were afraid

that they would fritter it away with gambling, drugs, and fast cars. I was the young lawyer who would go out and have a drink and talk them into signing the trust agreement that tied up their money forever. I was good at it. As a reward, the law firm decided to send me to Bermuda around tax time to get tax returns signed by several clients. The firm represented a number of very rich widows. So, the partners gave me four or five tax returns, a first-class plane ticket, and a room in an excellent hotel. The partners said, "Go spend a couple days to relax, get all this stuff signed, and come back."

I landed in Bermuda with a briefcase full of tax returns and a bathing suit. I was in for a shock. The rich clients saw that I was Jewish and had me sit in the kitchen with the other servants while they signed the tax returns.

I realized then that I was living my life as a highly educated tool of rich folks who treated me as just a skilled servant. I recall thinking that: "This is not what I was put on earth to do." I don't know whether it was my anger at not being allowed into their houses, or my increasing understanding that I was living a work life that was not consistent with my ideals. But in 1967, after three years, I left Wall Street. I just had to get out.

I lucked into a job at the New York Civil Liberties Union, the New York State affiliate of the ACLU.

Brotman: It sounds like this was the beginning of a major shift in your professional life.

Neuborne: It was. When I graduated from law school in 1964, there were only a few legal aid societies. There were only two full-time lawyers at the ACLU, so it never occurred to me that I could make a career in public-interest law. This is 1967. But I applied and, amazingly, I got the job. I still don't know why.

At my job interview, I was asked if I was a member of the ACLU. I said no. I admitted quite frankly that, until a couple of weeks ago, I had never heard of the organization. I was a kid from Queens, the first of my family to go to college. I knew about the union movement but I didn't know anything about the ACLU. As an undergraduate at Cornell in the late 1950s, I had attended meetings of the Student League for Industrial Democracy, which became SDS, but that was the sum total of my political education.

"Okay," the ACLU interviewer said, "you'll learn." Then they hired me. That's when I began to realize what the First Amendment could mean. My constitutional law classes at Harvard had been intensely skeptical about robust judicial protection of equality-based constitutional rights. Everybody I met at Harvard Law, from the dean to my fellow students, thought that radical change was illegitimate. The faculty made no bones about what they thought. In fact, I got a B in constitutional law (my lowest grade in law school) because I fought them. I kept writing radical reform stuff that the faculty didn't like. They would say to me: "That's very imaginative, but it's not law."

On June 1, 1967, I started at the NYCLU/ACLU, on a one-year leave of absence from my Wall Street law firm, to defend anti–Vietnam War demonstrators who were being arrested in massive numbers. Most didn't qualify for legal aid because they had a little money, but they also couldn't afford private counsel.

The ACLU made a lovely but rash promise that it would provide counsel to everybody who was arrested in a demonstration where they were engaged in protected activity. I was hired to fulfill that promise at the New York Civil Liberties Union, where massive arrests were taking place. That's how I learned how to be a trial lawyer. Before taking the ACLU job, I'd never been in court. For literally a year, I tried two cases a day. They were almost all simple disorderly conduct cases charging the defendant with obstructing traffic and defying a lawful order to disperse.

I soon developed a way to challenge cops' testimony. I quickly learned that the mass arrests were being carried out by loading the people to be charged onto buses. As the buses were unloaded, each protestor/defendant was assigned an arresting officer. If the arresting officer told the truth in court, the arresting officer could not testify as an eyewitness about the defendant's activities. So I would cross-examine the cop's testimony in the hope of getting a reasonable doubt dismissal from the judge.

Everybody knew what was going on. There were three kinds of cops. There were the cops who were embarrassed about the whole idea of mass arrests. It was easy to challenge their testimony. They would actually admit that they didn't see the defendant do anything but get off a bus.

Then there were the cops that didn't really care one way or another. They thought, "Hey, this is my job, I'll do what I can to get a conviction, but there are limits." There was a limit to the amount of lies they were willing to tell to get a conviction.

Finally, there was a relatively small group, I'd say 10 to 20 percent of the cops I dealt with, who believed that it was their job to lie, that these kids deserved what they were getting. If, these cops thought, the system was going to let them fall through the cracks because the arrests were poorly organized, there was something wrong with the system. They were determined to fix the cracks by making up whatever story they needed to secure a conviction. I earned my money by cross-examining this group of cops.

Brotman: It sounds like you were using procedural mechanisms to achieve substantive outcomes.

Neuborne: Exactly. That's essentially been the story of my career—the intersection of process and substance and the degree to which process shapes substance. Luckily, at the end of that year in criminal court, the ACLU had enough money to take me on full time. That's when I began to bring cases seeking to expand First Amendment protection of rights allowing people to assemble and to exercise free speech. I also began to think for the first time about First Amendment theory.

Among my early free speech cases were flag desecration cases. They all came out in New York in the late 1960s as the anti-war movement collided with the use of the flag to support the Vietnam War. It was my job to put together a theory that would close the gap between verbal and symbolic speech. In those days, speech meant only verbal speech. A lot of my early work was to explain why symbolic, nonverbal speech should be as protected as verbal speech, and then to try to build a theory that would enable us to argue that the flag-desecration statutes were unconstitutional as violations of symbolic speech. Symbolic speech seemed very important to me as a vehicle for the poor to express their concerns.

The ubiquitous statutes banning flag desecration forbade numerous uses or misuses of the flag, including flag burning. As a matter of strategy, we put flag burning last because I was sure that we didn't have five votes for it in the Supreme Court. I remember a conversation at ACLU headquarters on Fifth Avenue laying out a long-term strategy to reach flag-burning, but only once a strong foundation had been laid down.

Burt Neuborne 113

We started with cases in which verbal insults to the flag were forbidden, eventually winning a five-to-four victory in the Supreme Court. I then worked on a case where a kid sewed a flag patch on his ass and was arrested for casting contempt on the flag. With a straight face, I argued that the statute was "void for vagueness" because casting contempt could mean so many different things. I still remember the question: "Didn't your client realize that putting the flag on his ass was contempt?"

I said, "What my client actually thought shouldn't matter. You really need to ask whether the phrase 'casts contempt' is vague generally, whether it will deter large numbers of other people from engaging in protected speech." Of course, what I was doing at that point was doing what I have done throughout my life. That's to take First Amendment process (the ban on vague statutes) and use it as a way of expanding First Amendment activity (protest against the war). Another early case involved middle-class folks who put flag decals on their cars with peace symbols imprinted on them. Believe it or not, a Nassau County DA threatened to prosecute under the flag desecration statute.

Brotman: Were you always successful with these cases at the trial level?
Neuborne: We were often successful at the trial level, but not always. It made an enormous difference in which courtroom we were arguing the case. Sometimes we started in state court, by defending a pending criminal case; sometimes we began in federal court, by affirmatively going after a statute before an arrest had been made.

Along with several other lawyers, I pioneered such a federal preemptive strike strategy. Suing preemptively would enable us to be able to control what the factual record looked like. If you waited for an arrest, you never knew what was going to happen, you never know if someone's going to throw a punch. But if you could go in first—preemptively—you could shape the record and you could pick your client and your judge.

Those were the years when the procedural rules in federal court for assigning judges to new cases were not sophisticated enough to stop massive judge shopping by plaintiffs and the government. There were all sorts of ways to do it. Often, I filed late on a Friday afternoon, on the assumption that the judges I didn't want would be unavailable on the golf course. For example, take cases in Buffalo federal court, which is in the

Northern District of New York. There were two district judges there. All of the even-number cases would go to one guy, and all of the odd-number cases would go to the other. It was common knowledge. They were different politically. One was very conservative. One was quite liberal. So each got the cases they wanted. They knew just what they were doing.

I recall standing in line in the Northern District of New York clerk's office to file my complaint. The clerks were busy assigning cases consecutively, even numbers to one judge, odd numbers to the other. So I would stand on the line and crane my neck to see what number was being given out to somebody three or four places ahead of me. I would then use my rudimentary math skills to calculate whether I would draw an even or odd number. When I was going to get the wrong judge, I would have to go to the bathroom and then get back on line. My bladder would point back to the other judge. As a young lawyer, I quickly realized that the identity of the judge made a huge difference in what the law would be. Even if it shouldn't, it did.

Brotman: What about attitudes outside the courtroom that were influencing judges?

Neuborne: Public attitudes were very important. There's something I call the "psychic constitution." The "psychic constitution" is made up of people's beliefs and understandings about what life and law should be like. These are outside formal court lines. This is the legal zeitgeist. My experience was that it doesn't matter much what the written words in the text say if the psychic constitution doesn't believe it. You can talk about freedom all you want and equality all you want. But if you've got a psychic constitution of authoritarianism and racism, the law's just not going to work. That's the story of the failure of the equal protection clause in the years after the Civil War.

There was no psychic constitution deeply protective of free speech until the early 1960s. Until then, free speech protection was looked at grudgingly as a necessary evil to protect people who you didn't like very much, but who nevertheless should be allowed a degree of tolerance. These were the people that you would not invite to dinner but you didn't want to put in jail. So there was an anti-establishment element to the idea of free speech case.

Somewhere along the road in the 1960s, the moral force of the civil rights movement and the passion of the anti-war movement amended our psychic constitution about the importance of protecting free speech. All of a sudden, the speakers were us. There was also a great upsurge in popular pride in having our country become a bastion of free expression. More people became card-carrying members of the ACLU, or at least fellow travelers. Respect for free speech differentiated us from the bad commies, the bad Nazis, the bad totalitarianism people.

We, on the other hand, were the good guys who allowed this stuff to happen. We would be not just grudgingly tolerant of robust free speech protection as a necessary evil, but affirmatively proud of it. Free speech protection became an affirmative talking point in people's lives about what a great place this country was, about this sense of hope that was spreading about openness to needed change.

In the late 1960s, everything seemed to be opening; everything seemed possible. Free speech was one of the engines that would make that happen and one of the things that we cared enormously about. The Supreme Court was extraordinarily concerned with race in those years, and combined with this pride in the First Amendment, a legal doctrinal breakthrough occurred that was astonishing. The political movements pushed the First Amendment forward. It eventually culminated in the flag-burning cases, which are important because they were bipartisan and because they became iconic. They created a kind of psychological starting point. If flag burning is protected, the public could understand the power of the First Amendment. So could everyone around the world.

Brotman: I know that you were experiencing this at the same time as you traveled abroad.
Neuborne: In those years, I was doing a large amount of work speaking outside the United States, thinking I was defending American values. I thought that was what I was supposed to do as a young lawyer. I had no idea that my travel was being paid by the CIA. I had absolutely no idea that every one of those speeches was ultimately funded by the CIA.

When I spoke abroad, the very first thing anybody wanted to talk about were the flag cases. Everywhere. They wished their country could be like that. I was, of course, interacting with only a relatively small number of elite lawyers all around the world, but those flag cases resonated as something that everybody could understand, because you could take the symbol of the country and burn it in public. They used to say to me, "Oh, my God, how confident you guys have to be? How secure you have to be in order to do that." And I said, "We are confident and we are secure because we're right." How's that for smugness?

Brotman: How can this "rightness" be conveyed in a way that people can understand at an intuitive level?

Neuborne: Supreme Court justice William Brennan used to say that there are two reasons why we should care about the First Amendment. First, the "dignitary" reason, saying that's what differentiates human beings from everything else on the planet, this sense of being vested with individual dignity. It may be religious, it may be secular, where it comes from is unimportant. It's that we are committed to it, and that being an individual automatically includes the capacity to express oneself. So being faithful to the idea of human dignity requires you to protect the freedom to speak.

Justice Brennan also said there's another hugely important reason to protect speech. It's functionally critical to the proper functioning of institutions based on choice—like democracy and a market economy. Unless we allow people to express opinions freely, we will not get the free flow of information that's needed to allow a free marketplace of ideas to operate in politics or economics. Free speech is functionally important as a way of reinforcing the free flow of information needed for self-expression and informed choice. We can't allow the government to regulate speech because it's so important and because government can't be trusted to manage the flow.

Brotman: How influential was Justice Brennan in persuading others on the Supreme Court to decide First Amendment cases based on this line of thinking?

Neuborne: Very influential. What I call the "First Amendment Era of Good Feelings," in which both the left and the right were joined in his commitment to the free speech model, began to emerge in the late 1960s when the majority of Supreme Court justices adopted Justice Brennan's perspective. In the next ten to fifteen years, a tremendously powerful First Amendment doctrine emerged in the Court.

This was an era of unparalleled support on both the left and right for the idea of free speech. The left saw it as an engine of reform and as a way to fight for equality. The right saw it as a bastion of individual autonomy. They came together on free speech, and it became an overwhelming, powerful legal argument. But then, at some point after the campaign finance debacle, the left begins to say to itself, "Wait a minute, we thought free speech is a destabilizing idea; a way to attack an unequal status quo. Free speech is supposed to empower the people at the bottom to reach out and be able to organize to stop inequality." The left liked the idea of protected speech when it worked that way.

But it soon became apparent that robust free speech protection provides enormous individual autonomy protections too—protections of the power of the strong to speak, to keep themselves in power. The left learned that protected speech by the strong can lock in an unequal status quo. Thus, by the 1990s, the era of free speech good feelings disappears. There's no longer a common commitment to robust free speech. That's when you begin to get the speech wars.

The speech wars begin to break out in the 1990s over campaign finance reform; over hate speech, especially on campus; and over aspects of the commercial speech doctrine. You begin to hear people saying, "Wait a minute, wait a minute. If the speech is systematically harmful to large numbers of people, and they don't want to hear it, can the government force the speech down their throats in the guise of First Amendment protection?" That's when I believe the equal dignity and the individual autonomy wings of the Supreme Court came apart.

I began to realize that the First Amendment era of good feelings papered over very different reasons for supporting free speech. The conservative Republican Supreme Court justices were persuaded because they saw robust free speech protection as just another way of deregulating human behavior. "It's deregulatory jurisprudence. We love it." So they embraced the First Amendment.

Then, the left begins to realize that a powerful First Amendment may not be a path to an equal future. Maybe it's a reinforcement of privilege inherent in the status quo. Serious thinkers on the left begin saying, "Have we made a bad deal? Is this really a good bargain?"

118 The Conversations

Brotman: What's an example of a Supreme Court case that reflected this earlier period of good feelings?

Neuborne: The *Skokie* case occurred during the height of this era of good feelings. It involved Nazis wanting to have a demonstration in Skokie, Illinois, which was a suburb of Chicago. It was a Jewish suburb of Chicago, where significant numbers of Holocaust survivors lived. The Nazis picked Skokie on purpose. I think they picked it thinking that they would be denied the right to march so that they could be martyrs and make a big deal of it.

They were, indeed, denied the right to march. The ACLU jumped in and got a court injunction requiring that they be permitted to march. We lost half of our Illinois ACLU affiliate membership overnight—gone. There were also significant defections around the rest of the country.

At the ACLU, all agreed that if the organization had any reason to exist, then this case was the reason. I argued that if we can't handle this case, then maybe we should find some other way to advance social justice, but let's not pretend that we're a free speech organization. So the ACLU leadership took a deep breath and bet the future of the organization on Skokie.

If you go back to those days, it's entirely possible we were talking about the destruction of the ACLU as an organization. It was like doubling down in blackjack and coming up with a twenty-one. It was remarkable. We not only won the court case, but then when the Nazis were given the chance to march, they didn't show up. We called their bluff and there was nothing there. So the case went down in history as an example of being willing to bet the organization on a bedrock commitment to free speech.

Brotman: Looking back in retrospect, do you have any second thoughts about taking this case on in such a visible way?

Neuborne: It was a courageous thing to do. It was the right thing to do as an organization. Once the ACLU took the Skokie case, though, it was under pressure to "double down" all the time. Your job becomes protecting increasingly troubling free speech exercises. Such a dynamic is an important psychological force to keep pushing ahead. But it also sets the organization up by being forced to represent uglier and uglier people. Skokie begets Charlottesville.

Brotman: Skokie begat Charlottesville, Virginia, in 2017 with the Unite the Right white supremacist rally there. There, hundreds of neo-Nazis seek to march in force in an area where they are sure to be met with resistance in the streets.

Neuborne: Yeah, absolutely. The big difference in Charlottesville is that there you had a larger neo-Nazi movement that was capable of doing real harm and a real threat of violence. It's possible to argue that Charlottesville begat January 6 [the attack on Congress as the 2020 electoral votes for president were being certified]. But I would still support what the ACLU did in Charlottesville, supporting and defending the free speech rights of the most heinous people. I would not support what Trump did on January 6 in goading a mob to engage in a violent coup.

Brotman: So how did the free speech zeitgeist you talked about begin to change?

Neuborne: It changed because of the public discussion of the corrosive effect of money in politics and the horrible explosion of hate speech on the internet. There's strong public concern about whether, when speech is concerned, removing the government entirely as a mediating force risks destroying the village in order to save it. I think by the 2000 election, there was skepticism about where we were going on the First Amendment.

I began to think to myself, "Maybe the only reason for protecting it is that you just can't trust the government with this kind of power." So it's just a prophylactic reason. If that's why we protect free speech, it's a choice of which dangerous source of power you trust less—dangerous collections of private power or dangerous collections of public power? There are some speech settings where, with all its dangers of government overreach, I would rather be regulated by the public because at least I have a chance to fight against them. The powerful private regulator, like big tech, is absolutely beyond my capacity to do anything about. So now I'm much more ambivalent about First Amendment theory that completely insulates private speakers from government regulation while allowing the private speakers to regulate the speech of others.

I'm more troubled today than I was when I started back in the late sixties. I said to myself then, "Free speech doesn't have to earn its right to exist. It's a necessity because of human dignity." I now say, "But I have found it difficult to figure out why the idea of the dignity of a speaker includes a corporation, which has no soul." Corporations are legal fictions. They don't feel or aspire. The idea of dignity should not protect a corporation. There's dignity, of course, in the aspirations of individuals who make up a corporation—shareholders, management, workers, suppliers, customers, the surrounding community—and we should think and talk about their "dignitary" rights. But when you start talking about a collective abstract dignitary right of a corporation itself, I've never been able to link it to a dignitary theory of the First Amendment.

I've also come to realize that maybe I've been concentrating on the wrong person's dignity when I concentrate solely on the speaker. Maybe what we should be asking is, "Who's dignity should we be worried about—the listener's dignity? The dignity of the target?" Isn't that at least worthy of consideration as the speaker's dignity? Lately, we haven't been factoring it into our thinking. Maybe we've got to at least think a little bit about that, about a listener-centered free speech doctrine rather than an exclusively speaker-centered free speech doctrine.

Brotman: Is the younger, idealistic lawyer Burt Neuborne reconciled with the current version that has been tempered by time and experience?
Neuborne: I'm still as deeply committed to the First Amendment as a protection of the weak as I ever have been. I don't think we could ever hope to have peaceful change in this country unless you allow marginalized and weak people to speak freely. That requires erecting a secure barrier against government censorship. Once you allow government to disrupt the flow of information, you seriously damage the possibility of building a political and social movement that can be large enough and powerful enough to change things.

Brotman: I know that one of our nation's founding fathers, James Madison, holds a special place in your heart and mind.
Neuborne: Indeed. If you look back to Madison's work in the historic summer of 1789, when the first U.S. Congress met, he was given the principal responsibility for coming up with the draft of our Bill of Rights. Madison originally didn't want a separate Bill of Rights. He wanted to

Burt Neuborne 121

interpolate his various thoughts into the text of the original Constitution in a way that would limit the government's exercise of a particular power.

Eldridge Gerry persuaded him that our rights should be put into a separate set of amendments. The Bill of Rights starts with the First Amendment. The First Amendment needs to be first for a reason. It's first because it articulates the substantive goals of religious tolerance and free expression that Madison hoped would hold the society together. Everything else in the Bill of Rights is a series of procedural rules designed to identify and minimize perceived dangers to the First Amendment "City on the Hill."

The First Amendment is carefully organized—forty-five words and six ideas. The first idea is no government establishment of religion—to keep the government out of people's religious and conscientious lives. The second is free exercise of religion to assure freedom to behave in accordance with conscience. The third is free speech. The fourth is a free press. The fifth is free assembly. And the sixth is the right to petition the government for redress of grievances. Six luminous ideas—the only time in human history that those ideas have ever been put together in that order in a single document. They exist in other documents, of course, but not all of them and never in that order.

If you think about the order, it replicates the life cycle of a democratic idea. You start with the establishment clause, which is, after all, the protection of what goes on in the interior of somebody's mind, the freedom to think and to believe in a particular way and not be told by the state what to believe. Then the free exercise clause protects freedom to act in accordance with your conscience. Those two clauses are the absolute precondition for self-government. You can't have a self-governing people unless they are empowered to be able to think for themselves and believe what they wish, and to live their lives in compliance with their basic beliefs. If you crush that, you crush their sense of dignity, you crush their ability to act, and then you have squelched in advance any speech they want to be able to articulate.

Brotman: The power of speech is enormous.
Neuborne: Yes. And speech looks in both directions. Speech has a dignitary component, in that you're articulating the things that you have in

your mind. But it also has a functional component, because you're also articulating ideas that are necessary for the democratic process to function.

Then you have press, the idea of a free press as an amplification device. Only if speech is allowed to work on a mass scale will we be able to actually change things. That's what free press is about. Press freedom is the guarantee of speech on a mass scale. The amplifier, the conduit. The press can also be a speaker, depending upon its function. But you want to ask what function it's performing. Is it performing an amplification function or is it performing a speech function?

Then assembly, and it makes sense, because first you have freedom of thought, then you express the thought, then the thought gets disseminated to a mass audience through the press. Once it's disseminated to a mass audience through the press, the next logical step is to assemble. You couldn't put assembly first, since there would be nothing to assemble about. It's exactly where it's supposed to be in the half-life of a democracy.

In the late twentieth and now the twenty-first century, given communications, "assembly" is a virtual idea. You don't have to physically assemble. You can virtually associate on Facebook or be in a political party. Nevertheless, once you've associated or assembled in that way, the next logical step is to use your political power to go to the government and petition for redress of grievances. Fix it, put something or someone else in.

That's where I argue that the First Amendment right to vote is waiting to be discovered. The First Amendment right to vote is hiding in plain sight right there in the sixth idea—the petition clause. Without it, the last crucial part of the First Amendment's brilliant organization doesn't work.

So that's a summary of the thinking in my book, *Madison's Music*. I hope someday to persuade the Supreme Court to adopt it. As we go forward, evolving First Amendment doctrine must be shaped by the values underlying Madison's brilliant plan.

Brotman: How do you bring those values back into the psychic constitution?

Neuborne: You've got to have genuine political leadership. One of the tragedies of American life is that, once upon a time, the Supreme Court was a prophetic voice. When I was a young lawyer, the Supreme Court was the voice of moral prophecy, the voice of "We can be better, we are moving to a better place." Then, during and after the Reagan years, the voice of moral prophecy just stopped. It became the voice of selfishness—of pure self-interest. The Court became focused on rules. The Court seemed to reason that rules are better if they allow you to advance your selfish interests free from government interference. With the passing of Justice Ginsburg, the prophetic voice in the Supreme Court has been virtually extinguished. It lives on in an occasional dissent by Justice [Sonia] Sotomayor, but it must be reenergized. You have to build a political movement in order to affect the psychic constitution. And that can't be done without a voice of moral prophecy urging people onward.

The second problem in building a restorative political movement is that the founders' political system is badly broken. The founders envisioned a vast internal democratic braking system of electoral constituencies that would check each other. If they are large enough, every group checks every other group, and you wind up with compromises. A civic fuse box that prevents overheating. But the founders' checking system works only if you have large numbers of people voting. If only small numbers of people vote, let's say 30 percent of the eligible folks vote in a gubernatorial election, it means that only 16 percent of the population will be able to govern the other 84 percent.

The founders would be terrified at a system that allowed 16 percent of the population to govern. Not only can a small faction capture government, the small faction can then manipulate the rules to keep themselves in power. If, however, enough people vote, then a polity can't be captured by a small faction. They can govern with a legitimate democratic base, and they won't have to cheat at the margins to keep themselves in power. If enough people were to vote and rejuvenate the founders' conception of the correct way for democracies to operate, making it impossible for relatively small numbers of people to capture us, then all sorts of interesting things will happen.

Brotman: What about the role of mass media?
Neuborne: What the media has done—mass media—is they've managed to persuade the Supreme Court that they're really speakers, so they can deploy the First Amendment to fend off virtually all regulation. If we took the text of the First Amendment seriously, we would shrink the press clause into a kind of small appendage of the speech clause, where the speech clause does all the work and then the press clause is just along for the ride.

124   The Conversations

We would develop, instead, an independent jurisprudence of free press that would say, first of all, the press, as the organ by which we get information to the people, cannot be kept out of closed places. You can't keep reporters out of prisons, you can't keep them out of mental institutions. You can't keep them out of the places where, for years, horrible stuff has festered because nobody sees it. We've won the principle that you can't keep them out of court proceedings. I would use those same rules. I would say the press is the tribunal of the people and has to be their proxy, allowed in virtually everywhere, including the military.

Brotman: What would you do when the military argues that its classified information needs to remain secret?

Neuborne: The business about classified documents needs to be reformed. We have to deal with a ridiculously overclassified system. Vast amounts of information are classified by the government for no good reason. The press clause of the First Amendment is the wedge that I would use to break that open, recognizing that the press is the conduit for information. But that also brings responsibilities. The press gets something from my idea, which is much better access, but it gives something up. It gives up some autonomy about whether weak voices have to be heard.

Brotman: Doesn't social media create a much more level playing field for weaker voices?

Neuborne: Sure. Some might say that my thinking is trapped in the technology of the 1950s and 1960s and 1970s. The internet, they might argue, has changed all that. There are now cacophonous voices. The problem, of course, is that it reaches a point where a multiplicity of cacophonous voices is just as bad as having fewer voices. I'm not sure how to fix that. I think that it's no answer to say there's no problem now with media concentration because of the internet. I think there's a greater problem because the internet is so diffuse, it allows the concentrated media to have even more power by shaping people's ideas and by drowning out minor voices on the internet too.

Brotman: You had an upfront and personal role in a classic movie based on the First Amendment, *The People vs. Larry Flynt*, about the Supreme

Court case that sided with *Hustler* magazine's publisher in the name of free speech. Ironically, you played Norman Roy Gutman, who represented televangelist Jerry Falwell and argued that Flynt should pay damages after Flynt published a sex parody of Falwell.

Neuborne: I did play Roy Grutman. I loved his suits. I know what director Milos Forman was trying to do in the movie. He was trying to make a First Amendment movie that would inoculate people against censorship. The movie is an effort at mass education.

I once said to him, "Milos, this is a mistake. You treat would-be censors, like the guy I'm portraying, as cardboard figures. Your audience is going to love the movie, they're going to laugh, but they're not going to learn from it. Because when push comes to shove, the censor makes a ridiculous, utterly nonpersuasive argument. You should rewrite the script to give the other side better arguments for censorship and then defeat those arguments in strong intellectual terms." That's the only way to inoculate the audience. Foreman laughed and said, "Burt, you've gone so Hollywood. All you want is more lines for your character."

It was a joy to work with Forman. *The People vs. Larry Flynt* is a good movie. I thought that Milos Forman was one of the great artists of his day. But I still think he missed the boat. He could have made a deeper, more serious movie, especially because of his background. Milos grew up in a repressive society, communist Czechoslovakia. Every movie he made was a movie about what it meant to live in a repressive society. *One Flew Over the Cuckoo's Nest* uses an insane asylum as a metaphor for that society. *The People vs. Larry Flynt,* I think, was his effort to say something about the risk of censorship to a decent society.

Brotman: But you would have dug deeper in framing the story?

Neuborne: I would, yes. There's still no *12 Angry Men* for the First Amendment. There's no movie that manages to encapsulate its complex values. If it were made, it would be gambling with the good sense of the American people. It could backfire. The arguments could spark a countermovement to censor. But I don't think you can pretend that there's nothing on the other side. The only way you win an argument is to confront the other side, reason with them, and defeat them in the free market of ideas. We've got to get back into our free market of ideas and confronting each other. Not, "You're a racist," "you're a fascist." Let's confront each other with why arguments are right. We've got to find a way to get back to them.

Brotman: On reflection, and with both the present and future in mind, are you optimistic that the vitality of the First Amendment designed by Madison in the lyrical way you described can be sustained?

Neuborne: As a civil liberties lawyer, I've been happily running into stone walls for more than fifty years. I have no illusion that society changes overnight, or any illusion that the courts can fix things, or any illusion about reforming an economic system that is embedded in racism and injustice.

I was lucky enough though to see what can happen if the forces align. Maybe it was an accident of the [President John F.] Kennedy assassination, you know, an exercise in national expiation of guilt. But the sixties literally remade much of American life. American society has been living on what reformers achieved in the sixties for the last half-century. We have literally been mining that magnificent source of justice for half a century. I don't think it's beyond us to go further. We can build toward another moment when we can create a new set of values—a set of legal and moral and psychic rules that will enable us to move forward as a society.

I believe that I couldn't have been a civil liberties lawyer all these years without believing that social change always is possible. Otherwise, I would have never left Wall Street. I would have become cynical, probably made a good deal of money, spoken to my psychiatrist every day, and had three wives and kids who hate me—just a completely different life. I'll take the one I stumbled into.

David D. Cole

David D. Cole is the national legal director of the American Civil Liberties Union and the Hon. George J. Mitchell Professor in Law and Public Policy at the Georgetown University Law Center. He is also the legal affairs correspondent for The Nation *and a regular contributor to the* New York Review of Books.

He is the author or editor of ten books. Less Safe, Less Free: Why America Is Losing the War on Terror, *published in 2007 and coauthored with Jules Lobel, won the Palmer Civil Liberties Prize for best book on national security and civil liberties.* Enemy Aliens: Double Standards and Constitutional Freedoms in the War on Terrorism *received the American Book Award in 2004.* No Equal Justice: Race and Class in the American Criminal Justice System *was named Best Non-Fiction Book of 1999 by the* Boston Book Review *and the best book on an issue of national policy in 1999 by the American Political Science Association. His most recent books are* The Torture Memos: Rationalizing the Unthinkable *(2009) and* Engines of Liberty: The Power of Citizen Activists to Make Constitutional Law (2016).

Cole worked as a staff attorney for the Center for Constitutional Rights from 1985 to 1990 and continued to litigate as a professor. He has litigated many significant constitutional cases in the U.S. Supreme Court, including Texas v. Johnson *and* United States v. Eichman, *which extended First Amendment protection to flag burning;* National Endowment for the Arts v. Finley, *which challenged political content restriction on National Endowment for the Arts funding;* Masterpiece Cakeshop v. Colorado Civil Rights Commission, *in which the ACLU represented a gay couple refused service by a bakery because they sought a cake to celebrate their wedding;* Bostock v. Clayton County, *which ruled that Title VII bars discrimination on the basis of sexual orientation and transgender status; and* Mahanoy

128   The Conversations

Area School District v. B.L., *which protected a high school student's right to use profanity on social media outside of school hours. He has been involved for decades in many of the nation's most important cases involving civil liberties and national security.*

The late New York Times *columnist Anthony Lewis called Cole "one of the country's great legal voices for civil liberties today."*

Stuart Brotman: It might be useful to talk a little bit at the outset about how your First Amendment journey transpired. I have had others tell me about their experiences as student journalists or anti-war protesters, or talk about their formal education in the field, whether it's college or law school.

David Cole: I was an English major in college, and I went to law school wanting to be a journalist, not a lawyer. I was interested in women's rights in law school and worked for a number of women's rights organizations during that time. I went to the Center for Constitutional Rights (CCR) in the summer of 1983, to work with Rhonda Copelon, who was doing CCR's women's rights work then. But before I arrived, she left to become a professor, and there was no women's rights work at the center for me to do. So I got involved in legal work related to opposing U.S. intervention in Central America, in part defending activists who were targeted because of their opposition to U.S. intervention there. And that was my roundabout entry to First Amendment work.

Brotman: Let's just step back. You're in law school, you're interested in women's rights. What aspects of women's rights were your focus?

Cole: I was interested in feminism generally. I read a book called *The Mermaid and the Minotaur* by Dorothy Dinnerstein, which makes a psychoanalytical argument that traditional sex-role parenting, in which women do the lion's share of childrearing, is at the root of many of the problems we have in the world. I found it compelling. Of course, this was also the late 1970s and early 1980s, when feminism was at its height, so I was a product of the times. It's not surprising in retrospect that that was what drew me to public-interest work then.

So when there was no women's rights work to do at the Center for Constitutional Rights, I ended up doing this other work. And it took me in the direction of the First Amendment. My first trial was defending

Margaret Randall, a feminist who was facing deportation for having "advocated world communism" in her writings, most of which were about Central America. This was 1984, but it might as well have been 1954. From that point on, I represented many dissidents of one type or another. Flag burners. Documentary filmmakers who were penalized because the Reagan administration deemed their films critical of the United States. Travelers who had their diaries and datebooks seized and copied by Border Patrol agents upon returning from Nicaragua. I represented Gay Men's Health Crisis in a successful First Amendment challenge to a regulation limiting its ability to use federal funds to talk about safe sex as part of AIDS education. We challenged the federal gag rule that barred Title X family planning clinics from discussing options with respect to abortion. And I represented performance artists Karen Finley, John Fleck, Holly Hughes, and Tim Miller when the NEA [National Endowment for the Arts] denied their arts grants because their art was too controversial. My litigation docket quickly became a First Amendment docket. But in retrospect, it was serendipitous. I didn't set out to be a First Amendment lawyer, but rather to defend causes that CCR supported: anti-war, feminist, gay and lesbian-friendly, and the like.

Brotman: How did you come to think that you wanted to litigate to get relief through the courts as opposed to using other means?
Cole: I went to law school really thinking I wanted to be a writer. I was only dissuaded from that view by my last job as a student, which was at CCR. I'd taken time off from law school to pursue journalism. I interned at the *Atlantic Monthly*. I had planned to intern at the *Nation* during another semester off. But in between, I worked at CCR and loved it. It was a bold, progressive, and exciting place to work, and they gave me a lot of responsibility. I saw that I could direct my interest in writing toward social justice through law.

CCR used the courts to advance progressive social movements, defending people who were being targeted because of their political views, or using litigation to develop law or provide focal points for social activism and education around issues both at home and abroad.

Brotman: Were any of your law school professors influential in shaping your thinking about these issues?

Cole: In law school, my most influential professors included Burke Marshall, who taught me First Amendment, federal courts, and a seminar called "The Limits of Law," and Owen Fiss, who was a brilliant teacher, passionate about social justice, and a devoted mentor. No one did more to inspire me about the promise of law than Owen Fiss. And with Professor Fiss's encouragement, I also took a class in the English Department graduate school on Freud, taught by Harold Bloom. As a law student, I wrote an article applying Harold Bloom's theory for interpreting poetry to the First Amendment tradition reflected in Supreme Court jurisprudence.

Brotman: Sounds interesting. What was your analysis in that piece?

Cole: The basic argument was that law, like poetry, develops in part through a kind of misreading of precedent. Bloom focused on the anxiety that the great poets struggled with, anxiety about how to overcome the influence or shadow of their great predecessors. In Bloom's view, the great poets are the ones that break from the influence of their predecessors and create a new way of doing poetry. And when they are successful, they require us to read the old poets through the lens of their work. To be great, Bloom argues, a poet must strongly "misread" his predecessors.

I applied that concept to constitutional law and First Amendment doctrine in particular. It's an odd fit because in the law you are obligated to follow precedent, not break from it. A judge is legitimate if he or she follows and applies precedent. But when you think about the great Supreme Court justices, they tend to be those who broke from precedent and forged a new path. So while legitimacy in the law requires that one follow precedent, the great justices are often those who broke from it in influential ways. And I thought, what better area to trace that than the First Amendment tradition, where the principal decisions that define our understanding of the First Amendment today are the dissents of Justices Oliver Wendall Holmes and Louis Brandeis. Their dissents eventually become the majority view of the Supreme Court, through a series of "misreadings" of prior precedents that claimed not to be overruling but in fact changed the law dramatically.

Brotman: You were arguing that radical change could be accomplished by dissent first and persuasion later.

Cole: Yes. That was really my first First Amendment piece. Then I built upon that. I think my English major background was valuable. There's an affinity between a love for literature and for freedom of expression. Censors insist that the works they seek to suppress have fixed and often reductive meanings; the object of a critical reader is to find multiple meanings, to find ambiguity. But that very ambiguity, and the freedom it represents, is the enemy of the censor. My background studying poetry made me sympathetic to that.

Brotman: How did this play out in the First Amendment cases you litigated?

Cole: Some of my cases were fairly traditional, such as the notion that you should not be deported for advocating communism. Seems like a no-brainer. The notion that you should not be thrown in jail for expressing your views by burning the American flag also seemed pretty straightforward (although the Court split five to four, so not so obvious for some). I think the more cutting-edge cases I litigated in this area involved challenges to restrictions on what people could say when receiving government subsidies. These included the right to talk about safe sex in federally-funded AIDS education, the right of documentary filmmakers to receive customs benefits even if they criticized the United States government in some way, the rights of performance artists to create art freely with government funding, and the rights of federally subsidized Title X family planning clinics to counsel their patients about abortion.

I also litigated a number of cases addressing whether the First Amendment should protect immigrants to the same degree as citizens. Clearly, you could not throw a citizen in jail for having advocated communism, yet several of my early cases, including that of Margaret Randall, asked whether that right extended to noncitizens as well.

Brotman: These cases started at the trial level, so you were involved right at the beginning.

Cole: Yes.

Brotman: And then all of them were ultimately appealed.

Cole: Many but not all, yes.

132 The Conversations

Brotman: What sort of reaction were you getting from judges at the federal district court level?
Cole: Most of these cases we won in the lower courts but they were not always upheld on appeal.

Brotman: Tell me a bit about the landmark flag-burning cases that went to the U.S. Supreme Court.
Cole: It was a real privilege to work on *Texas v. Johnson*, the case that established that the First Amendment protects flag burning. That case reinforces the fundamental First Amendment notion that the fact that people being offended by a speaker's message is not a justification to suppress the speech. And as a doctrinal matter, it is particularly important for identifying how courts assess the regulation of expressive conduct or symbolic speech—conduct that communicates. The Court in *Texas v. Johnson* made clear that if the government's interest in regulating conduct is related to what the conduct expresses, then it requires First Amendment strict scrutiny. If the government's interest in regulating the conduct has nothing to do with what the conduct expresses, by contrast, courts would apply a deferential form of intermediate scrutiny. So a law that banned all public burning without a permit could be applied to the burning of a flag, because the interest would be in regulating fire and smoke, not speech. But when the government singles out the burning of the American flag, it is plainly doing so because of what burning the flag expresses.

In other words, courts don't look at the conduct and ask, "Is it more speech or is it more conduct?" There's no principled way of answering that question because so much conduct is potentially expressive. Instead, courts look at the government's interest in regulating. *Texas v. Johnson* established that.

We relied on just this distinction in *Masterpiece Cakeshop v. Colorado Civil Rights Commission* just a few years ago. There, the baker was saying, "My baking of this wedding cake for a same-sex couple is expressing my art." Our rejoinder was that that is not the question. The courts should not ask whether the cake is more sugar and icing or more speech. It's both.

Instead, you ask why the government requires the baker to sell the cake to a gay couple. And the government imposed thar requirement

David D. Cole   133

to advance equal treatment in public accommodations, regardless of
whether the business was "expressive" or not. Its interest did not turn on
whether the cake was expressive, but on the fact that the baker had opened
his business to the public, and therefore, like all other public businesses,
could not discriminate. That interest has nothing to do with the fact that
your cake is expressive. If you're selling hammers and nails, you would
not be able to deny them to a gay couple. The same is true for cakes.

Brotman: Why do you think the Supreme Court didn't buy that argument?
Cole: Actually, the Court didn't directly address the argument. It avoided
the issue by concluding that the Colorado Civil Rights Commission had
evidenced anti-religious bias in some of its comments, and that was a
distinct free exercise violation. In the end, the Supreme Court ended up
not deciding the core question regarding discrimination.

Brotman: Some of the people I've spoken with think that it's important to have some sort of an overall analytic framework about the First
Amendment and then develop it over time. Others say this framework should evolve case by case. Your thoughts on these two different
approaches?
Cole: I think it's important to think about why we have a First Amendment
and then relate the rules that have developed on a case-by-case basis to
that overarching purpose. The marketplace of ideas is hardly perfect, but
it's a preferable system to one in which government censors determine
truth. That is critical because the First Amendment at its core is as much
about checking government abuse as it is about individual self-expression.
It's what protects civil society, the web of citizen associations that operate
to advance and defend values that people believe in, and that operate as a
check on government power.

   If that's the case, we need to be very skeptical of government efforts to
control what is said and who you are permitted to associate with. To me,
this is really core to understanding the First Amendment. From that, you
get notions such as no prior restraint, skepticism about content discrimination, and the like. We should be highly skeptical about any effort by the
government to regulate the content of speech and should have a particular concern when that regulation is targeted at political speech, precisely

134   The Conversations

because of the role the First Amendment plays in checking government abuse and advancing democracy.

Brotman: How much of the marketplace of ideas should be determined by the economic marketplace?
Cole: I think that there is a real risk that the economic marketplace, supported by those who are powerful, can come to dominate the marketplace of ideas—simply by virtue of their wealth, rather than by virtue of the strength of their ideas.

That concern is presented most starkly in the campaign finance context. I do think that campaign finance regulation should be subject to heightened First Amendment scrutiny, but that doesn't mean that campaign finance cannot be regulated. I know, some people say money isn't speech, so campaign finance laws need not satisfy First Amendment scrutiny. I don't think that's right. When the government controls how much money you can spend on speech, that's a speech issue. If the government said you could only spend one hundred dollars on books this year, we wouldn't say that's not a regulation of speech, that's just the regulation of money.

Campaign finance rules regulate how you spend your money on political speech. So it's a speech issue. But the fact that it's a speech issue doesn't mean there can't be any regulation. It just means the regulation has to be tied to an important government interest. I think the Supreme Court has been—and this is me speaking personally and not for the ACLU—as an institution narrow in its understanding of the compelling interests that might justify government intervention in the marketplace of ideas to try to reduce some of the effects of the economic concentrations of power.

For example, federal law required corporations that engaged in campaign expenditures to create a separate political action committee to which people voluntarily give, to ensure that the corporation's spending did not reflect funds that they've generated through selling widgets or cars or computers—nothing to do with the power of their ideas.

That seemed to me an appropriate regulation because it doesn't target particular viewpoints or particular content. It simply tries to neutralize the distorting effect of concentrations of wealth on the electoral debate. But the Supreme Court ruled that the only compelling interest that justifies the regulation of campaign finance is a concern about quid pro quo corruption, or bribery, and not a concern about concentrated wealth distorting the debate. But government ought to be able to respond to the corruption that ensues when politicians are far more responsive to the interests of a few very wealthy constituents than to their many not-so-wealthy constituents. To me, that's a form of corruption as well. If you recognize that broader form of corruption, then a broader set of campaign finance laws can be justified.

There's another form of First Amendment interest that people are beginning to talk about now. We should be breaking up those corporations that exercise undue influence in the marketplace, and in particular social media. The Facebooks and Googles of the world not only have tremendous capital, but they also control the platforms on which the conversations are happening.

For some of the same reasons that we're concerned about the federal government having the power over what can or can't be said, I have similar concerns about a handful of private entities having that power. One way of responding to that would be, "We're not going to try to regulate the speech, we're just going to break up entities that have that power so that there's more competition."

Brotman: Let's turn to the issue of defamation lawsuits by government officials.

Cole: I think *New York Times v. Sullivan* was rightly decided. When it comes to public officials, the interest in ensuring that people have the freedom to criticize government officials overrides the interest in the reputation of those officials, absent an "actual malice" standard—knowing something is not true or recklessly disregarding whether something is true.

Brotman: How did you decide to make the transition from active litigator to law school teaching?

Cole: I loved my job at CCR, but I also still wanted to write. I felt that by going into teaching, I could have it both ways. I could write. I could still litigate. I could teach, and I would have a more balanced life and career. But I loved my litigation, so I kept almost my entire docket and even kept my office at CCR for several years. I continued to litigate for my entire career at Georgetown Law School, often with CCR, sometimes with the ACLU, and sometimes with both. Almost all my litigation activities have been *pro bono*.

Brotman: It seems like you have been operating in a legal ecosystem of sorts.

Cole: I suppose so. That ecosystem is what I would call civil society. It's private citizens coming together and supporting causes that they believe in, and then using the tools that our Constitution provides to advance or defend those values. That's true of the Center for Constitutional Rights, Planned Parenthood, the National Rifle Association. That's true of the ACLU. We're all part of that.

There are differences in focus and emphasis, but everyone has a part to play in protecting democracy and advancing civil liberties and civil rights. The Center for Constitutional Rights has always seen itself as an arm of the progressive movement, whereas at the ACLU, in some sense, our client is the Bill of Rights. CCR will generally not represent those with whom it fundamentally disagrees, whereas the ACLU will, if the principle deserves defending. We will defend people with whom we strongly disagree, such as the Nazis in Skokie or the alt-right in Charlottesville. But at the end of the day, both organizations are committed to protecting constitutional rights through litigation, legislation, education, and citizen engagement.

Brotman: You make that argument in your book *Engines of Liberty: The Power to Make Constitutional Law*.

Cole: Yes. I argue there that constitutional law doesn't change because clever lawyers make clever arguments in the Supreme Court, justices hear them, and are convinced. That's part of the story to be sure. But I think when you look closely at any significant development in constitutional law, you'll see that what really made the development possible is a concerted effort by civil society organizations like the ACLU, the NRA, the Federalist Society, or Planned Parenthood.

These organizations have worked over the long haul through incremental change in multiple forums, whether they be legislative or executive or judicial, whether they be local or state or federal, or even in some instances international. I think in order to understand how to be an effective constitutional lawyer, you have to understand how this process operates.

Legal briefs are a small part of the story. I think a much bigger part is the work done to educate the public, to develop law incrementally outside the Supreme Court altogether, so that when an issue gets to the Supreme Court, the justices are just kind of recognizing that the law has changed, rather than making the change themselves. In the book, I show how that story of institutional incrementalism in multiple forums explains both marriage equality and the individual right to bear arms. It doesn't necessarily go in a liberal or conservative direction. But it's how the law moves. And it's the First Amendment in action.

Brotman: What do you think of arguments that the First Amendment protects too much speech, especially when it comes to hate speech?

Cole: Some people on the left today seem to question the value of protecting free speech, especially when it comes to hate speech or speech by the powerful. But I say be careful what you wish for. If we were in fact to empower government officials to decide whose speech deserves protection and what ideas can be expressed, and you had people like Donald Trump and Mike Pence making those choices, I think people on the left would quickly see the value of not empowering government to decide whose speech is sufficiently inoffensive to be tolerated and whose isn't. What government does in the name of regulating hate speech might very quickly turn people around on that question. Those on the right may see that value too, if the decisions were being made by politicians that they disliked.

Brotman: What about imposing some limits on social media?

Cole: In the ether, lies get propagated and spread like a virus. Counter speech on social media is much less effective. The internet has challenged notions of the marketplace of ideas. [Justice Oliver Wendell] Holmes's idea was that the exchange in the marketplace would move in the direction of truth, revealing falsehoods for what they are. But an entirely unregulated marketplace, driven by algorithms to favor conflict, seems a recipe for spreading falsehoods as much as truths. So social media challenges our frameworks and our assumptions. But at this point, social media raises more questions than it answers. What do we do about disinformation and unrestricted propagation? How do you solve the problem without creating other problems? Who should regulate social media and by what metrics? We will be grappling with these questions for a long time.

Brotman: Now you are at the ACLU having to grapple with these questions.
Cole: Yes. And what better place to do so?

Brotman: How did you wind up there at this point in your career?
Cole: My predecessor in this job, Steve Shapiro, stepped down after twenty-five years as the ACLU legal director. He was a tremendously talented lawyer. The ACLU's executive director, Anthony Romero, urged me to apply for the job. You have to realize this was the spring of 2016; the world looked very different then. Anthony basically said, "David, how can you not apply for the job—you've been litigating and writing about constitutional law for thirty-some years, under a conservative-majority Supreme Court? Just think what it would be like to lead the ACLU, and especially its Supreme Court practice, under a liberal-majority Supreme Court?" At this time, of course, everyone knew that Hillary Clinton was going to win the 2016 presidential election, and that meant she would get to appoint Justice Antonin Scalia's successor. For the first time in forty years, we would have a liberal majority on the Supreme Court. So it sounded like a good deal to me. And then on November 8 of that year, the job changed dramatically. Donald Trump was elected president of the United States.

Brotman: Your thinking must have required a quick U-turn.
Cole: Yes. But in many ways, the ACLU became even more important. Going back to something I said before, I think that the core idea of the First Amendment is protecting civil society so that it can perform a checking function on government. This means that an organization like the ACLU is most needed when we have a president like President Trump, who posed such a multiheaded threat to civil rights and civil liberties.

We've never been just a First Amendment organization. We are probably the preeminent First Amendment organization, but we are also—and always have been—a defender of civil liberties and civil rights across the board. We protect the rights of free speech and association, but we also protect the right of privacy, equal protection, and reproductive freedom. We fight national security incursions on civil liberties, we advance religious liberty, and we fight the establishment of religion. And we push for voting rights, immigrants' rights, racial justice, LGBT equality, women's rights, the rights of the criminally accused and incarcerated, the rights of people with disabilities, and of minority groups generally.

None of that is new. We've always covered this range. We are a bigger player these days than we ever were before. I think, relatively speaking, we probably devote more resources now to civil rights than to civil liberties. But we haven't reduced our efforts on the First Amendment side. We've just expanded our efforts on the civil rights side, I think.

Brotman: What ACLU issue seems to be one that keeps you awake at night?

Cole: I think campaign finance regulation is probably one of the most important questions that we need to get a handle on if we're going to save democracy from itself. There's the question of whether tolerating hate speech is a First Amendment fault line. I think we should be tolerating speech that we disagree with, even if it's deeply offensive, and obviously that principle still has to be vigorously defended. But everyone doesn't accept it as given. The power of private platforms to control the marketplace of ideas is deeply troubling. The question of how we deal with disinformation in the social media age is a very challenging one. I think the extent to which the Supreme Court is going to allow the First Amendment to be a general deregulatory instrument on behalf of business to fight all sorts of economic business regulation is also one of the key questions that we will be looking at with interest. And these are just the questions in the First Amendment realm. There is quite plainly so much work to be done to achieve a more just and equitable society for African Americans, Native Americans, and so many other historically subordinated groups.

Brotman: What about First Amendment restrictions in the name of national security?

Cole: Obviously very important but not particularly new. I think the questions about terrorist groups and providing material support to terrorist groups, for example, that have come to the fore since 9/11 are really no different than the questions about supporting the anarchists in the early twentieth century or about supporting or associating with the Communist Party and its various affiliates from the 1920s through the 1960s.

I don't think the answers really need to be rethought. I think what we need to do is hold fast to the principle that you have to have a very close nexus between speech and illegal conduct before you can actually criminalize the speech, and that guilt by association is impermissible. National security—there's always going to be a risk that government will say that in order to stop some catastrophe from occurring. That was true with anarchism, communism, and terrorism.

What's sad to me is that we don't seem to have carried over the lessons of the anti-communist era to the present. By the end of the McCarthy era, the Court had developed very protective First Amendment doctrines around speech and association, precisely because of the abuses that anti-communism brought. But holding fast to those principles in the face of new threats has been a challenge.

Brotman: Can you imagine a period of time where the Supreme Court starts to walk that back?

Cole: To some degree it already has, as in the Court's treatment of "material support" of designated "terrorist organizations," even where the support consists solely of human rights advocacy. But I think that if the government were to actually start prosecuting people, as they did during the McCarthy era, or if they start using the power that Congress has given them in a broad way, snaring lots of innocent and sympathetic people, there would be a course correction.

Brotman: How closely should the text of the Constitution be considered the law of the land?

Cole: I think everybody starts from the text of the Constitution, but most of us don't stop there because the text is written very broadly, with an understanding that it's going to guide the country for centuries. We shouldn't be restricted by the imaginations of the people who either drafted it or ratified it.

If you ask yourself, "Why would we today agree to be bound by the particular specific views of people who've been dead for two hundred years?"

It's hard to answer that question. If you instead say, "That's not how the Constitution works. People got together as a nation, tried to articulate a set of principles in broad strokes with an understanding that, over time, they would be developed through interpretation and application." That to me makes sense. That's a living Constitution.

It's not that we make it up every day. We are guided by what went before. We take seriously the lessons of the past and the principles, but we recognize that due process, free speech, equal protection, and unreasonable searches and seizures are open-ended principles precisely so that we can ensure that the Constitution that we are bound by today reflects *our* deepest commitments, not just the commitments of a people who've been dead for over two hundred years.

Brotman: Do you think we are doing better with First Amendment and civil liberties protections than in recent decades, including the formative period of the 1960s?

Cole: I don't know that we are doing better. Some of the basic protections, in cases such as *Brandenburg v. Ohio* and *Scales v. United States* and *New York Times v. Sullivan,* are now long established. But in part for that reason, I worry that some have begun to take these freedoms for granted, forgetting that they were forged by decades of struggle on behalf of political activists, union leaders, civil rights organizers, and dissidents.

In that regard, public education is critically important. The education of young people about the core values of our constitutional democracy is essential. What I don't have a sense of is really comparatively speaking, did we do it better at any other time than today? I think that every poll I've ever seen on constitutional issues from any period suggests a great deal of misunderstanding on the part of many people in the country. So I see it more as a constant deficit rather than some new deficit.

Brotman: How can government help reduce this deficit?

Cole: Government has a role in promoting the values of the community, particularly in the education of citizens. I don't think you can educate effectively without some commitment to the importance and value of freedom of inquiry, thought, and speech.

But we can't rely on the government alone to educate us about the importance of checking the government, and therefore of the First

Amendment. So it also has to be the job of the civil society institutions that the First Amendment protects.

Brotman: Do our political leaders need to step up here too?

Cole: It's certainly important for leaders to defend core principles of our democracy when they are under attack. I don't really have a sense of who those political leaders are, which maybe is an answer to your question.

That's one of the things that I think is so exciting about the ACLU. It is an organization that draws people to it because they believe in the values of the Bill of Rights. First among equals is the First Amendment. We grew from 400,000 members before Donald Trump was elected to 1.8 million after his election. And we were not alone. Planned Parenthood has never had greater support. The *New York Times* and *Washington Post* never have had higher subscription numbers than during Trump's presidency. The American people evidently understand that citizen engagement is critically important to defending the liberties and the values that we care about when they are under threat.

The Women's March, the March for Our Lives, the #MeToo movement, and the Black Lives Matter protests were all examples of individuals coming together and using the First Amendment to defend the principles and values that they see under attack. To me, that's where our salvation lies, if there is a salvation. It is in the fact that people in this country understand, in a deep way, the importance of living with the First Amendment, by which I mean engaging in political action to defend the values and beliefs that they hold most dear. That's what the First Amendment is ultimately about.

Brotman: I sense that you are reflecting some rays of optimism.

Cole: I think we have a robust civil society and a deeply ingrained understanding that if you don't like what's going on, you don't just sit back and moan. You stand up and get engaged. Use the tools of democracy, use what the First Amendment guarantees, which is your right to be critical, to join with others to write about it, to speak about it, to demonstrate about it, to petition about it. That's the First Amendment in action.

Brotman: What would you say to those who may be dispirited now about the direction of our country?

Cole: I understand the feeling. The news can be terribly dispiriting. The challenges are immense. But history underscores the importance of continuing to engage and to use the First Amendment to fight back. At the end of the day, that is the tool that we have. It is the tool of politics. It is the First Amendment that protects our ability to gather together and object to injustice and to demand justice. That's what we have short of a revolution. And I'm not a big fan of revolution.

Lucy A. Dalglish

Lucy A. Dalglish is dean of the Philip Merrill College of Journalism at the University of Maryland. She served as executive director of the Reporters Committee for Freedom of the Press from 2000 to 2012. The Reporters Committee is a voluntary, unincorporated association of reporters and news editors dedicated to protecting the First Amendment interests of the news media. The Reporters Committee has provided research, guidance, and representation in major press cases in state and federal courts since 1970.

Prior to assuming the Reporters Committee position, Dalglish was a media lawyer for almost five years in the trial department of the Minneapolis law firm of Dorsey & Whitney. From 1980 to 1993, she was a reporter and editor at the St. Paul Pioneer Press. *As a reporter, she covered beats ranging from general assignment and suburbs to education and courts. During her last three years at the* Pioneer Press, *she served as night city editor, assistant news editor, and national/foreign editor.*

Dalglish was awarded the Kiplinger Award by the National Press Foundation in 2012 for her service to journalism. She was also awarded the Wells Memorial Key, the highest honor bestowed by the Society of Professional Journalists, in 1995. A year later, she was one of twenty-four journalists, lawyers, lawmakers, educators, researchers, librarians, and historians inducted into the charter class of the National Freedom of Information Act Hall of Fame in Washington, D.C. Dalglish appears frequently in print, online, and broadcast stories about issues involving the media and the First Amendment.

She has been a national leader in supporting open-meeting and open-records laws at the state and federal levels, as well as a key player over the past ten years in the effort to pass state and federal reporters "shield laws." She served on the boards or advisory committees of the National Freedom of Information Coalition, the National Center for Courts and the Media, the Sunshine in Government Initiative, and Openthegovernment.org.

Dalglish serves on the board of the News Leaders Association. She was named the Journalism and Mass Communication Administrator of the Year in 2021 by the Scripps Howard Foundation and the Association for Education in Journalism and Mass Communication.

Dalglish earned a juris doctor degree from Vanderbilt University Law School, a master of studies in law degree from Yale Law School, and a bachelor of arts in journalism from the University of North Dakota. While attending North Dakota, Dalglish worked as managing editor of the Dakota Student *and as a reporter and editor for the* Grand Forks Herald.

Stuart Brotman: You were a little girl living in a relatively remote part of the United States. What is your earliest memory of a personal encounter with the First Amendment?

Lucy Dalglish: I was raised in North Dakota. I grew up in Grand Forks, about three blocks from the University of North Dakota. I had a very progressive sixth-grade teacher who thought that one of the best ways to teach kids was to have them put out a weekly newsletter newspaper.

It was always competitive to see who was going to get to be the editor. We worked on a newspaper covering national political events, local news. We put it out every Friday and sold it on the playground. We had subscriptions to families—one for three cents or two for a nickel. This was a very innovative thing to do. I don't know that a teacher could do it now.

The first assignment she gave us that morning was that everybody had to write an editorial. By that afternoon, she had read through all these things the sixth graders had done. She picked me to be the editor. I had to make assignments every Monday morning. We had a business manager, we had an art director, and we had students who were in charge of selling the subscriptions. We were diligent, and this was a fabulous learning experience.

Brotman: Sounds like it. What were you writing about as a sixth grader?

Dalglish: I wrote editorials about pollution. Eighteen-year-olds getting the right to vote. The Vietnam War. The draft. All of these things. I remember Nixon was president. I wrote an editorial about women's liberation. I came out against it. Live and learn.

I wrote an editorial about TV violence, and I criticized my own father for his judgment about what I could watch on TV. I came home for lunch that day and my dad was there and he was upset. He took me aside and he said, "You don't get to write editorials criticizing your father in the neighborhood newspaper." I said, "Well, it is freedom of the press." He said, "The school may give you freedom of the press. But the First Amendment doesn't apply at home."

He said it wasn't fair of me to do that without telling him first. So I was grounded for a week.

Brotman: What about learning of the First Amendment in a more formal way in the classroom?

Dalglish: I'm sure that part of the learning experience in sixth grade was our teacher. She was explaining to us free speech and free press. I had had several teachers in elementary school who were very good at teaching social studies, what you can do in this country. I guess we hadn't quite come to ethics yet.

I didn't spend that much time thinking that I was going to be a journalist. I also edited my student newspaper in junior high school and then I was the co-editor of my high school paper. Again, had a fabulous teacher who defended us when we wrote controversial things. We went to Bismarck to cover the legislature. But I wasn't much thinking, "I'm going to be a journalist or I'm going to be a lawyer." I was still in that exploration stage. I probably thought I was more likely that I would become a lawyer.

Brotman: What were some of the hot issues you were covering as a high-school journalist?

Dalglish: Teenage pregnancy was a big one. Drugs too.

Brotman: Any issues about how vigorous your reporting could be about them?

Dalglish: I remember finding a couple of kids in the high school who were single mothers and talking to them, persuading them to go on the record. The principal didn't say we couldn't do it, but I remember him asking our advisors, saying, "Can you wait until after the bond referendum gets

148   The Conversations

approved? Can you publish this story next month?" I do remember that. That seemed like a reasonable compromise because I was also very active in music and theater. And I wanted a new auditorium.

Newspapering just sort of seemed to be a fun thing to do. For me, it was a good way to find out what was going on in the world. I didn't feel that everybody needed my wisdom in editorials. I was curious about things. It was a great way to meet people and have an excuse to go and talk to people. I always wanted to know what was happening in the world. I also had this feeling that by doing journalism, you can shed light on some things that people might need to know about and that they might not otherwise know. When I got to college, I fell in with the crowd at the student newspaper. I went to the University of North Dakota.

Brotman: So another chapter of your journalism journey began.
Dalglish: I started taking journalism classes right away, as a freshman. The editor of the *Grand Forks Herald* came to talk to one of our classes. I drilled down and asked him questions about a controversial photograph that had been published a couple of weeks earlier. They were removing a dead child from a swimming pool. It was a neighborhood I was very familiar with. You could see this little toddler's feet. I remember my parents having a fit. I just started asking him all sorts of questions like, "Why did you think it was appropriate to actually show a picture of this dead baby?" The next thing I know I'm being called to the director of the journalism school's office, and they said, "Tom Shoemaker wants to know if you want a summer job." He was the editor in Grand Forks.

I spent the summer there, between freshman year and sophomore year. Then the following year, I worked very hard with the student newspaper and met another student who was very interested in First Amendment law. The director of the program taught a First Amendment law class. I was just enthralled by that class.

Brotman: You remembered what you wrote about in elementary school and high school. How about when you were at the *Grand Forks Herald* during college?

Dalglish: I remember they had fairly easy crime stories and easy community stories. They also had a supplement that they were trying to sell on college campuses in that general area. I remember writing stories about what was going on in those various schools. It was not really an advertorial but it was a special section. I wrote almost everything for this special section. When I could get my mom's car, they sent me on the road. I'm like eighteen or nineteen at this point. It was fun.

I was the managing editor for the student paper and then eventually worked part time at the *Herald* until I graduated. I graduated in three years. I had three years of very intense journalism. Tom Shoemaker called his counterparts at the *St. Paul Pioneer Press* and *St. Paul Dispatch*. They were two separate papers at that time, both owned by Knight Ridder. He said, "I think you should hire this kid."

So I ended up in St. Paul, which was my dad's hometown. I moved there for the summer and was living at my grandma's house. It was really good experience on many levels. Along the way, as a young reporter, my favorite stories always took place in the courthouse. Back then, there were beat reporters who could just go and spend time walking around the halls talking to people. I was assigned to Dakota County, which includes the southern suburbs of Minneapolis and St Paul.

Brotman: Lucy Dalglish is finally a full-fledged cub reporter on the beat, right?

Dalglish: I covered everything. You could go to the courthouse and dig around and find great stories, because everything in society at some point, whether it was crimes, bank robberies, murders, mayhem, or civil disputes over boundary lines—everything ends up in court in some way.

I was fascinated by that. I also did a project with a partner where we were investigating condemnation cases in the path of the interstate freeway. We found a bunch of, let's just call it conflicts of interest, in who was deciding values on those properties and all their interrelationships. We did this big story. I got sued for libel. It took seven years to have that case dismissed.

Brotman: This probably didn't endear you to your employer. Did the *St. Paul Pioneer Press* also face legal liability?

Dalglish: The newspaper also was sued. My partner and I were the star witnesses. I was deposed over two days, four or five years into this. Unlike other people who were kind of freaked out by it, I thought it was fascinating.

I should also mention that after about six years, I applied for a fellowship to law school, because the Knight Foundation used to support five journalists a year going through the first year of law school. The idea was you would learn about the law and go back to your newsroom and cover the law, as well as teach people in your newsroom how to cover the law.

I was awarded this fellowship, got one year's worth of law school credit, and I earned a master's degree from Yale Law School. A fantastic opportunity. I went back and covered federal courts for a year until I became an editor. I covered federal justice issues—also fascinating.

Brotman: Let's talk a little bit about your Yale Law School experience. Any influential professors?

Dalglish: I took Owen Fiss's First Amendment class, which was kind of an eye-opener. He was so provocative, and it was hard. I was used to dealing with pretty classic news journalism-related First Amendment issues, and this was more classic speech. Allowing freedom of press for some stifles the speech of others.

Brotman: It probably was a very quick year. With diploma in hand, did you just go back to your reporting life?

Dalglish: Yes, then I went back to the newsroom. There were some issues going on. I was editing by that time. There were some leadership changes in the newsroom. I looked around and thought, "People here have spent their entire career in this newsroom. Is this what I really want to do?"

I only had maybe a year left where I could take all of my Yale Law School credits and transfer them. I thought maybe someday I'd like to teach. I wasn't really interested in doing the Ph.D. thing. I would much rather be a lawyer. So I applied to a variety of law schools as a transfer student.

I should also say that during this time, I had gotten heavily involved with the Society of Professional Journalists. I was on the national board. I became its national freedom of information chair. I was testifying in front of Congress on various open-government issues. I would come to

Washington, D.C., and do a lobbying trip every year. I wanted to continue doing that.

And when I was accepted at Vanderbilt Law School, I just packed up, quit my job at the *St. Paul Pioneer Press*, and moved to Nashville. Loved it. Got to hang out with those guys from the Freedom Forum when they were getting the First Amendment Center set up at Vanderbilt and helped them work on programs they were doing.

After graduating, I went back to Minneapolis to work at a big law firm. I got to work on a handful of media cases. I basically knuckled under and also learned how to do construction arbitrations and insurance defense, including some libel cases.

I was a litigator. I don't think I would have done anything else. Then my firm had this program where it would loan lawyers for four to six months to the city attorney's office prosecuting gross misdemeanors. I then was a prosecutor for six months, something like that. A fascinating experience. Then the job to head the Reporters Committee for Freedom of the Press in Washington in Washington, D.C., opened up.

Brotman: You packed up again, now leaving Minnesota for good, and began yet another new chapter of life at the Reporters Committee.
Dalglish: I was there for twelve years. That really kind of jumped me into the national scene. I was familiar with people involved in these issues, mostly from newsrooms. I really made it a point to get to know the lawyers all over the country who did this kind of work, as well as get a closer relationship with the advocates in Washington, D.C.—not only those doing media-related advocacy work but also nonprofits like the Project on Government Oversight and Government Accountability Project and the Center for Responsible Politics on issues regarding government transparency. We had common interests.

Brotman: I know you worked diligently there to protect the rights of journalists to use confidential sources.
Dalglish: The founding of the Reporters Committee for Freedom of the Press was directly tied to reporters' privilege issues. After 9/11, there was a spate of subpoenas on journalists. Some ended up going to jail. The first one who went to jail was a woman named Vanessa Leggett in Houston. She had gotten a jailhouse interview with a guy who was a suspect in a

murder. She ended up going to jail for 248 days or something like that, for protecting her source. She was a journalism professor trying to write a book. The local media were not all that supportive of her.

Brotman: You also have been very involved in open government as a broad area. When did you begin to sense that there were some potential barriers between what a reporter might like to get and the information that government held, which might make it difficult for a reporter to uncover?

Dalglish: There were always skirmishes locally, when you were trying to do some investigations and then one agency or another wanted to make your life more difficult. I always have related to the fact that bureaucracies have difficulty having people come in and ask for things. They're not used to it.

This is pre-internet. Mostly what I remember being more of an issue was how expensive it was to get copies of things. In the courts, you just had a really good sense of what was public and what was not.

I realized that in Minnesota, we had it pretty good, actually out in the West generally. The states where they really had a nasty time tended to be on the eastern seaboard. A lot of those states didn't have good open-meetings and open-record laws. Pennsylvania, not so. New Jersey was terrible; Massachusetts was awful.

Brotman: Why do you think there was such bad behavior by some of these states?

Dalglish: Sometimes it was ignorance, sometimes it was willful. Heck, that still goes on. In some states, we got a lot more clarity adopted. It was fun to work with the people who were on the ground in those states. We were doing legislative advocacy and litigation at the same time.

While all this was going on, I started getting involved with the National Freedom of Information Coalition. This is a coalition that was largely funded by the Knight Foundation. All these state transparency groups would meet a couple of times a year to exchange language and talk about best practices and try to get some uniformity in the law. I ended up later on becoming the president of that organization.

Lucy A. Dalglish

Brotman: Combing through paper records in a municipal building may seem a bit romantic for a journalist, but it also seems like ancient history now.

Dalglish: Having the internet began to change access to information, access to records, and maybe the thinking about open government and open records since the technology made all this information available.

Just because the internet was out there doesn't mean that government agencies had the money to upgrade to an online system. That took decades. Didn't mean right away that you could dive in and get everything else in the files. It took time; on the state side, it took even longer. Now that the internet is out there and virtually everything about everybody is public, ironically there's a lot of the openness that we had worked for which is being taken away now for privacy reasons.

Privacy is a lot more complicated than it was twenty years ago. Probably the biggest impact the internet had was not so much in getting access to information but an ability to disperse it in ways you could never disperse it before. Mugshots are a really good example. Most states let you have access to criminal mugshots.

On the federal side, we lost the battle. They will only release mugshots if it's in the FBI's interest. Now more states are rolling back on access to mugshots. On the one hand, I can see why, because a lot of people who have their picture taken in a mugshot are never charged with anything. But public records are still public records.

Brotman: Your work at the Reporters Committee for Freedom of the Press seemed to require a military-like level of precision.

Dalglish: We always lined up lawyers ahead of time in the local jurisdiction when there was a national political convention, whether it be Los Angeles or St. Paul or Tampa. We would have somebody set up for a hotline. If you got grabbed covering a protest, there was somebody available to go in and extricate you as soon as possible, so you can be back on the street reporting.

We also would be giving them tips: "If a cop tells you to back off, back off. Do not expect to not be arrested. And if somebody with a gun tells you to do something, then just do it and we'll argue about it later. But if they take your SD card out of your camera or take your camera, let us

154   The Conversations

know immediately. They can't do that." We worked every once in a while with the Committee to Protect Journalists. The safety issues there are a lot more scary now.

"If somebody around you is throwing a brick through a window, don't pick up the brick. Quite honestly, in the midst of mayhem, do what you can to extricate yourself from the situation as soon as possible. In the height of a demonstration, they don't care if you have a press pass around your neck." Today, people have cellphones. Everybody considers themselves to be a journalist. So it's become a lot harder for journalists to operate and cops are just arresting everybody.

Brotman: There is considerable debate now about who qualifies as press for purposes of freedom of the press.
Dalglish: I've always had the broadest possible definition of what freedom of the press covers and obviously sometimes it overlaps with freedom of speech, particularly nowadays. I think the best way to look at this is when we were in front of Congress in 2009 and 2010. We got really close to having a federal shield law enacted. The House had an occupational test or an institutional test for who was a journalist, and the Senate had a function test. The House version presumably would have covered someone who makes their livelihood, who works for a bona fide verified news organization. On the Senate side, they would have looked at what you were doing, what your intention was at the time. Were you engaging in journalism?

Brotman: Which of these two tests do you prefer?
Dalglish: I will always prefer the function test. If you are a blogger, you can always fit into the function category. The same if you are someone who is gathering information independently, not just aggregating news from others. If it is original material and it is something routine, that's a really easy case in my view.

Brotman: What about someone asserting freedom of the press by virtue of Facebook postings?
Dalglish: If it is a regular Facebook posting, and this is Facebook providing the template for you to do this, and this is something you regularly

did, and it was original or mostly original material, I would probably say, "Yes, you are a journalist." If I were a blogger, that's probably where I would publish.

Brotman: It would be interesting to get your perspective on where you think that state of investigative reporting is going.

Dalglish: A lot of foundation philanthropy is looking at ways to promote investigative journalism. They're very concerned. Local news organizations can't afford to do it anymore. So they're trying to partner with organizations like ProPublica to do local things. The Scripps-Howard Foundation has decided the way it would get involved in all of this was to set aside money to create investigative reporting centers at journalism schools to train the next generation of investigative journalists. We are one of two schools, along with Arizona State University, that got a separate $3 million grant.

We're trying to educate a new generation of investigative journalists. If you go to an investigative reporters' and editors' conference these days, you're going to be astonished at how young that crowd is. The ones that are there are really good at it. We're all having to beef up our digital and our data reporting. This has just exploded in the last couple of years. You're going to see mainstream news organizations that stay healthy work with each other more often. These freestanding investigative reporting operations will pair up with local news organizations.

Brotman: In large part, journalism is no longer a money-making proposition, even for longstanding news enterprises.

Dalglish: At some point, we're going to have to figure out how to get some money returned to journalism. We're not going to be able to rely on philanthropy forever. This is a much bigger issue that I'm not directly involved in but I keep tabs on.

Advertisers are still very happy to pay for content. The problem is they're no longer paying the content creators, they're paying Facebook and Twitter. But those folks are not paying for the content.

Brotman: Let's talk about your role now as the dean of a major journalism school. What are students like these days in terms of how they're thinking about the First Amendment generally, and in particular how they're thinking about free press issues?

Dalglish: My school has a majority of out-of-state students. They come in as freshmen, and they've had some pretty awesome high-school journalism teachers. So they come in with a pretty good base of knowledge about the First Amendment and how it works. They end up having a pretty sophisticated idea of press freedom rights and ethical responsibilities. They really get a healthy dose of that here.

I've had a really eye-opening experience. Our president and our general counsel and I have had numerous conversations about this. The year before, we had a murder here on campus and it still hasn't come to trial. A white Maryland student stabbed a Black student here. They were coming out of a bar and they came to a bus stop that was on campus. It was commencement weekend, so if everybody else had been on campus, it probably would have been a lot more dangerous. The assailant has been charged with a hate crime. Students then came back to school really upset. Of course, the first thing they want to do is to ban all offensive speech on campus.

Brotman: Where would you draw the line here, if at all?

Dalglish: If somebody draws a swastika in chalk on the sidewalk in front of the library, they should not be kicked out of school for doing that because that's offensive. Our president here, who's a lawyer, appointed me to be the co-chair of a taskforce on inclusion and respect. We were supposed to come up with recommended policies on what can and cannot be done.

I got screamed at night after night after night by students, who were justifiably distraught but who thought the only way was to change longstanding policies about speech on campus. What they had a very hard time comprehending was that we don't get to just make that stuff up. We're actually following the law. "We don't care," they said. "You should be courageous and violate the law" is essentially what their argument was. It was night after night after night of this. I've had a lot of educating I had to do with my taskforce members about what we could and couldn't do.

We ended up coming up with a policy that is uniform as far as it applies to students, faculty, and staff on targeted hate speech. If you're able

Lucy A. Dalglish

to identify the individual who was targeted, intimidated, or harassed, then it may be hate speech.

Brotman: How do you think more sensible free speech policies should be adopted on college campuses?

Dalglish: Peer-to-peer seems to work the best. You can't just make students take a diversity class, and you can't make them take a free speech class. You have to infuse this stuff campus-wide through a speaker series and orientation programs. We need to get more than just the journalism school involved in this. That's really hard to pull off.

I'll tell you the most effective thing that happened. There were a couple of female students who just lit into us at an open forum at the library. They were viciously saying, "You need to just ban all of this stuff."

There had been a kid in the back of the room, he had almost a Mohawk. He was very dark skinned and very tall. He was pacing back and forth in the back, which was standing room only. I could tell the cops in the room were just watching this kid and waiting for him to go off because he was so agitated. He finally came up to the microphone. He said, "You don't get it. That is not what you want. This is exactly how dictatorships form. You don't want to eliminate the right of free expression." He gives this free speech defense that was really quite brilliant.

I went up to him afterward. I'd never laid eyes on this kid before. He was kind of mingling in the back of the room. "Can I just ask, is your family from a part of the world where you have firsthand experience with this?" He said with obvious sarcasm, "Yeah, Ethiopia. It's a democracy there, right?" He then remarked, "They don't understand what they're talking about." This kid's family had lived it, you know. They were fairly recent immigrants. Freedom resonates when it comes from their own experiences, especially based on a lack of it. He understood that a university is a place that should be a marketplace of ideas.

The funny thing is, faculty in other places have a pretty good appreciation and belief that they have all this academic freedom. They don't understand that academic freedom really isn't a law. It's not actually as strong as the right to speak, but they think they can have all this freedom. They don't necessarily want the kids or the staff or anybody else to come

158 The Conversations

out and diminish that notion. That's the other thing with free speech. Everybody thinks they should be free. You know, ten years from now, somebody's going to come up with another notion of what's offensive and will want to put that on the list of offensive things.

Brotman: Does a free press also mean an ethical press?
Dalglish: There are a number of people who talk about the notion of a free press, a responsible press. I don't think that is inherent. If you read back at the time our Constitution was being developed, what some people were publishing back then, there was nothing fair about a lot of it. This notion of fairness is a relatively new development, probably going back to maybe World War I. I think it's a good one. I think it's important. We certainly teach it here. But it's not a requirement.

When I was at the Reporters Committee, somebody would call with an ethical question. My response was, "I'm sorry, I'm a lawyer. I don't do ethics." What we teach our students is that if you behave ethically, you usually don't get into legal trouble. And if you behave legally, you usually don't get into ethical trouble.

Brotman: How are you teaching this to students in journalism school?
Dalglish: We try to teach them that there is journalistic responsibility because it's a good thing. Here's why: this is what society expects in general. We're all better off if we behave responsibly. But is it required? No, it's not really inherent in the First Amendment. It's just not.

I would argue that because the bulk of mass communication over the previous hundred years came through news organizations that have been fair and responsible, by and large we were able to show a certain amount of respect and facilitate civil discourse. One of the things I'm most concerned about in our society right now is polarization and a leadership that does not behave in a fair and responsible and truthful manner. Everybody then thinks it is okay to behave that way.

In our country, what are we united on these days? Baseball? Twenty-five years ago, when the internet was getting going, all of this seemed so wonderful. Self-actualization. People will be able to express themselves. I didn't quite count on some of them behaving as badly as they behave now.

I worry so much about bloggers and folks like that, along with social media platforms like Twitter. People have really been damaged. That's not to say that people haven't been damaged by mainstream press occasionally over the years. They have. I'll acknowledge that. But now we have more damaged individuals, I think, more regularly. It's also led to a polarization of society. I don't know how we're going to get it back. I don't know how we're going to get back some of those basic notions of democracy.

There's a guy who gave a speech at a political science academic conference recently. He basically said, "Congratulations, we've passed the height of democracy. The heyday of democracy was 1981. Now it's going down. Now with all this self-actualization and free speech, the dictatorships are coming back. The rise of authoritarian governments corresponds with the rise in the internet." It was a really interesting talk to hear.

Brotman: The bloom seems off the internet rose now.

Dalglish: I think we might have passed this new Age of Enlightenment. I really think, as fabulous as the internet has been, technology has harmed our ability to accomplish a lot of those goals. While the potential for greater good is amplified, the potential for damage is amplified as well. Because the bad things are so much, we pay so much more attention to them. I think the good things sometimes get lost.

Brotman: Can we be doing a better job of teaching about the First Amendment? You seem to have benefited from such early exposure in school.

Dalglish: Civic education is happening in extremely isolated pockets. There are some high schools out there doing amazing things, worrying about amazing things. I think the Student Press Law Center helped enormously to protect what those kids can do or say. But for financial reasons or because school districts figure they have to focus on STEM [science, technology, engineering, mathematics], a lot of those programs are being eliminated. That scares me.

Brotman: What about support at the grassroots level?

Dalglish: I think we're going to see some community groups getting a lot more agitated. I think this is going to help opportunities for leadership too. I worry about communities, because if you look back on the line of cases that have supported the public's right to know, or the rights of the news media, if you look at the captions, that was almost always going to have the name of a local newspaper in it.

They're still litigating some of those things but not as much. They don't have the money. They have to pick and choose their legal battles a lot more carefully these days. But I think also you find some pockets of folks like the big media forces—the *Washington Post,* the *New York Times*, and the *Wall Street Journal.* They've got some pretty gifted lawyers and editors who're going to have to speak out for the rest of us. The electronic media has not been involved as often. It's largely a financial issue, a huge financial issue. Everybody's trying to scrape by.

I'll tell you where the broadcasters still get involved—in things having to do with access to demonstrations. They've been involved in court proceedings. They actually got live audio coming out of the Supreme Court in a decision. That's progress. I mean kudos to everybody who worked on that. I didn't think they would, I thought maybe they would tape it and then release it, but live, that's really remarkable. So we're only one step away from visual. It may be a big step, you know. I've never really understood that because the states that have cameras in the courtroom seem to do just fine.

I think the fears people have about that access, about cameras in the courts, are overblown. They really are. I was speaking to some federal Ninth Circuit judges. Some of them are just crying for reporters to show up again and start covering this stuff because people don't have enough exposure to what the courts do. One benefit to society surely is having that high level of exposure.

Bob Corn-Revere

Bob Corn-Revere is a partner at the law firm Davis Wright Tremaine LLP in Washington, D.C. He has long been a leader in advising clients in the areas of media, communications, and information technology law. He is a tireless advocate for client First Amendment rights, with particular experience applying these protections to new communications technologies. As a former Federal Communications Commission official, he has helped clients navigate complex regulations and administrative proceedings, and as a former journalist he assists media organizations in their ability to gather and disseminate information.

Corn-Revere has advocated for his clients in courts across the country, including all of the federal appellate courts and the U.S. Supreme Court. He has won landmark First Amendment victories that extend full constitutional protections into novel areas. He served as counsel in the U.S. Supreme Court in United States v. Playboy Entertainment Group, Inc., *and* United States v. Stevens, *setting important First Amendment precedents. He also represented CBS Corporation against the FCC in the Super Bowl "wardrobe malfunction" case, forcing the agency to pay back fines it had assessed.*

He has litigated over a dozen cases involving the First Amendment rights of public university students and faculty members as outside counsel for the Stand Up for Speech initiative of the Foundation for Individual Rights in Education. He successfully petitioned Governor George E. Pataki to grant the first posthumous pardon in New York history, to the late comedian Lenny Bruce, in a landmark pro bono *case.*

Corn-Revere is a former president and national chairman of the First Amendment Lawyers Association, is a member of the Media Institute First Amendment Advisory Council, and previously served on the board of the American Library Association Freedom to Read Foundation.

162 The Conversations

Stuart Brotman: How did you begin getting involved in issues related to free speech and free press?

Bob Corn-Revere: In high school, I started writing for the local town newspaper. I grew up in a small community. Fifteen-year-olds don't often get columns in newspapers. The Charleston, Illinois, newspaper would publish on its back page on Saturdays the newspaper for Charleston High School. I had a friend who would write for it. I told him they should have a column from my high school, which was in an adjacent town but in the same county. He talked to the publisher, and they offered me a gig as a paid writer. I made the princely sum of three dollars a week.

I started out writing about school events and things like that. I quickly got bored writing about just what was going on in school and so started writing opinion columns about things like [the killing of student protestors by Ohio National Guardsmen at] Kent State and Vietnam War protests. The following year, they stopped publishing the Charleston school newspaper in the town paper, but they called me and said, "We'd like you to keep writing these things." So I continued writing the columns without having to connect them to high-school life.

Brotman: Then you go off to college.

Corn-Revere: Yes, but a very short distance away. I attended Eastern Illinois University, which was only ten miles away from my hometown. So during summers, I stayed with the newspaper as a reporter covering the city council, the county board, and the school board.

Brotman: When did you begin to veer off from journalism toward an interest in law?

Corn-Revere: I always had plans eventually to go to law school. At one point, a good friend who was a fellow reporter said, "Did you know there's such a thing as media law?" I thought that was interesting. He planted a seed that stayed in the back of my mind. The other thing too is that I've always hated bullies. I've always hated the authoritarian mindset, so that was sort of a natural background for getting involved in First Amendment issues as well.

Brotman: You also were involved as a college debater, right?

Corn-Revere: I got involved in debate beginning in high school. I did various kinds of forensic activities including debate—individual events like original oration and extemporaneous speaking. I went to a lot of tournaments and got a scholarship offer to continue doing debate in college.

Brotman: Were there any experiences you had during that period where you saw examples of interference with free speech or free press?

Corn-Revere: I saw things that I thought were abuses of power, which as a reporter I always wanted to uncover and write about when I became aware of them.

Brotman: And did anyone stop you from doing this?

Corn-Revere: I was never the target of anyone trying to prevent any of those kinds of publications.

Brotman: What about the ability to get information from government?

Corn-Revere: You try and cultivate as many sources as you can to get information, and I had my local go-to sources. But at that time, I knew nothing of the Freedom of Information Act or the state sunshine laws.

Brotman: But in the end, you left Illinois behind to attend law school in Washington, D.C.

Corn-Revere: I guess you'd say I took the scenic route from high school through law school because I was in no rush. I squeezed four years into five for my undergraduate studies, pursuing a double major in communication studies and journalism. But I spent probably 90 percent of my time during college on debate and my newspaper reporting job. After graduating, I was offered a graduate assistantship at the University of Massachusetts in Amherst. I coached the undergraduate debaters and focused on graduate work. By that time I knew I really wanted to go on to law school and get involved in media law. So I focused my studies on broadcast history and regulation. I started learning the background of the Communications Act, the FCC, and the regulation of electronic media.

After that, I came to D.C. and started law school at the Catholic University of America. One of the reasons that I went there is because

164   The Conversations

Harvey Zuckman, a professor there, was starting a communications law program. I ended up working with Harvey as his research assistant on a reference book that summarized the law of mass communications. That ultimately led to being asked by him to be a co-author of a larger treatise on modern communications law. So by the time I finished law school, I was pretty well steeped in media law.

Brotman: Who were some of your other intellectual influences in the First Amendment field?

Corn-Revere: One early inspiration was Mike Royko, the legendary columnist for the *Chicago Daily News*. That actually goes back to even before high school, because I was a newspaper carrier as a kid. I would deliver the morning *Chicago Daily News* in my small downstate community. I got hooked on reading Royko's columns, talking about the abuse of City Hall and the Mayor [Richard J.] Daley regime. This was in the mid-1960s. It really kind of hooked me on what journalism can do in standing up to power.

Later, another major influence was Nat Hentoff, with his *Village Voice* columns and his books. He was a very big influence. Then, as I was studying in law school, I came across the writings of Professor Geoffrey Stone at the University of Chicago Law School. And Burton Joseph, a lawyer who had a long association with the ACLU and also *Playboy* magazine. Judith Krug, who for a long time ran the intellectual freedom office at the American Library Association, was another big influence. She really had the First Amendment in her bones.

Brotman: Some of these people were leading anti-censorship advocates. How did this meld with your thinking about media law?

Corn-Revere: Well they go hand in hand. I began to see cases of censorship that had a real-world impact on people's lives. In law school I learned about Mary Beth Tinker in Iowa standing up to the authorities in her high school. They didn't want her to have this gentle little protest against the Vietnam War by wearing a black armband to school. First Amendment stories like this help illuminate the principles that protect freedom of conscience and free expression.

Brotman: Why do you think this was perceived by school authorities as being such a threat?

Corn-Revere: It was only through time that I began to wonder more about not just the mindset of people who are trying to vindicate their rights or establish these principles but the mindset of those who were trying to suppress speech. That became really fascinating to me. And it tied into my natural aversion to authoritarian modes of thought.

Brotman: This sounds like a deeper-held feeling, maybe from childhood?
Corn-Revere: I was an avid reader of comic books as a kid growing up. They were pretty well sanitized already because the controversies over comic-book censorship started in 1948 or so and went through about 1955. That's when the Comics Code Authority was adopted.

By then, the comics that I read as a kid were the ones with the seal of the Comics Code Authority, certifying that they meet the decency standards that were established by the industry. I grew up reading both DC and the Marvel Comics—Superman, Batman, Green Lantern, Spider Man, Thor. These mainstream, standard comic books were all that was available to me as a kid in the early to mid-1960s. I thought the seal meant someone said these comics are okay, but I had no idea what they meant. When I went into a movie theater in the late 1960s, there were industry movie ratings. And when I watched TV, at the beginning of a broadcast day, there was yet another seal of approval, issued by the National Association of Broadcasters. This was all just part of the background that we lived in, with an assumption that some authority is going to be in control of what we view or read, that someone is going to make these decisions for us.

It was only later, as I learned about the First Amendment and media law, and the ways in which these private ratings systems are sometimes driven by threats of government coercion, that I became aware of the interplay between authority and free expression. In a free society, the natural order isn't that someone's going to make these decisions for us. The natural order under the First Amendment is that as individuals we make these decisions for ourselves.

Brotman: Why do you think people are interested in censoring the communication of others?
Corn-Revere: It starts as a way to promote a cause that motivates them. It may be a single issue. I don't think anyone grows up aspiring to be a censor. I think what happens is that people develop, for whatever reasons,

a set of ideas that they believe are so self-evident that they must be true, not just for themselves but for everybody. And once you have that level of certainty, that level of absolute conviction that you are right, then you begin to think that that is something that can be imposed by the government.

I think that's where this mindset begins. That's exactly what you see in the rise of Anthony Comstock, who was the first professional censor in America. I guess if he were growing up in the dot-com era, he would be following the advice of dot-com entrepreneurs—create your own job. That's what Anthony Comstock did.

He had originally been from Connecticut, served in the Civil War, then moved to New York and became a dry-goods clerk. But his hobby was to be an anti-vice vigilante. He felt that the salacious publications of the time were ruining young men. So he started his own endeavor of raiding booksellers and magazine peddlers to make citizen's arrests, and he would invite reporters to come along. Given the publicity, his rise was almost meteoric. He did his first raid and got some coverage for that in 1872.

This brought him to the attention of the YMCA, which formed a committee to further Comstock's endeavors—a Committee for the Suppression of Vice. Some of the rich benefactors in New York helped support this. They authorized Comstock to travel to Washington, D.C., to see if he could persuade Congress to adopt a new federal obscenity law.

Brotman: Was he successful there?
Corn-Revere: Absolutely. By March 1873, there was a new law, the Comstock Act, elements of which are still part of the U.S. federal code. He gave up being a dry-goods clerk and went into enforcing morals full time. He was the secretary of the New York Society for the Suppression of Vice and also was a special agent of the Post Office. For the next forty years he essentially set the moral agenda for what could be published in America. Although he was not a government official—just a quasi-government official with a badge—he could make arrests. He essentially got a commission from Congress but he was not on the government payroll.

Brotman: Wow!

Corn-Revere: The committee that he had helped form for the YMCA was rolled into its own organization—the New York Society for the Suppression of Vice. Do you know what the seal for the New York Society for the Suppression of Vice showed? It had a Victorian gentleman with a top hat, dropping armloads of books onto a bonfire. So it wasn't just a job, it was a point of pride that he was a book burner. He would not only burn the books but he would melt down the printing plates to make sure that they couldn't be reprinted.

Brotman: Quite a horrific image.

Corn-Revere: There's more. Comstock drove a number of people, some say at least fifteen different people, to suicide. He was proud of that fact and even publicized it. And later on, he would try to suppress classic literature. He went after authors such as Walt Whitman and George Bernard Shaw, among many others.

Nothing was too small to escape Comstock's attention. Censorship literally consumed him. On one occasion he was seen on subway cars covering up parts of posters that he thought were too salacious. Comstock is the one who set the tone and decided what speech government could suppress. That's why the mindset of the censor is something that I became very interested in. What does it take for someone to believe that they are so right about how people should live, how they should think, that they would impose their will on everyone else?

He was pretty indiscriminate—he would not just target works of fiction. Comstock also prosecuted political and philosophical works, and even medical textbooks.

There was one particular doctor who created a sort of home health manual that became very popular at the time. Comstock thought that it went too far in discussing sexual matters. And so he brought an action against its author, Dr. Edward Bliss Foote. Foote and his son, Dr. Edward Bond Foote, became strong opponents of the Comstock Act as a result. Along with all this, Comstock was opposed to anything that even discussed contraception. As a matter of fact, the Comstock Act itself was designed to specifically prevent the transmission through the mails of any printed information that involved contraception.

168   The Conversations

His last case was to prosecute Margaret Sanger, a turn-of-the-twentieth-century advocate for birth control, and the driving force behind what became Planned Parenthood. He wanted to put her behind bars for her activities in supporting birth control. She had gone to England to avoid prosecution, and while she was there, Comstock did a sting operation and arrested her husband. He also served as the chief witness for the prosecution. With high-profile cases like this, Comstock got as much press as P. T. Barnum. At the time, Comstock was one of the most famous men in America. He died just days after the Sanger trial ended, and his obituary ran on the front page of the *New York Times*. Comstock is largely forgotten today, but he set the moral agenda for this entire period, from the early 1870s until 1915, when he died. And his influence continued thereafter for decades.

The prevailing constitutional doctrine from the Comstock era didn't get overturned by the U.S. Supreme Court until 1957. So we're talking about an eighty-year period where the notion of national censorship was pioneered in the 1870s at the behest of largely one man.

Brotman: He surely had accomplices though.
Corn-Revere: Sadly, yes. People responded to what we now call a "moral panic." There is a tendency for politicians to propose simplistic answers to complex problems, particularly when they want to avoid scrutiny. In 1873, Congress needed something to divert attention from the Crédit Mobilier scandal and passing the Comstock Act that year was just the ticket. Another tried and true tactic is adopting measures from whatever activists claim is a threat to children in some way. You know, you can never politically go wrong by saying that you're going to protect children, in whatever form that happens to take. Comstock didn't just target obscenity; he campaigned against dime novels, newspaper accounts of crime, "salacious" art, and even home medical guides, claiming they would corrupt the youth of the day.

Eventually, his act wore thin. Comstock had gone too far and became the subject of ridicule. Students at Princeton, at one of his campus appearances, glued flannel leggings to a statue on campus—*The Gladiator*—because they said they didn't want Comstock to be too offended by seeing it undressed. Comstock increasingly was lampooned in political cartoons, particularly after his forays into censoring art. George Bernard Shaw popularized *Comstockery* as a term connoting prudishness and excessive zeal. The culture changed around Comstock, and eventually the law of free expression caught up. However, this didn't happen until long after Comstock's death.

Brotman: Was Comstock a precursor of Senator Joseph McCarthy, who in the 1950s sought to root out communists in the United States, whether real or imagined?

Corn-Revere: There are parallels between Comstock and Senator McCarthy. Both men exhibited the type of absolute certainty about their causes that intimidated their adversaries. Whether their certainty was real or used for show, it is a tactic frequently used by the type of person who strives to seize power and impose their will on others. And when such people successfully exploit a moral panic, they often get little pushback from the rest of society—at least at first.

Brotman: But then the tide turned.

Corn-Revere: Beginning in the late 1950s, as First Amendment doctrine developed, society changed with it, although a little bit behind.

Brotman: Censorship remains a social norm after all these years.

Corn-Revere: The drive toward censorship will never go away. We'll always see it in one form or another. Moral panics haven't stopped, and certain people will always promote causes that they think are so important that they can impose their will on the rest of us. Comstock and his followers ruined the notion of censorship as a profession. Because Comstock became such an embarrassment, nobody today wants to be called a censor. They'll try and find some other label to describe what they're doing. They'll try to justify their actions using various ways, or they'll say what you're doing isn't really speech or it's not speech that the Constitution protects. For example, Dr. Fredric Wertham called his proposals to ban the sale of comic books to kids a "public health measure," and he bristled at being called a censor. But in the end, those who advocate speech restrictions want to do the same thing—to impose their will on others about what they ought to read.

Brotman: What about when an entire industry then adopts this based on the notion that either it will keep censors off their backs, or it will actually be a good business decision?

Corn-Revere: The situation with comic books I just mentioned illustrates this phenomenon. After World War II, there was a moral panic regarding comic books. Starting in the popular press, the question was raised whether reading comics was good for kids. Comics were wildly popular then to a degree that is hard to appreciate today. And a few in the medical community—most notably Dr. Fredric Wertham, who I just mentioned—began to claim that crime- and horror-themed comics caused juvenile delinquency. Wertham even claimed that Superman caused a disrespect for authority and comics like Batman and Robin and Wonder Woman turned kids gay. State and local lawmakers had great difficulty coming up with a law that could survive constitutional review, so they did what often occurs in this situation: they applied pressure on the industry through congressional hearings and threats of legislation. After notorious hearings in 1954 in which Dr. Wertham testified, the comic book industry adopted a "voluntary" code of self-regulation. It devastated the comics industry, which didn't recover until the 1970s and 1980s. Now, all the hysteria about comics just looks foolish, and Wertham has been roundly discredited.

This is a scenario that repeats itself all the time. It didn't start in the 1950s. We saw moral panics like this in the nineteenth century and probably even before that. Then, there were cheap, sensational theater productions, called penny-dreadfuls, that were blamed for causing crime among lower-class children in London. Toward the end of the nineteenth century in the U.S., cheap paperbacks about crime or cowboys, commonly known as dime novels, were likewise blamed for inspiring wayward youth. In the early twentieth century, there was moral panic surrounding jazz music, and a few decades later, we saw the same thing with rock-n-roll. When hip-hop was becoming popular, we saw this cycle repeat itself.

A lot of the panic focuses on youth culture—whatever the kids are interested in that scares or confuses the parents. More recently, we see the same reaction with things like video games, electronic media, and social media. The cycle repeats itself over and over again.

Brotman: At least now there is well-developed First Amendment law that can help society dampen moral panic. Your thoughts?

Corn-Revere: First Amendment jurisprudence certainly is much better developed now, but courts historically were slow to adapt traditional First Amendment principles to newer technologies. While the printing press was contemplated by the framers of the Constitution, the courts still had to figure out what the "free press" meant. At least they knew that whatever it meant, it clearly applied to the printing press.

When newer technologies developed, like cinema and radio, the courts were baffled as to how to deal with them. When the first cases arose that asked whether these technologies were protected by the First Amendment, the courts said "no." The Supreme Court in 1915 held that cinema isn't the "press" and therefore falls outside the First Amendment. It said that cinema is just entertainment, and that it's probably pretty dangerous and should be regulated. This ruling upheld state licensing boards for movies, which required preclearance before movies could be exhibited. The same approach affected radio a couple decades later, and radio was licensed by the federal government.

Brotman: So we went from Comstock, who was a private citizen who had developed some sort of crazy governmental role, to the government itself actually asserting certain powers over free speech.

Corn-Revere: That's right. Those powers continued through most of the twentieth century. But as First Amendment law began to develop through the mid-twentieth century, and to achieve more doctrinal coherence, the courts became more comfortable applying First Amendment protection to newer technologies.

The Supreme Court in 1997 dealt with whether the First Amendment protected the internet. For the first time in history, the Court right out of the box said "yes, this new technology is fully protected by the First Amendment." Since then, courts have been increasingly comfortable applying full First Amendment protection to the newest communication technologies.

I don't mean to suggest that we have now resolved all these difficult free speech issues. That 1997 decision I mentioned—*Reno v. ACLU*—invalidated a federal law that tried to apply so-called indecency regulations to the internet. The Court held that the First Amendment protects speech on the internet, but also that the test for indecency was too vague as a restriction on speech. Just to be clear, indecency is a body of law that was "borrowed" from rules that regulate broadcast radio and television. The Supreme Court has not yet struck down indecency rules for radio and TV (although it came close in 2012), and lower courts increasingly have taken a hard look at FCC decisions in this area. I think it is safe to say the days are numbered for the FCC's ability to regulate in this area, but it is still trying to keep its options open. It continues to do so even as the rise of streaming video and the proliferation of various subscription models for video programming make the indecency rules irrelevant or obsolete. Yet the doctrine still exists.

Indecency is essentially the embodiment of what obscenity law was under Comstock in the nineteenth and early twentieth centuries. Indecency is related to obscenity in that it is a regulation of expression related to sex or excretory activities, but it doesn't deal with hardcore depictions of sexual activity, as is the case with modern obscenity law. Indecency law just deals with "bad words" or can be a reference to images of sex or nudity. The test the FCC developed for indecency is almost indistinguishable from the test for obscenity in Comstock's time. That test was imported from Victorian England in a case called *Regina v. Hicklin*, and it held that if the tendency of speech might corrupt the morals of a vulnerable person who was exposed to it, then it should be prohibited. There was no need to consider the entire book—an isolated passage was enough for a conviction—and the literary or artistic merit of the work was irrelevant. Courts didn't consider the potential impact of the material on the average person but on the most vulnerable, and contemporary community standards did not apply. Under that standard, under which Comstock thrived, any reference to sex in a book could be considered obscene. Publishers of information on birth control and even doctors who published home health guides were prosecuted and convicted. Under that standard, courts would refuse to permit the entire book to be submitted in evidence because it was considered to be too "salacious" to be in the court's docket, and in some cases held a book's title alone was enough for a conviction. This law of obscenity was finally overturned in *Roth v. United States* in 1957, but the essential focus of the *Hicklin* rule lingers on in the FCC's law governing indecency.

Brotman: It sounds like the shadow of Anthony Comstock still is visible.
Corn-Revere: Sad but true. During his time, Comstock had a massive impact not just on the culture but on individual lives. He claimed to have convicted enough people to fill a train sixty cars long with sixty passengers in each car, and a sixty-first car almost full. He also claimed he had destroyed 160 tons of obscene literature and 4 million pictures. Comstock kept meticulous records for the number of books that he had destroyed and provided a tally every year in his annual reports for the New York Society for the Suppression of Vice.

The constitutional doctrine under which Comstock operated remained the law until the Supreme Court overturned it in 1957. *Roth v. United States* and subsequent cases established that for something to be obscene, a work had to appeal primarily to the prurient interest and be utterly without redeeming social value. To find something obscene, courts also were required to consider the work as a whole, not just isolated parts.

As the law was developing, there was still a significant risk that valuable speech would be suppressed. The pathbreaking comedian Lenny Bruce was arrested and prosecuted for doing his routines in comedy clubs in the 1950s and early 1960s. Henry Miller's book *Tropic of Cancer* was being prosecuted as obscene. So was *Lady Chatterley's Lover.*

In 1973, the Supreme Court, after a series of subsequent cases, articulated the standard for obscenity that exists today, in *Miller v. California.* The law of obscenity is still no model of clarity, but due to cultural changes it has far less of an impact on art and entertainment today.

Brotman: It seems like there is a residue of thinking about obscenity in this even more nebulous area of indecency.
Corn-Revere: Indecency is this sort of "obscenity-lite" concept, and as I said before, the test for indecency is essentially the same one that Comstock applied to obscenity. Courts don't look at the work as a whole and don't look at whether the work has serious merit. The only question is whether or not this is material that a government official believes might be bad for a young person to see. This is the standard for indecency that the Federal Communications Commission continues to apply today.

Brotman: A little FCC history lesson would be helpful here.

Corn-Revere: The FCC attempted to define indecency in the 1970s. The counterculture comedian George Carlin had a routine called "Filthy Words" that popularly became known as the "seven dirty words" routine. This became the subject of a landmark Supreme Court decision in 1978, *FCC v. Pacifica Foundation*, which upheld the FCC's ability to enforce that legal standard for radio and TV.

Brotman: There also seems to be a connecting line between Lenny Bruce and George Carlin, right?
Corn-Revere: Yes, Carlin had many of the same comedic characteristics of Lenny Bruce. He too was a caustic social commentator. If you were tracing the family tree of comedy and the law, you would see a direct line between Lenny Bruce and George Carlin.

Brotman: Let's go back to the Carlin broadcast indecency case. Why do you think the FCC was interested in this?
Corn-Revere: Many things were changing in the 1960s, and the FCC was trying to get a handle on how to handle radio. FM radio began to develop in the late 1960s almost as a separate medium, particularly for airing music and spoken-word comedy.

At the beginning of the 1960s, there was a very conservative, very staid view of what could be said on air. A station actually lost its license because one of its misdeeds was having a radio personality who would say things like "Let it all hang out." That was considered to be beyond the pale. But by the end of the 1960s, with all of the cultural change, including the development of FM radio, there were on-air interviews with people like Jerry Garcia of the Grateful Dead, who was dropping the word *fuck* every third word in an interview.

The FCC then had to decide how to handle that phenomenon. It needed to develop a standard for indecency because the term was already written into the statute but no one had ever bothered to define it. So the FCC decided to come up with a standard that wasn't the obscenity standard but was something else—as I said before, "obscenity-lite."

No one could say for certain what indecency meant. When George Carlin did his routine on one of his comedy albums, listing the seven words that you can never say on radio or TV—shit, piss, fuck, cunt, cocksucker, motherfucker, and tits—the FCC decided to make this routine the subject of its test case after the bit was aired on New York City's Pacifica radio station, WBAI-FM, in the afternoon.

The broadcast received only one FCC complaint in all of metropolitan New York. A member of an activist group, Morality in Media, claimed to have been driving in his car listening to the station and heard the broadcast. He claimed in the complaint this took place at two o'clock in the afternoon on a weekday with his young son in the car. As it happened, this "young son" was fourteen or fifteen years old, and why he was out of school nobody knows.

Brotman: How did the FCC respond to this complaint?

Corn-Revere: At the time, the FCC tried to be a little bit circumspect. It didn't issue a fine to the Pacifica station. It simply placed a letter of admonition in the station's file. Such a letter could be used as ammunition if someone were to challenge renewal of the station's license in a future proceeding. Or if a station has other violations, then such things as a letter of admonition could be a factor that could provide some basis for imposing a higher fine. Having such a letter in the file is a black mark that no licensee that depends on the government for license renewal wants to have. For Pacifica, it was worth fighting the decision for that reason and also for the principle of free speech.

Brotman: The stage for a court appeal then was set.

Corn-Revere: Yes. The FCC defended its standard and lost in the court of appeals, in the D.C. Circuit, which held that this standard couldn't be intelligently applied.

The Justice Department looked at this decision and agreed not to appeal further, since it felt that the indecency standard was beyond redemption and would be a loser in the Supreme Court.

But the FCC decided to appeal to the Supreme Court on its own. No one was more surprised than the FCC that it won this decision on a five-to-four vote, which upheld its legal authority to enforce this indecency standard against broadcasters. The new chairman of the FCC at the time, Charles Ferris, announced within a week of the Supreme

Court's decision that the FCC was not going to become the nation's censor. It was going to apply the test for indecency very narrowly.

Brotman: How narrowly?

Corn-Revere: In essence, the FCC decided it was going to apply the test only to the seven words of the George Carlin monologue. For nine subsequent years, that was the law. As far as I can tell, George Carlin is the only standup comic ever to have created an actual legal standard. And it's funny to boot.

Brotman: Let's go back just a little bit, because during this period we have an evolution of a new type of talk radio, which is essentially people calling in and talking about sex topics. That was not covered by the enforcement of the indecency standard, but it was something that the FCC was sensitive to in a different way.

Corn-Revere: The FCC chairman at the time was Dean Burch. He was really upset about this phenomenon, dubbed "topless radio," which was very popular with housewives at the time. These were typically call-in shows during the afternoon. People would talk about their sexual problems or their sex lives or whatever. In March 1973, Chairman Burch gave a speech at a National Association of Broadcasters convention that basically said the FCC was not going to put up with this, and he threatened to take action against broadcasters that failed to get in line. Within a matter of weeks, this very popular radio format disappeared.

This isn't uncommon for licensed media. It goes back to that issue of how technology is treated differently under the First Amendment and what anomalies that creates. But the framers of the Constitution knew they were dealing with a business institution when they said they were protecting the press. That was the new technology of their era. That's one of the reasons why, given the history of press licensing in England, it was considered to be understood that the First Amendment prohibited licensing of the press.

When newer communication technologies were introduced in the early twentieth century, this question was reconsidered. We now have an arguably more powerful medium than print, an electronic medium that suddenly the government decides it can license. We can talk about the

Bob Corn-Revere

historic reasons for that, like spectrum management, but I think it's not obvious that government licensing had to be the solution for broadcasting.

There could have been a system of spectrum leasing or spectrum ownership, but we ended up with a system of press licensing. What comes with that is a more fraught relationship between electronic publishers and the government. When you have a format like topless radio, all it takes is a speech from the head of the agency that licenses broadcasters and suddenly that kind of speech disappears.

Brotman: There are other examples of this "raised eyebrow" regulation that doesn't even need to be written into a regulation or law in order to take effect.

Corn-Revere: The same thing happened in the early 1970s with drug lyrics, where the FCC had a public notice that went out, which attached a memo from the Pentagon. The memo said, in essence, "Here are songs that are being played on the radio that we think glorify drugs."

They included songs like "Puff the Magic Dragon" by Peter, Paul, and Mary, and "The Pusher," a Steppenwolf song that was actually an anti-drug message. But it didn't matter because, suddenly, this memo from the Pentagon became a de-facto do-not-play list.

That's the ghost of Comstock rising again. Where government has the authority to affect the lives and livelihoods of publishers, it is understandable that people will bend their will to these officials. Cases like that almost never get litigated. Regulation by raised eyebrow is insidious, and it often is beyond the reach of the legal system because it takes place outside the judicial process.

Brotman: Let's talk about indecency as it has been applied in the post-Carlin era. In particular, other contexts such as fleeting expletives during live broadcasts or fleeting depictions of nudity, sometimes only a second or two on TV.

Corn-Revere: After the *Pacifica* case, at least broadcasters had some guidelines. They knew that the seven words from the George Carlin monologue were going to be prohibited. There was a clear, bright line.

The price of that clarity was the fact that you had a rule that really didn't do anything. It's no coincidence that for the nine years after the

Pacifica decision came down, there were no indecency enforcement cases at the FCC. But then a new round of complaints arose from certain activist groups, and some even picketed outside the FCC.

The FCC responded by changing its indecency standard very slightly. As I mentioned, one of the reasons why the Supreme Court upheld the FCC's indecency standard is because the FCC promised to use its power very carefully. It basically said, "We're really only enforcing it against the verbal shock treatment of the Carlin monologue." Among other things, it wouldn't bring an enforcement action if the words were fleeting or were broadcast by accident.

That's where this "fleeting expletives" exception to the indecency standard was created. If the slip was brief and unintended, the FCC's position was "no harm, no foul." The indecency standard also did not impose a prohibition on speech, as does obscenity. Instead, the FCC said indecent speech had to be channeled to late night when kids presumably aren't in the audience. With those reservations, and limiting the indecency concept just to those seven words, there was a small area of potential prohibition, or at least this late-night zoning.

Brotman: What changed?

Corn-Revere: There's a lot of edgy stuff you can air that can offend many in the audience that doesn't include the seven Carlin words. Consequently, the FCC started getting more complaints in the late 1980s, and it decided to adopt what they called a "generic" indecency standard. This meant the FCC would return to a more general description of indecency. Under the generic standard, indecency *could* (and almost certainly would) include the seven prohibited words, but it also could include anything else that could fit within the general description. Still, however, indecency wouldn't include fleeting expletives and inadvertent on-air utterances or images, such as someone blurting out something on a live broadcast. And the FCC pledged to enforce the generic standard with restraint.

That was the compromise. Indecency was no longer limited just to the Carlin words, but the FCC still claimed the policy was narrow because of the exceptions for fleeting expletives and channeling indecent material to late night. That approach held for another twelve years or so. There were some court cases challenging the generic indecency standard, but none of them made it to the Supreme Court.

Brotman: Then the twenty-first century began, and along with it the FCC began to change its thinking in this area.

Corn-Revere: In the late 1990s and then in the early 2000s, political interest in this area began to build. In a January 2003 live broadcast of the Golden Globe Awards, Bono of the band U2 showed a tad too much exuberance when accepting a Golden Globe for the band. He exclaimed, "This is really fucking brilliant!" The "fucking" part failed to get bleeped out by the network standards and practices folks, and it went out over the live broadcast. At the time, the FCC said that it understood that fleeting expletives like this were not actionable under its indecency standard and so the staff initially didn't find that Bono's slip of the tongue was a violation.

Brotman: That didn't end the matter, did it?

Corn-Revere: No, it didn't satisfy Congress or the people who were complaining about it. More importantly, it didn't satisfy the activist groups, the so-called morality police. The Parents TV Council was chief among them. These people are the spiritual descendants of Anthony Comstock.

They wanted to eliminate the fleeting expletives exception, and they managed to persuade Congress to hold a hearing on the FCC staff's Golden Globe decision and on indecency enforcement generally. The FCC dispatched the head of its enforcement bureau testify, and he promised the FCC was going to change the standard. This was the beginning of 2004, and it already was a hot political issue during an election year.

No one realized at the time that this issue was going to go nuclear very soon. Three days after the Golden Globes hearing, the Super Bowl "wardrobe malfunction" happened. During the live broadcast of the Super Bowl halftime show with Janet Jackson and Justin Timberlake, at the end of the performance there was an unscripted and unanticipated move. Timberlake pulled off a piece from the bodice of Janet Jackson's costume, revealing for nine-sixteenths of a second her bare left breast.

Brotman: What happened then?

180   The Conversations

Corn-Revere: All hell broke loose, starting with more congressional hearings. The FCC and its leaders were hauled before Congress to explain what they were going to do. Record fines were levied against the broadcasters by the FCC. Congress revised the law, multiplying the level of fines by ten times. Television station groups were forced to reach settlement agreements with the FCC, in some cases for millions of dollars.

CBS, who I represented after the Super Bowl incident, was fined $550,000 for the "wardrobe malfunction." The FCC knew, and we provided them with all of the information following a complete investigation, that the incident was totally unplanned and unauthorized by the network. This was not part of the script. It was something the performers came up with after the rehearsals and before the show.

None of that mattered. The FCC had Congress breathing down its neck, so it decided to hold the network responsible, fining it $550,000. We ended up in litigation for eight years and ultimately prevailed with the Federal Third Circuit court deciding that the FCC had violated the due process rights of CBS. It reversed the fine and forced the FCC to pay back the $550,000.

Brotman: As a political matter, regulating indecency to protect children seems to have a widespread appeal.

Corn-Revere: Yes, the entire focus of the indecency standard is on youth, and its entire reason for being is to prevent exposure by young people to mainly sexual words or images. Obviously, there's a reasonable argument that younger people may need more protection from exposure to certain content, and the government may have a role to play in that area.

That notion has been embedded into law—children are not adults, that they need some kind of protection. Normally, we rely on parents for that. But as media has grown up, there are certain areas of law that have allowed government to support this parental role. For example, if a kid were to go into a bookstore, the government may require that girlie magazines or adult books must be kept on a blinder rack. This attempts to strike a balance between protecting children and allowing adult access to material they have a right to obtain. The idea behind blinder racks is that you don't impede the ability of adults to buy the material, but kids will not be exposed to the covers in the store.

Bob Corn-Revere

With electronic media, it is harder to strike the same balance of protecting kids without unduly restricting speech. One-size-fits-all solutions, like the FCC's indecency rules, are too cumbersome. Only one-third of American households have kids under eighteen, yet indecency regulation restricts speech in 100 percent of households.

This issue also came up in the context of internet regulation. The first law Congress adopted to deal with the internet was the Communications Decency Act (CDA), which was part of the 1996 rewrite of the Communications Act. The CDA attempted to extend the indecency standard by importing it from broadcasting to the internet. Had this effort succeeded, George Carlin's seven dirty words (and much more) would be banned from the internet, if you can imagine that. Fortunately, the Supreme Court held that applying any indecency regulation to the internet violated the First Amendment.

This was the very first time in history the Supreme Court, when confronted with a new communication technology, accorded it full First Amendment protection. It wisely struck down the indecency provisions of the Communications Decency Act that attempted to regulate the internet as if it were broadcast radio and television.

The indecency standard itself was so amorphous that the Supreme Court found it could not be applied in an intelligible way. The Court also noted that online media enables individual households to filter out unwanted content, allowing parents to be more selective about what comes into the home. Equally as important, the Court observed that the government could not apply standards that have been used for radio and television to this new medium.

Brotman: We've talked about broadcasting, a medium based on receiving signals through antennas. But most viewers now watch television through cable, not broadcasting. These indecency restrictions have not been applied to cable TV, right?

Corn-Revere: Cable TV originally started in the 1940s and 1950s as a way of serving communities that couldn't get good reception for over-the-air television signals because of terrain issues. Entrepreneurs in these areas began to put an antenna up on the mountainside and then feed a

182 The Conversations

cable down into the community so people could receive broadcast TV in their homes.

Beginning in the 1970s, unique content began to be offered for cable TV. New networks sprang up where for the first time people were seeing uncut movies in their homes. Some of this content, particularly on subscription networks, included nudity or other content that if you aired the material on broadcast television, it would be sanctioned for indecency by the FCC.

This led to court challenges to determine whether the government could regulate cable TV in the same way as broadcast TV. This started mainly at the state and local level. Various ordinances were adopted to prevent cable operators from being able to show uncut movies. Those ordinances were struck down by the courts as violating the First Amendment.

Brotman: But the desire to regulate cable television continued in a different way then.

Corn-Revere: Yes. By then, there was a mature cable industry with adult networks offered as separate subscription channels. In the Telecommunications Act of 1996, Congress included a provision to regulate adult cable networks, because even on scrambled channels, the possibility that some of the content would bleed through the signal existed. People might either hear sounds or see some hazy visual content. These adult channels were already scrambled—encrypted—so that only those people who had paid the subscription price would receive the channel.

This is a business model where people pay for content. For those who don't pay, there must be an ability to block the channel from unauthorized reception. On the earlier cable systems before digital technology, there were analog systems where sometimes the scrambling was imperfect. It could be affected by many things, such as by weather, the cable installation at a particular household, or even by the particular TV set in a subscriber's home. Because of these diverse circumstances, sometimes some of the content would bleed through. With this new law, Congress tried to regulate adult cable networks where the scrambling isn't perfect by treating it like broadcast TV.

Under this law, the cable operator would be required to turn off its adult network signal for two-thirds of the broadcast day. As a consequence, the affected adult channels could be on only after 10 p.m.—during those times when the FCC assumed children are not going to be in the audience. This legal restriction was applicable to all households because of the possibility that in some households, some adult content might get past the scrambling technology.

Brotman: The race to court for a challenge on free speech grounds was inevitable.

Corn-Revere: Indeed. This was the challenge that Playboy Entertainment Group brought, which ultimately went to the Supreme Court. This occurred around the same time as the challenge to the CDA's internet indecency regulations we discussed. The lower court in this case first issued a temporary restraining order barring enforcement of the law, but ultimately it was allowed to go into effect.

The law had a very predictable impact on channels like Playboy TV. The network basically was turned off by many cable systems at the time because it wasn't economic for a system to have an affiliation with a channel if the cable system couldn't transmit it full time.

The decision allowing the law to go into effect ultimately was reversed by a three-judge panel, but the federal government took the case to the Supreme Court for a final resolution. In a five-to-four vote, the Supreme Court struck down that law as a violation of the First Amendment.

Brotman: I know you argued that case. What was your strategy in getting the justices to understand the differences between broadcast and cable television?

Corn-Revere: Knowing that cable had elements that looked like broadcasting, I knew that the Supreme Court justices might think, "Well, cable TV seems like broadcasting, so we will treat it like broadcasting." That is one of the difficult things about evaluating different communication technologies under different constitutional standards.

Cable and over-the-air television provide the same type of content through the same appliance into the same household, and yet they're treated differently under constitutional law. I give presentations where I will ask an audience to imagine five TV video monitors at the front of the room. All of them have an identical picture. Then I'll ask them, "To what extent can the government regulate or ban that image?"

184   The Conversations

The answer is, "It depends." It isn't based on what picture is in the box but rather how the picture got into the box. In this hypothetical, one TV monitor is playing a videotape on a VCR. That medium is essentially un-regulated, at least no more than traditional obscenity laws. Certainly, indecency laws wouldn't apply there. But if that same image was transmitted to the TV monitor via an over-the-air broadcast, then indecency regulations would apply. You would get different answers depending on whether the hypothetical monitors were fed by cable, the internet, or some other source. My task in persuading the Supreme Court was to get the justices to focus on whether it made sense to deviate from traditional First Amendment protections because of the transmission technology involved.

Brotman: How difficult was that to do?
Corn-Revere: By that time of the argument, fortunately, case law had begun to develop, with other courts holding that cable television could not be regulated in the same way as over-the-air broadcasting because regulation wasn't based upon the use of licensed spectrum. Cable is a subscription medium and wasn't broadcast over the air to everybody. Given the cases in the lower courts exploring that issue, I had an intellectual foothold for how to approach it at the Supreme Court.

Brotman: The differing First Amendment treatment for these five TV monitors still remains as a legal norm today.
Corn-Revere: Yes. And this is a strong argument for why the indecency standard should be revisited by the Supreme Court. It simply isn't sustainable given the many changes in technology, and in traditional constitutional terms can't be justified. Today there is a greatly enhanced ability to tailor media use on a household-by-household basis.

When William Howard Taft was chief justice in the 1930s, the Supreme Court was asked to decide how to treat radio under the First Amendment. But Chief Justice Taft considered radio as akin to the occult, and he sought to put off deciding the issue. So the Supreme Court for years didn't deal with the constitutional status of broadcasting. We see that phenomenon happening again today, where it looks like the Supreme Court will look for ways to kick the can down the road without ultimately deciding the status of the broadcast indecency standard.

This remains a significant issue for broadcasters, whose business depends on the approval of federal regulators. This is what makes licensing of a medium an anomaly in the United States, because we have a First Amendment that is grounded on the opposition to press licensing. Ever since the beginning of broadcasting, it has been an uneasy accommodation between regulatory goals and preserving First Amendment values. The tension comes to the fore with regulations like the broadcast indecency rules. They impose regulation of content on this medium that is not permitted for any other medium. The late Supreme Court Justice Ruth Bader Ginsburg, among others, had long been skeptical about the indecency rules, which she believed should be reconsidered for the twenty-first century. She could not persuade most of her fellow justices to do this, however.

Brotman: How is the FCC dealing with broadcast indecency complaints today?

Corn-Revere: For the most part, it isn't. After the courts rejected the FCC's efforts to crack down on indecency almost a decade ago, the FCC has had little to say about what the standard should be. In 2013, the FCC dismissed a backlog of complaints that had been languishing in its files and issued a public notice asking people to comment on how the indecency standard should be reformed. The FCC also announced that it was only going to enforce the regulations against what it called the most egregious cases, but without saying what that meant.

Now, years later, the FCC never acted on that public notice and never took any further action to redefine broadcast indecency. Do indecency regulations apply to news? Well, the FCC has gone both ways on that. What about serious films? We still don't know. Justice Elena Kagan joked during a Supreme Court that the FCC seemed to be applying a Steven Spielberg exception to its indecency rules. That's because films he directed, like *Saving Private Ryan* and *Schindler's List*, appeared to be spared the FCC's heightened enforcement standard but without any explanation for why they were treated differently. The FCC's inconsistent and unexplained standard remains in place today.

Brotman: Let's talk about another new technology which is now actually more old than new. Video games have similarities to books and comics, obviously, and affect a lot of young people too. Then some government regulations involving the sale of video games to minors began to be put in place.

Corn-Revere: Yes. This really started in the 1990s, as local communities adopted various regulations trying to ban certain kinds of violent video games or tying age restrictions to them.

Anthony Comstock strikes again. Comstock was an equal-opportunity censor. He was plenty worried about sex, anything that had the slightest hint of sex. He was against it. But he also went after dime novels because he saw them as training grounds for youth crime.

Video games are a descendant of Comstock's concern over dime novels and their potential to affect behavior. The concern with video games was essentially imitative behavior and also a desensitization to violence. The other thing that was happening at the time was a rising crime rate in the United States. Since video game sales were increasing at the same time, some people pointed to rising crime rates among youth and concluded that the games were the cause of youth crime.

But correlation is not causation. Another problem with the assumptions that were being made is that crime rates started dropping significantly beginning around 1993. So there was no real-world corroboration for the assertion that games cause crime. Plus, outside the United States, societies that had a high intensity of video game usage by youth also had low crime rates—places like Japan. In spite of these facts, various states started adopting restrictive video game laws.

Brotman: The court battles began again to challenge these restrictions.

Corn-Revere: And an interesting thing happened. Courts by now were increasingly applying First Amendment protections to new technologies. Video games were not just new but they also are interactive. The cases that emerged in the early 2000s were uniform in striking down these regulations, many of which suffered from the same conceptual difficulties as the broadcast indecency standard.

The various regulations typically sought to apply age restrictions on who could buy or rent a video game. The affected games were defined based on violent content and in some cases sexual content, with no clear definitions for what was meant by those terms. The laws sought to apply a "harmful to minors" theory to justify regulating sales or rentals to minors. "Harm to minors" is a doctrine somewhere in between obscenity and indecency. It is the legal doctrine that has been used to justify such measures as "blinder racks" that I mentioned before.

Brotman: But there was no definitive Supreme Court ruling on this yet that lower courts would be required to follow.

Corn-Revere: After California adopted a video game law that restricted sales to minors, the Supreme Court decided to take up this question of how to regulate violent video games. This was unusual because all the circuit courts to address such regulations up to this point had held the laws were unconstitutional. Usually, the Supreme Court will not take a case where all the circuit courts are in agreement.

There was great concern at the time about what the Supreme Court was going to do. The concept of "harmful to minors" always had been limited to sexual matters like indecency. But with the video game laws, the states wanted to extend that to regulate violence. It is hard to imagine what a definition could be of violence that would address the asserted concerns but also limit what content the government could regulate. Another challenge was the interactive nature of the medium. Would allowing such regulation mean there might be a lower level of First Amendment protection for media because they are more engaging, more robust?

Fortunately, the Supreme Court held the California law was unconstitutional. Unlike with broadcast indecency, it is settled law that video games receive full First Amendment protection. Yet going back to my five TV video monitor hypothetical for what constitutional standard to apply, if you transmitted a video game through one of those technologies, it still might be subject to a differential constitutional standard because of its interactivity. Thankfully, the Supreme Court rejected the theory that interactive media receive less constitutional protection.

Brotman: Do you think there will be a point in time when we will begin to rationalize these different standards, or are we basically always going to be in the cycle of new technologies developing and having to look at them individually?

188   The Conversations

Corn-Revere: Think of the communication technologies that I listed so far: cinema, cable television, the internet, and video games all receive full First Amendment protection. The only outlier is broadcasting. As I mentioned before, the Supreme Court has been reluctant to revisit this for a long time. I think while we're making progress, there is still that anomaly.

I also think that there will always be those who demand censorship. It just depends on what the issue is, whatever the latest moral panic happens to be. And if we don't remember the lessons from the past and the reasons why we came to the level of First Amendment protection we have now, then we risk making some of the same mistakes again.

The values of free speech and free press are embedded in our cultural and political DNA. It is a key part of the American identity. Rejection of authoritarianism goes hand in hand with this. Yet this coincides with a strong drive for censorship, mainly driven by people who have a particular axe to grind. There is always going to be a tension between those two forces.

Brotman: Let's close by talking about the current and future tensions you perceive. College campuses seem to be living laboratories where these tensions are palpable. They don't really involve technologies or any of the things we talked about, but rather involve some of those basic issues that started in the 1800s and then moved through the twentieth century. But they still are here. In particular, certain individuals or groups on campus want to impose what's called a heckler's veto.

Corn-Revere: Yes, we see efforts to close down speech on many campuses by those who purport to know what speech is acceptable and what is beyond the pale. For them, it is not enough to voice their opposition to ideas of forms of expression they find disagreeable. Their purpose is to silence "evil" speech. This mindset harkens back to Anthony Comstock, who was absolutely certain he knew what ideas must be prohibited. But as Justice Oliver Wendell Holmes wrote, "certitude is not the same thing as certainty."

Brotman: Restricting speech on college campuses is a hot-button issue. Like all of our politics, it is highly polarized. Some on the right want to show up on campus and offend as many people as they can. Then there are some on the left who want to restrict any speech that they consider to be offensive.

Corn-Revere: The concerns from both sides are understandable. If you look at historically marginalized populations, many of these people are from groups that were underrepresented on college campuses in years past. They're there now, trying to make sure that the campus is welcoming for everybody from all backgrounds.

Yet at the same time, those who are advocating for traditional protections for free speech have valid concerns. What's interesting is that so many of the demands for limiting speech on campus now are coming from the students instead of the administrators. In years past, these were driven from the top down instead. We also have an explosion of social media, which tends to drive people further into their respective corners.

Brotman: Looking ahead, do you have a sense of optimism in terms of First Amendment protections, particularly in the free speech and free press areas, or do you think that some of the repressive cycles that we've talked about will continue to repeat themselves? Are we just in a perpetual hamster-wheel situation?

Corn-Revere: I don't think it's a binary choice between optimism or pessimism. I also think that the repressive cycles will continue. In some ways, these cycles must continue because no issue is ever fully settled or resolved. I think we're writing on sand. And our future will depend on the actions we take in response to these cycles.

You can establish a precedent for one day or one year. But then you'll have to defend it again down the road. We're operating in a dynamic system where we have to continue to reestablish and reaffirm the principles on which we all will operate. There always will be a demand by some to restrict some types of speech as the latest threat to mankind.

We have to continue pushing back against those demands as we move forward. That doesn't make me pessimistic. The very premise of the First Amendment is that no question is ever fully settled. The First Amendment is why we have free inquiry, because everything is open to questioning, including the value of free speech itself. All I can really do is try to uphold the principles that I believe in and try to win the next censorship battle when it comes along.

Rick Jewell

Rick Jewell is the Hugh M. Hefner Professor of American Film Emeritus at the University of Southern California (USC) School of Cinematic Arts. He also served as an Academy Film Scholar of the Academy of Motion Picture Arts and Sciences.

At USC, he taught courses on American film history at both the graduate and undergraduate levels, plus classes on film censorship, film genres (the western, the gangster film), film style analysis (RKO and the Studio System, the James Bond films, Stanley Kubrick), and seminars on national cinema (Italian cinema; American film, 1939–45; American film, 1967–72).

Jewell is the author of The Golden Age of Cinema: Hollywood, 1929–1945, *and the definitive two-volume studio history:* RKO Radio Pictures: A Titan Is Born *and* Slow Fade to Black: The Decline of RKO Radio Pictures. *He has published articles in numerous journals including the* Historical Journal of Film, Radio and Television, Film History, *and* Film Quarterly.

He estimates that he's been included in the special features of more than thirty-five feature-film DVDs, including collections showcasing Fred Astaire and Ginger Rogers, Bette Davis, and Humphrey Bogart.

Stuart Brotman: How did you get interested in the area of film censorship? **Rick Jewell**: I came to USC in 1972 to do my Ph.D. At that point, I was entranced, as many people were back then, with international cinema, particularly what was happening in Europe, plus Japanese cinema. [Akira] Kurosawa was always one of my favorites. I thought that I would work in that area. But very quickly, I changed my mind. I began to see American cinema in a much different light.

I wanted to do a more in-depth study of American film history. I became particularly fascinated by the history of the film business and ended up writing my dissertation on a studio that went out of business in the 1950s—RKO. The heyday of RKO was the so-called Golden Era, the classical period of Hollywood cinema in the 1930s, 1940s, and 1950s. Of course, you can't look at that era without encountering all of the censorship issues that faced filmmakers back then, and that faced movie studios as well.

I quickly became interested in how the best filmmakers like Billy Wilder found ways to make great films despite the restrictions placed on them by the Motion Picture Production Code, the Catholic Legion of Decency, and other censoring agencies. So that's how it happened.

Brotman: Let's go back to early American cinema history. I think that in the early 1900s, Chicago enacted the first film censorship law.
Jewell: Right. As far as I know, that was the first municipal censorship law in the country. It was set up by the police department in Chicago. The police commissioner would look at films and say okay for release or not okay. I think the Chicago censorship board was started around 1907. In 1909, there was an important court case, *Block v. Chicago*, concerning a couple of films distributed by the Block Company that had been denied exhibition licenses by the Chicago police chief. Block lost that case.

The court decided that what Chicago was doing was just fine, and those two films, which supposedly contained too much "malicious mischief," should not be allowed to screen in the city. This was the kickoff of many legal cases that would follow.

Brotman: Then in 1915, D. W. Griffith's *Birth of a Nation* is released.
Jewell: One of the most important films in movie history for its cinematic innovations. The main issue with *Birth of a Nation*, from a censorship point of view, was its dramatization of D. W. Griffith's belief that the outcome of the Civil War had not been a good thing. And that the Reconstruction period had had a terrible impact on the South.

Griffith made this movie based on a book called *The Klansman*, whose hero was the Ku Klux Klan. As one might expect, the movie quickly became very controversial. There were protests against it in cities like New York, Philadelphia, and Boston. That did not slow it down. Actually, it added to public interest in the movie, and it became the first great blockbuster in cinema history. The great irony of *Birth of a Nation* is that it's much harder to see the film today, at least in any kind of public screening, than it was when it was first released.

From the very beginnings of cinema, certain people voiced concerns about the effects movies could have, particularly on young people but also on society as a whole. Many citizens came to believe that movies were a dangerous, corruptive influence on their lives and their communities.

In 1897, before there were even projectors and screens, a peep show parlor in Atlantic City offered a fleshy belly dancer performing her specialty. It was entitled *Dolorita in the Passion Dance*. Rather quickly, an outcry against this scandalous exhibitionism followed. Thus, protests against moving image entertainment began even before actual movies existed. There always have been men and women troubled by moving images and their alleged aftereffects.

Brotman: But the First Amendment predated all of this.

Jewell: Yet no significant film censorship case made its way to the Supreme Court until 1915. In that year, *Mutual v. Ohio* appeared on the Supreme Court docket. Mutual was a film distributor that operated in the Midwest, including throughout Ohio. By that time, there were state censorship boards, as well as municipal censor boards, in a number of places. Ohio had its own state board, as did at least half a dozen other states, such as Pennsylvania, Kansas, and Maryland. Mutual decided to mount a legal challenge to the Ohio board.

I read the legal brief. I thought the arguments of the Mutual lawyers were pretty strong. Their main contention: censoring movies violated the First Amendment of the U.S. Constitution. People should have the right to express themselves freely in any artistic medium, including motion pictures. Thus, it was un-American to censor movies. The Supreme Court disagreed, and in a unanimous decision to boot. The Court held that the movies were not an art form. They were a business, "pure and simple," and therefore not eligible for First Amendment protection, unlike book publishers, for example. On top of that, the Court claimed movies were "capable of evil." They might influence people in ways that were corruptive and damaging to society. This was strong stuff. The decision meant that commercial films were vulnerable to all manner of censorship, including by municipal and state censorship boards.

Brotman: Let's talk a little bit about the movie industry's reaction to that case.

Jewell: The movie industry was already being continually bedeviled by state and local censorship boards. These boards would block exhibition or allow it based on their own notions of what was proper. They also dictated ways a film would have to be altered to gain their approval.

One unfortunate thing was that most boards did not have written rules about what narrative content was okay and what was not. Thus, a film company producer was never quite sure what would pass muster. A film that might be fine in Pennsylvania might not be acceptable in Kansas.

Producers had little choice; they did what was necessary to gain the release of their product. But this often led to cuts that rendered their stories incoherent. No producer wanted to receive a report from a theater owner stating, "My customers hated your movie. It was stupid. They didn't understand what was going on."

Most censorship boards were staffed by political appointees, particularly the state boards. It was a pretty sweet job. You spent your day watching movies and made a nice little salary from it. Did these censors care much about the quality or artistic ambitions of the films they watched? I doubt it.

Brotman: Did any of these censorship boards talk to each other? If something was banned in Detroit, for example, would that increase the likelihood it was going to be banned in Chicago or Atlanta or Boston?

Jewell: I don't know how much give and take existed between the different boards. But they certainly talked to the producers. All the companies had staff members who dealt with boards around the country, got a sense of what would play in Boston but not in Atlanta or Memphis or wherever, and tried to guide their filmmakers accordingly.

Brotman: How early did these boards get involved in reviewing scripts or film footage?

Jewell: I don't know that the boards ever required the movie studios to submit scripts or even ideas for movies. That came later in a different form. In 1922, the Motion Picture Producers and Distributors of America (MPPDA), an industry trade association, set up its own apparatus to work with the censor boards. Former Postmaster General Will H. Hays became the first president of that organization, and the MPPDA soon became known as the Hays Office.

Right away, Hays's staff began working to minimize the impact of these boards. A couple of years later, they came up with "The Formula"—a distillation of all the problem areas that films had been encountering across the country. According to Hays, The Formula was developed to be helpful to the different studios in their choice and treatment of material. It might have helped if filmmakers had actually paid attention to it.

Most didn't want to be restricted in their creative endeavors. They also were very interested in making movies that reflected the times. This was the Roaring Twenties, the Jazz Age. A lot of things were changing, like Prohibition, which ushered in bootlegging, bathtub gin, and speakeasies. The many changes, especially in urban society, were not readily embraced by conservative members of society. But many moviegoers expected to see contemporary stories and characters on their screens.

They wanted stories about nightclubs, jazz dancers, flappers. They wanted tales reflective of more liberal attitudes toward sexuality that were then taking hold in the country, particularly in big cities. And Hollywood responded with films like *The Sheik* and *It,* starring Rudolph Valentino and Clara Bow. As a consequence, the censorship boards stepped up their hectoring of the studios, despite the efforts of Will Hays.

Mr. Hays soon realized that he would never be able to sanitize Hollywood. He personally backed away from censoring and became the principal cheerleader for motion pictures instead. His real strength was public relations. He constantly sang Hollywood's praises, emphasizing all the good things the movies were doing for the United States. But he knew that criticism of Hollywood product was a sensitive area that had to be addressed. So he hired more people to develop solutions and tried, as best he could, to remain above the censorship wrangles.

Brotman: The Hays Office was also involved in looking at literary properties that might be made into movies.

Jewell: That's right. The Formula also focused on certain literary properties that the studios were interested in buying, mostly novels that would likely cause trouble once they were transformed into movies. These books were racier, more open about sexuality, and so on. The Formula regularly circulated an updated listing of books that studios should avoid purchasing, thus saving them both money and censor difficulties. But believing these stories were presold moneymakers, studios went ahead and bought most of them anyway and made them into movies.

Brotman: Were there other movie industry groups dealing with the censor boards?
Jewell: Indirectly. The Independent Theater Owners Association represented thousands of movie houses in the U.S. They were seeking government intervention in the exhibition arena.

Brotman: Why so?
Jewell: By the mid- to late 1920s, the five biggest movie studios had added theater chains to their production and distribution arms. Naturally, they gave preference to their own theaters when releasing top films. Independent theater owners were plenty unhappy about that. They felt it was unfair that a big Paramount movie would always open in a Paramount theater or a Warner film in a Warner Brothers theater.

Another aspect of the business that they hated was block booking. The major companies didn't sell their movies one at a time. They sold them in large blocks. If your theater customers preferred the MGM stars, you generally had to buy a whole year's worth of product from that company, sight unseen. Mr. Theater Owner had no idea if these films were going to be good, bad, or indifferent, or contain content that might offend his loyal customers.

The theater association believed block booking was an unfair, monopolistic business practice and lobbied the government to outlaw it. One argument was that their inability to reject certain films left them open to angry complaints from loyal customers upset about the content of certain pictures. But block booking was a cornerstone of Hollywood distribution strategies and thus an important aspect of the business that Will Hays had been hired to protect. And he did protect it, but his efforts had censorship implications.

Throughout the 1920s, cries for government censorship of the movies grew increasingly louder, and studio executives grew fearful that the government might begin to police the content of their movies. Plus, this might lead to regulation of their business practices as well. In the end, Hays's connections in Washington paid dividends. He was able to fend off government censorship and was generally successful in preventing government intrusion in the film industry during the rest of his tenure at the MPPDA. He retired in 1945.

Brotman: Let's talk a little bit about the role of the Catholic Church during this period as well.
Jewell: The Catholic Church was initially supportive of Hollywood efforts to fend off censorship. But over time, certain films upset the church hierarchy and moved them in the opposite direction.

Brotman: For example?
Jewell: The presentation of Irish Americans in *The Callahans and the Murphys*, made by MGM in 1927, got the church's attention. This comedy contained scenes of Irish characters drinking, fighting, and working as bootleggers. It even showed mothers drunk at an Irish picnic.

The picture crossed a line, depicting members of the faith in ways that were considered highly offensive. Consequently, the church attacked MGM, attempting to have the picture pulled from theaters shortly after it was released. A shocked MGM called back the prints, recut it, and added a prologue saying something to the effect that the picture is a celebration of the grand tradition of Irish humor.

But the damage was done. As time went on, the Catholic Church became more critical of movie content and more determined to dictate what parishioners might see in their neighborhood theaters. Basically, the church said to the industry, "You'd best pay attention to us because there are a lot of Catholics in this country. We can discourage them from going, not just to certain movies but to all Hollywood pictures."

Brotman: Did the church come up with its own production code?
Jewell: Yes, in effect it did. It created the Legion of Decency. They managed to convince good Catholics in dioceses throughout the country to sign pledge forms saying they would join the Legion of Decency in its crusade against immoral movies. Members agreed to boycott any film

the church decided was immoral. The emphasis was certainly on sexual content, but attention was also paid to other onscreen elements that disturbed church ideology.

Brotman: What role, if any, did the Catholic Church play in influencing the development by the Hays Office of the Motion Picture Production Code?

Jewell: Martin Quigley was publisher of an industry trade paper, the *Motion Picture Herald*. He was also a good Catholic. He knew that the Catholic Church was getting more militant about movies, so he went to Will Hays and proposed that he, with the help of professionals, draft a code of cinematic right and wrong. This document, he believed, would not only mollify church officials but also alleviate the ongoing difficulties with state, local, and foreign censorship bodies.

Working with a Catholic priest from St. Louis, Father Daniel Lord, and several studio executives, Quigley created what came to be known as the Motion Picture Production Code. This was a prescriptive document outlining proper screen morality. The code had twelve different sections. The most expansive ones dealt with the presentation of criminality on the screen and, of course, sexuality. In March 1930, the code was adopted with great fanfare by all the studios. But its authors neglected to include a crucial component—some kind of mechanism for enforcing its precepts so that filmmakers would actually have to abide by it.

Brotman: It sounds like the Catholic Church actually was very influential since it also could organize a boycott of specific films through the Legion of Decency on its own.

Jewell: To clarify, the Legion of Decency did not come into existence until 1934, four years after Hollywood adopted the Production Code. Indeed, one of the main reasons for its creation was, as I implied, filmmakers flagrantly ignored the Production Code. And why did they follow this self-destructive path? Because the adoption of the code happened to coincide with the onset of the Great Depression. Like most other industries in the country, the movies quickly felt the sting of hard times. Within a year, admissions declined 30 or 40 percent. Suddenly, companies that had been raking in money began to consider bankruptcy.

RKO and Paramount went into receivership in 1933. By then, most of their competitors were teetering on the edge of disaster. Studio production chiefs realized that they had to give spectators more "cutting edge" content to get them back to the box office. In short order, an explosion of shocking material entered the movies, content that people had not seen on screens before: more immorality, more violence, more sex, even nudity. As expected, this fueled the determination of reformers, and particularly religious reformers like the leaders of the Catholic Church, to do something about it.

As I mentioned, in 1934 the Legion of Decency began rating motion pictures. The initial rating system was ABC, a fairly simple system: A was fine for everybody. B was objectionable, perhaps okay for adults. And C was immoral—boycott this movie. The Legion certainly got the attention of Will Hays and the studio moguls. They knew they had to do something—and quickly. So the Production Code Administration, the PCA, was established to enforce the Production Code. This began in midsummer 1934.

Brotman: Were the individual municipal and state censorship boards also interacting with the Hays Office in any way?

Jewell: Absolutely. By that time, they're working overtime, rejecting and forcing damaging cuts on the so-called pre-code movies. This naturally does not endear them to Hollywood's content providers. I suspect most censorship boards were not just in favor of greater content oversight by the PCA, they were delighted to see it happen because it would make their lives easier and less contentious. Will Hays must have been feeling the lion's share of the pressure because talk of government censorship had ramped up again. He understood that Hollywood couldn't get away with any more empty promises. I suspect the PCA would never have been born if Hays and the studio heads hadn't felt the industry was about one step away from Washington taking control of their business.

Brotman: Let's talk about some of the major studios, how they reacted. Did MGM, Warner Brothers, and Paramount all have different responses to how they would comply with the Production Code, now that the PCA was there to enforce it?

Jewell: I think the big shock was to the people who worked for those studios. In the pre-code period, Paramount brought Mae West to Hollywood. She immediately became very popular, but her gusto for sex, open admission of multiple lovers, and genial attitude toward lustful behavior shocked many strait-laced souls. Nevertheless, movies like *I'm No Angel* raked in box office lucre; some argue her movies saved Paramount Pictures from ruin. But the onset of the PCA robbed Mae of the very qualities that made her so appealing to a segment of the audience, quickly ruining her career. Overnight, Paramount couldn't make a true Mae West film anymore.

Warner Brothers had been the gangster film studio, with stars like James Cagney and Edward G. Robinson and films like *The Public Enemy* and *Little Caesar*. Now suddenly, they could not produce films featuring so-called sympathetic gangsters. In fact, gangsters were not even supposed to be movie protagonists anymore. These examples suggest the enormous content earthquake brought on by the hegemony of the PCA; every studio had to make dramatic adjustments that affected its particular box office strengths.

Brotman: Did it affect MGM in any way?

Jewell: They had so many top stars who could be cast in a number of ways—drama, comedy, even musicals. Jean Harlow was MGM's answer to Mae West, and they had to rein her in. Less so Joan Crawford, Norma Scherer, or Clark Gable. The PCA affected MGM less than Paramount, less than Warner Brothers, and maybe less than Fox.

But they had all been making movies that were in violation of the Production Code. No question about that. Every one of the studios was impacted when the PCA started to enforce the code. A note on penalties: if a film was released without a PCA seal, the studio now had to pay a $25,000 fine. Moreover, that film couldn't play in any theaters owned by one of the Big Five companies: MGM, Paramount, Warner Brothers, Fox, and RKO. These company-owned theaters were situated in the big cities of America. They were the great movie palaces of the era. If a company tried to release a grade-A film that could not play in these theaters, that film was doomed. That studio couldn't get its money back. This was the principal deterrent.

Brotman: During this period, there were renegade filmmakers like Howard Hughes who were testing some of these censorship boundaries.

Jewell: Exactly. Mr. Hughes was the ultimate bad boy of early 1930s Hollywood. He made films that were controversial and disturbing to many people. Hughes considered himself a Hollywood outsider and great advocate of the First Amendment. I'm not so sure he was personally committed to free speech. I think he saw an opportunity to produce screen stories he wanted to see and, because of their excessive content, might make a lot of money.

His first big movie that fired up the censors was *Scarface* in 1932, directed by Howard Hawks. It was the most violent film made by an American company up to that time and contained overtones of incest as well. It violated the Production Code in every way you can imagine. Hughes fought a pitched battle with the censors, particularly the New York State censorship board, one of the most powerful because it controlled access to New York City theaters.

The censors forced Hughes to make many cuts and add a prologue to *Scarface*. He even changed the ending so it could play in New York. In Manhattan theaters, Tony, the vicious gangster played by Paul Muni, is hanged, demonstrating that the law had brought him to proper justice. But in New Jersey, across the Hudson River, the same film played with another ending. There, Tony was shot down in the gutter instead.

Brotman: Then Howard Hughes basically got out of the independent production business, until the early 1940s. How had things changed when he came back to make movies?

Jewell: Hughes left the business before the PCA began its work. But it was at the peak of its powers when he decided to make a western called *The Outlaw* in 1940. Hughes naturally entered into an extended battle with the PCA, which had plenty of problems with *The Outlaw*. When he failed to get any significant accommodations from them, he appealed their decision and lost. He then cut the film to satisfy the PCA but strangely sat on the film for three years.

In 1943, Hughes did release *The Outlaw* in one theater in San Francisco. It was supposedly the approved version, but he had Jane Russell, his bosomy "discovery" and the film's main star, put on a stage show before its showings, which I assume was pretty sexy. That got people's attention. But the thing that really got their attention was something else.

Along with the Production Code Administration, there existed the Advertising Code Administration, which approved the advertising that could be used to sell a movie. All of movie posters, billboards, and other advertising materials had to be okayed by them. Accompanying the San Francisco release of *The Outlaw* was scandalous, unapproved advertising, which predictably outraged some of the locals but provided the picture an overdose of publicity. After the film's run ended, Hughes pulled it back, supposedly to recut and improve it. But, once again, he waited three more years before its wide release.

All that time, people were talking about this "sensational" movie, which wasn't really sensational at all. But he had managed to generate a lot of attention for his film. When it finally came out in 1946, spectators showed up just to see this "incredible" new Howard Hughes production.

Brotman: By the late 1930s, there was a feeling that the United States could become involved in armed international conflict. There certainly was a notion of national feelings, and these were expressed on the screen too.

Jewell: American citizens definitely were concerned about what was happening in Europe, most particularly in Germany and Italy. And a lot of the people who worked in movies also became concerned. They were displeased with Hitler and Mussolini and wanted to use the medium at their disposal to attack Nazi and fascist ideology. But the studio heads were doing business in those countries, exporting films there. Would it be a good idea to make movies that upset the leaders of Germany and Italy, likely causing their pictures to be barred from those lucrative markets? Or were they going to antagonize their creative talent by backing away from stories that took strong stands against the Nazis and fascists?

Brotman: Was pressure placed by the Production Code Administration on the studio heads?
Jewell: Absolutely. Several studio heads resisted the desires of their creative people—their writers, producers, and directors who particularly

wanted to make anti-Nazi movies. Plus, the PCA was no fan of such agitprop. MGM bought an anti-fascist novel and play by Sinclair Lewis called *It Can't Happen Here*. Louis B. Mayer and the other MGM execs must not have read it before they paid $50,000 for the rights. But the PCA informed MGM that it could not turn the drama, about the takeover of the U.S. by a fascist dictator, into a film. MGM had to eat its investment—it never made the movie.

MGM did film *Idiots Delight*, based on Robert Sherwood's play, in 1938. The play was an indictment of Italian fascism. But the PCA once again intervened. They invoked the National Feeling section of the Production Code, which demanded movies show respect for the flags, institutions, and patriotic feelings of foreign nations. By the time the studio finished excising content that disturbed the PCA, one couldn't tell the movie had anything to do with Italy, or fascism for that matter. Recognizing how committed the PCA was to making sure no one could accuse the movie business of trying to steer America into the next war, many committed movie makers gave up, believing they had no chance to take a stand against European despotism.

Brotman: Did any studios resist the power of the Production Code Administration then regarding these types of films?
Jewell: To this day, I admire Harry and Jack Warner because their studio made *Confessions of a Nazi Spy* in 1939. The PCA once again tried everything to halt production of this film. Its efforts failed because no one could claim the film was fiction or an unfair depiction of actual events.

In the previous year, a group of Nazi agents had been rounded up on the East Coast by the FBI. They were brought to trial and convicted of espionage against the United States, then sent to prison. The film was unusual for its time, made in a semi-documentary style that stuck very close to the facts of the actual case. Thus, it became the first hard-hitting, no-holds-barred anti-Nazi film made in Hollywood. The Warners had taken a stand against the Nazis three years before. They stopped doing business with Germany in 1936. Every other studio hung in there until the Nazi government pulled the plug on American movies in the early 1940s because of pictures like *Confessions of a Nazi Spy* and Charlie Chaplin's *The Great Dictator*.

One more example—when I was doing my RKO research, I discovered that George Stevens, arguably the top director under contract to the company at that time, wanted to make an anti-fascist picture in 1939. He was told that George Schaefer, the president of the company, had vetoed the idea. "He's afraid to commit us to any picture that is propaganda against anything," reported studio chief Pandro Berman.

Brotman: Then the United States enters World War II. It also sets up the Office of War Information.

Jewell: Yes, this is the first and only time that the government did stick its nose directly into Hollywood. The belief in Washington was that movies had to be part of the great crusade against our enemies. President Roosevelt fervently believed movies could help America win the war.

Therefore, the Office of War Information (OWI) set up a branch in Hollywood. Its job was to read scripts and provide suggestions, and look at finished movies and make sure they were going to make positive contributions to the war effort. Interestingly, after all these years of fearing intrusion into their businesses, the studios had no problems with OWI. It didn't have much impact at all.

Why? Because Hollywood folk were just as patriotic as everybody else in the country and had been chafing at the content restrictions placed on them for years. Conservative or liberal, Hollywood filmmakers wanted to use the powerful communications medium to attack our menacing antagonists in Japan and Germany and Italy.

Very quickly, an avalanche of films poured out that were pure propaganda. That's why, with some exceptions like *Casablanca*, World War II Hollywood product does not hold up well today. Even people who love that period quickly tire of films featuring unalloyed American heroes fighting brutish Germans and savage Japanese.

Nearly all the World War II films emphasized people doing their part for the war effort. There were westerns with cowboys fighting Nazis. Tarzan and Lassie battled the Nazis. Obviously, many of these films were ridiculous, but audiences ate them up. And the studio heads had perpetual smiles on their faces because the Great Depression was over and people had jobs and money in their pockets. Everybody went to the movies. They adored these silly propaganda movies.

The OWI never was a threat to Hollywood. It actually helped the producers. For example, if a studio wanted to shoot on a military base, the OWI tried to facilitate access.

Brotman: Now we're into the 1950s.

Jewell: Two things happened in the late 1940s that impacted censorship in the 1950s. One was McCarthyism. After the war was over, some Hollywood filmmakers wanted to make more realistic movies, movies dealing with social problems in the country. Between 1945 and 1949, several were made: *Crossfire*, *Pinky*, and *The Snake Pit* come to mind.

Then Senator Joseph McCarthy from Wisconsin rose to prominence by convincing many Americans that communists were infiltrating American society in an effort to take control of the country. Under the dark shadow cast by McCarthy and his minions, even a great movie like *The Best Years of Our Lives*, the Academy Award winner of 1946, began to appear suspect, even subversive to some. It focused on soldiers coming back from combat and their problems adjusting to civilian life.

After the House Un-American Activities Committee hearings on communism in Hollywood in 1947, the heads of the movie companies became frightened. They began to engage in self-censorship, afraid to make certain harder-edged, realistic movies. The era of the witch hunt had commenced and people in Hollywood began losing jobs left and right, accused of being communists and injecting communist propaganda into films. Nobody felt safe in that environment, particularly if one wanted to make a film critical of some aspects of the "American way of life."

Brotman: Was the FBI involved in investigating Hollywood during that period?

Jewell: Definitely. It was a very paranoid era in the movie capital. J. Edgar Hoover and his FBI had their eyes and ears out for what they considered seditious activities in Hollywood, especially among writers and directors.

Brotman: You mentioned that there were two problems with film censorship that began in the late 1940s and extended into the 1950s. What was the second one?

Jewell: The other problem kicked off in 1948, when the government, which had been concerned for a number of years with movie industry business practices, forced the studios to begin selling off their theater chains. Most companies had done this by the early 1950s. They abandoned exhibition, concentrating solely on production and distribution.

From a censorship point of view, what no one apparently considered was that those theaters were key to the enforcement of the Production Code. Now those houses were being bought up by companies that had made no commitment to showing only PCA-approved pictures on their screens. Savvy individuals started to consider what might happen if a film was released without a code seal. It could soon be possible to get an unapproved film into a lot of good theaters because the big studios didn't own them anymore.

Brotman: It also might be great publicity to advertise a film that seemed a little bit forbidden.

Jewell: That's exactly what happened. The director Otto Preminger made a silly romantic comedy called *The Moon Is Blue*. United Artists released it without a code seal, and it was a huge success. You look at the film now and wonder what was all the fuss. The picture is about a seducer, played by William Holden, and a "prospect" (Maggie McNamara) who outsmarts him every step of the way. Needless to say, he never gets her into bed. It includes words like *seduction* and *mistress,* words that were verboten according to the Production Code. Big deal.

Following along the same path, RKO released *The French Line* starring Jane Russell. The PCA refused to provide a seal of approval, but RKO, then run by Howard Hughes, opened it in St. Louis with outrageous advertising: "Jane Russell in 3D. It'll knock both your eyes out." I assume it was successful. Other films then came out without Production Code seals. The censorship apparatus in Hollywood was starting to break down.

Brotman: Sounds like the time was ripe for a direct legal challenge to the power of the censorship boards.

Jewell: Indeed. That brings us to 1952. Joseph Burstyn, a distributor of foreign films, bought an anthology film from Italy to market in the U.S. One of the parts was *The Miracle* made by Roberto Rossellini, the great neorealist filmmaker. Its story, about a woman seduced by a vagrant who becomes pregnant and believes this is the second Immaculate Conception, was considered blasphemous by many Christians.

Naturally, the Catholic Church and its Legion of Decency were appalled, and the New York censorship board eventually banned the movie. Burstyn challenged this, and the case went all the way to the Supreme Court. In a total reversal of the 1915 *Mutual* decision that we discussed earlier, the Court decided the movie deserved free speech protection. Overnight, the First Amendment could be applied to the movies—a truly monumental change.

Consequently, in the 1960s, a lot of the state and municipal censorship boards began to scale back or go out of business. The 1960s were an era of tremendous change in Hollywood, including a remarkable freeing up of screen content. The odd thing to me, quite frankly, is that the Production Code continued to exist throughout most of the decade. This seems amazing because, by then, hundreds of movies were being released that violated the code. The PCA responded by revising it every two or three years in order to keep it on life support.

Finally, Jack Valenti took over the Motion Picture Association in 1966. Initially, he instituted another revision of the code. But he quickly realized that the code was not just an empty vessel; it was a joke. The only thing to do was to get out of the business of attempting to shoehorn morality into screen stories. Instead, the MPA decided to provide information about the movie so that potential patrons could decide if this was something they wanted to see or allow their children to see. Censorship was out; education was in.

Valenti unveiled the new movie rating system in 1968; it is still very much with us today. The system has also been controversial over the years, and some people have suggested the ratings are actually a subtle type of censorship. But at least the antiquated Production Code finally disappeared after shaping what people could see for decades.

Brotman: Did the courts give up too, after the *Burstyn* case solidified the free speech protection for movies?

Jewell: Not quite. In the early 1960s, another Supreme Court case involved the Chicago censorship board. It was challenged for imposing

208   The Conversations

prior restraint on a film. In this case, the Supreme Court said that freedom of speech is not absolute, and prior restraint of a movie is not always inconsistent with the First Amendment. The Court left matters open to deal with individual cases of movie prior restraint as they came up.

This case played against the broadening First Amendment protection that the *Burstyn* case seemed to promise. A severe limit on allowable prior restraints against newspapers and print already had been established as a red line that couldn't be crossed. Not so with films, which still could be reviewed and restricted on a case-by-case basis.

Brotman: What's an example of a case that was brought to challenge the application of prior restraint on a particular film?

Jewell: During the 1960s, a lot of films were imported from abroad. They were viewed differently from domestic product because they were subject to customs restrictions. Films like *I Am Curious Yellow*, a sexually explicit film from Sweden.

Europe was much more open, especially in terms of nudity and sexuality, than America had ever been. These films became a big issue with the censors, who questioned whether works from outside of the United States should even be imported into the country. A customs violation was a criminal violation. The movie importer presumably could be indicted and go to jail if convicted. *I Am Curious Yellow* essentially challenged the customs ban. It was definitely an exploitation film, banned initially in Massachusetts. But the courts ultimately decided the film was not obscene, freeing it for domestic exhibition and opening the floodgates for more foreign film imports, and for more nudity and sexuality in American films as well.

Brotman: We talked before about the Office of War Information. Obviously, they didn't have much of an effect. They could review, for example, if someone wanted to do a location shoot on a military base. Have there been any residual aspects of that in contemporary cinema, where films need to get government permission or need to depict a government agency favorably, like the FBI? Is government involved at all now in granting that type of permission?

Jewell: As far as I know, the answer is yes. If you want to shoot on a military base today, you have to give the base commander your script beforehand. The officers go over it and make sure they feel the presentation of the military in the story is generally positive. But there have been plenty of anti-military films too. Whether those filmmakers managed to circumvent the rules, or simply avoided military base location shooting, is not well known.

But you raise a really interesting question about the FBI. Some years ago, one of my students wrote a paper about *The FBI Story*, a Warner Brothers film from the late 1950s. Jimmy Stewart was the star. She demonstrated that the real producer of the movie was J. Edgar Hoover, not the studio. He had complete control. Every aspect of the picture had to receive approval from Hoover. I don't believe that could happen today. There have been films since then that were not positive portrayals of government agencies, like the CIA and FBI. I suppose Jack Warner wanted the FBI and Mr. Hoover to back his picture, so he gave him full control. Obviously, that period has passed away.

Brotman: What lessons have been learned by looking back at the long arc of cinema history? Are these purely historical artifacts, based on the time the people that were involved in the studio system? Or are there any larger lessons in terms of censorship today?

Jewell: I think there's very little that's going on now that would apply in terms of either government, the Catholic Church, or the industry censoring movies. That's really changed enormously. Let me say a couple of things about that. First, I'm not an advocate of censorship. I think censorship is highly damaging to creative expression. We're fortunate to live in the U.S. because censorship is a straitjacket in many other countries of the world, especially in the movie and television industries of those countries.

We're also fortunate that we eventually transcended the censors. Not that total freedom is necessarily a good idea. As parents, for example, I believe we should be careful about what our kids are exposed to at a young age. Also, I have come to realize that censorship is not an altogether bad thing. One of my surprise discoveries while researching classical Hollywood was that in some ways, the censors prompted

210 The Conversations

filmmakers to be more creative. During the pre-code period they had a great deal of freedom. Then the PCA arrived and slammed doors in their faces. And yet many wonderful films were made in the 1930s, 1940s, and 1950s. One reason is that the true artists found ways to suggest, rather than show, delicate subject matter, and the results were often delightful. They developed subtle solutions to PCA problems, and subtlety can be highly desirable.

Brotman: What's an example?

Jewell: A good example comes from *The Big Sleep*, which Howard Hawks directed in 1946. Based on a Raymond Chandler novel, it stars Humphrey Bogart and Lauren Bacall. The dialogue, written by William Faulkner, Leigh Brackett, and Jules Furthman, with input from Hawks, is superior throughout, but one scene stands out. Bogart and Bacall are in a bar discussing horseracing. However, they're not really talking about horseracing. They're talking about getting together and going to bed. The scene is not only witty and romantic; it thumbs its nose at the Hollywood censors.

Brotman: I assume the audience understood what was going on in the film.

Jewell: Maybe not all of them, but I'm sure more sophisticated members of the audience got it. The writer-director Billy Wilder was brilliant at this sort of thing in movies like *Double Indemnity* and *Some Like It Hot*. He found ways to be provocative without hitting you over the head.

Brotman: Today, obviously, you can hit people over the head without any restrictions.

Jewell: Yes, but ironically, I believe there's more self-censorship going on in Hollywood now than there ever has been. I'm totally bored by the blockbuster, superhero movies. They substitute action and special effects for character development, sharp dialogue, subtlety, or provocative ideas. But that's what young people seem to want, and the studios do well financially by giving it to them.

I believe the studios sell young people short. They can handle complicated human relationships and edgy stories that make them look at life from different perspectives. But they won't find such material in today's mega-cinema. Nothing that could possibly disturb, offend, or confuse audience members. There are no prohibitions against inspired content anymore, but corporate thinking rules: "Keep it simple ... and loud!"

Brotman: Do you think that any type of government censorship board could arise from the ashes of history, now or in the future?
Jewell: The censorship boards are long gone. The last municipal censor board was Dallas, which closed in the 1990s. It seems incredible that it lasted that long. They were, I believe, mostly concerned about blasphemy at that point. But anything's possible. A censorship resurgence is not out of the question.

Congress came fairly close to doing something about TV a couple of decades ago. Senator Joseph Lieberman and others wanted to crack down on the evolving content of programming. Too much sex and violence to their liking. You never know. Pro-censorship voices will never be completely silenced.

Brotman: I know you had a longstanding professional relationship with Hef over several decades, given your common interest in film history and film censorship. How did that begin?
Jewell: Hef got in touch with the USC School of Cinematic Arts, where I was a professor. He said, "I know about your school. And I'm wondering, do you teach a censorship class there?" At that point, we did not, because Arthur Knight, the professor who had first taught the censorship class, was no longer on our faculty.

We replied, "Well no, not at the moment. But we have one on the books and we would like to revive it. It's an important subject, and we have several professors interested in teaching it." Hef then said, "I'll donate $100,000 to support the class if you revive it." Then the question arose—who was going to get this plum assignment? I was really busy but wanted to teach it badly. Another colleague of mine, Drew Casper, had similar interests but was already teaching an overload of courses. So, Drew and I got together and agreed to co-teach the class. We didn't want anyone else to do it.

Brotman: What was the next step to get this class going?

Jewell: Hef threw a kickoff party for the class and invited some of us out to the Playboy Mansion. We were already five or six weeks into the first offering that fall semester. Just before the party was held, we received a message from Hef's assistant: "You can bring five students from the class to the party."

Then we were in a bind, since the class had more than twenty students, all undergraduates. We thought, "How are we going to choose five students?" Serendipitously, we had just given a midterm exam. The top grades were two A's, two A-minuses and a B-plus. Everybody else had performed less well on the test. So that nobody could accuse us of favoritism, we simply took our top students to the Playboy Mansion. It was wonderful.

Brotman: How did you convince Hef not just to support the class financially but also to become an integral part of it?

Jewell: Drew and I had already decided to invite Hef to the class. We thought he would be the perfect topper to end the semester. We certainly knew his ongoing commitment to the First Amendment and to the movies and felt he would be a terrific addition. So we approached him at the party.

It was the first time we had met. His response to our request was, "No, no, I don't do things like that." We were a bit depressed, but I came up with one of the best ideas I ever had. We assembled our five students and told them Hef had just turned us down. "He won't appear in your class. But we have a feeling if you guys ask him and tell him how much it would mean to you and to the other students, who couldn't be here this evening, he'd have a hard time saying no to you."

They asked and I was right. Hef melted immediately and said yes. He came to campus and did a Q&A during the last class of the term. He was just fantastic. And our students were really good. They asked him great questions. Mary O'Connor, Hef's longtime personal assistant, called me not long afterward to say that Hef absolutely loved the experience. "And if you want him to come back in the future, you've got him." You bet we wanted him, and he was true to his word. He never missed "his" class session for the next twenty years. Finally, his health began to fail and he couldn't do it anymore, but it was an amazing run.

Rick Jewell 213

There was a time I particularly remember. Hef was invited to receive a special award in London. I'm sure it was prestigious, and I'm sure he wanted to go and accept it. But it conflicted with our class. He said, "No, I can't go, I can't miss my class."

So very quickly, Drew and I started calling Hef the third professor. He taught our students so much. He didn't lecture, it was always Q&A. He was quite brilliant, and the students loved it. Not surprisingly, "Censorship in Cinema" quickly developed a reputation and grew in size. Soon, we were attracting over one hundred students every fall. His appearance was an event we all looked forward to, and other professors from our school and around campus would often show up to see him in action.

He was involved in other ways too. Early on he said, "I must see the syllabus." We sent the syllabus for the first two or three years, and he would pepper us with questions, especially about some of the films we had chosen to screen. Then I guess he decided we knew what we were doing because he didn't ask to see the syllabus anymore.

I particularly enjoyed the sessions in the early years when feminist critics had leveled their big guns at Hef and *Playboy*. Some of our students were aware of these attacks and wondered if they should question him about them. We always told them, "No holds barred. He wants you to ask him tough questions."

And so they did. He was fabulous in terms of the way he answered their questions, the respect he gave to them. We could just see the students' minds turning over when he was there.

Over time, feminist criticism of Hef and his magazine started to ebb, and the student questions grew less contentious. I especially miss those early classes when there was more of a rough-and-tumble atmosphere. Students always wrote a paper in the class on topics they chose. We did our best to open them up to as many issues related to film censorship as we possibly could.

Brotman: When Hef was doing the class, what were his points of sensitivity? Was it mostly about sexuality or were there other issues?
Jewell: Every session was different. I kick myself that we didn't record each class. Hef liked to talk a lot about the censorship problems

he had to surmount in the development of the magazine. A lot of the kids were pretty knowledgeable about *Playboy*, but he increased their knowledge tenfold.

He also loved to talk about the movies because the movies were so important to him in his life. He used to say that Hollywood movies provided the dreams that motivated him when he was growing up in the 1930s and 1940s, during the Production Code era. The code was a revelation to him—how movies were being controlled. He said he could sense it without knowing specifically how it was being accomplished.

Hef would discuss anything that was on the students' minds. He frequently would talk about battling the postal censors in the early days of *Playboy,* drawing parallels to the foreign film censorship battles with the customs inspectors.

Brotman: At what point did Hef decide he was going to endow a professorial chair at USC?

Jewell: I think it was about three years after the beginning of our censorship class. Our dean Elizabeth Daley and director of development Marlene Loadvine began discussing potential chair donors, people who already had provided some financial support to the School of Cinematic Arts. Hef was one of the names that popped up. They knew he loved coming to our class, so they approached him with the big "ask." They told me that among all the patrons of endowed chairs, and now there are over thirty of them in our school, they never received a quicker "yes" than the one that came from Hugh Hefner. He said, "I want it to be a chair in American film, because American movies have been so important in my life." I consider it a great honor to have been the initial holder of the Hugh M. Hefner Chair for the Study of American Cinema.

The Hugh M. Hefner First Amendment Awards, 1980–2020

Information for subsequent years is available at www.hmhfoundation.org /about-the-awards. The awards are not always presented annually, which is reflected in the chronology below.

2020 WINNERS

David E. McCraw (Law): Deputy general counsel of the *New York Times,* for his book *Truth in Our Times: Inside the Fight for Press Freedom in the Age of Alternative Facts.* McCraw has led the *Times*'s fight for freedom of information since 2002. From Chelsea Manning's leaks to Trump's tax returns, McCraw is central to the paper's ability to fulfill the public's right to know.

Andrea Dennis and **Erik Nielson** (Book Publishing): Authors, for their book *Rap on Trial: Race, Lyrics, and Guilt in America*, a groundbreaking exposé about the alarming use of rap lyrics as criminal evidence to convict and incarcerate young men of color.

Omar Jimenez (Journalism): Journalist and CNN correspondent, for representing the power of consummate professionalism during his on-camera arrest while covering the George Floyd protests in Minnesota.

Christina Clusiau and **Shaul Schwarz** (Arts and Entertainment): Documentary filmmakers, for their successful battle to overcome the U.S. government's attempts at censoring their film *Immigration Nation* and delaying its release until after the November presidential election.

Michael Frazier (Education): Student at the University of Kentucky, LGBTQ and First Amendment rights activist, for working to eliminate free speech zones on campus and successfully leading the effort to draft and enact the bipartisan Kentucky Campus Free Speech Protection Act.

Ira Glasser (Lifetime Achievement): Former director of the ACLU, for his fierce defense of freedom of speech and expression during his twenty-three-year tenure as executive director of the ACLU. He is widely recognized as building the robust infrastructure that is today's ACLU. By the time Ira retired, the ACLU had a $30 million endowment, offices in every state, and was more powerful than ever. Additionally, he saw earlier than most the disproportionate racial consequences of the War on Drugs.

2020 JUDGES

Theodore J. Boutrous Jr., partner at Gibson, Dunn & Crutcher LLP, and global co-chair of the firm's Litigation Group.

Kyle Pope, editor-in-chief and publisher of the *Columbia Journalism Review*.

2019 WINNERS

Jonathan Haidt and **Greg Lukianoff** (Book Publishing): Haidt, a social psychologist at NYU's Stern School of Business, and Lukianoff, president and CEO of the Foundation for Individual Rights in Education (FIRE), for their book *The Coddling of the American Mind: How Good Intentions and Bad Ideas Are Setting Up a Generation for Failure*.

Grace Marion (Journalism): Former editor-in-chief of her high school newspaper, *The Playwickian*, for her fight against an especially heavy regime of school censorship and for her investigative reporting on the school's lack of sexual misconduct records for its teachers.

Theodore J. Boutrous Jr. (Law): Partner at Gibson, Dunn & Crutcher LLP, and global co-chair of the firm's Litigation Group, for successfully representing CNN and Jim Acosta in bringing First Amendment and due process claims against President Donald Trump, forcing the White House to restore Mr. Acosta's press credentials.

Dr. George E. Luber, **Ph.D.** (Government): Former chief of the Climate and Health Program in the Division of Environmental Hazards and Health Effects at the National Center for Environmental Health, Centers for Disease Control and Prevention (CDC), for his outspoken defense of science education and climate change, despite the risk of termination.

Christian Bales (Education): 2018 valedictorian of Holy Cross High School and an openly gay and gender nonconforming student, for creatively and inspirationally expressing their free speech rights in delivering their valedictory speech with a bullhorn following the commencement ceremony, after the school tried to suppress it by refusing to let them speak during graduation.

The Hugh M. Hefner First Amendment Awards, 1980–2020

Floyd Abrams (Lifetime Achievement): Senior counsel, Cahill Gordon & Reindel LLP, for his lifelong devotion to constitutional law. Abrams has argued numerous significant First Amendment cases in the U.S. Supreme Court. Many arguments he has made orally, and in his briefs to the Court, have been adopted by it as binding precedents protecting freedom of speech and of the press from infringement by the government.

2019 JUDGES

Neal Katyal, the Paul and Patricia Saunders Professor of Law at Georgetown University, a partner at Hogan Lovells, and former acting solicitor general of the United States.

Michael B. Keegan, president of People for the American Way and People for the American Way Foundation.

Karen Tumulty, a columnist and former national political correspondent for the *Washington Post* who writes frequently on free speech and the First Amendment.

2018 WINNERS

Laura Kipnis (Book Publishing): Cultural critic, essayist, and professor of media studies at Northwestern University in the Department of Radio, Television, and Film, for her book *Unwanted Advances: Sexual Paranoia Comes to Campus.*

Jamie Kalven (Journalism): Writer and executive director of Invisible Institute, for resisting a subpoena demanding he reveal a source after breaking the story of the fatal 2014 police shooting of seventeen-year-old Laquan McDonald in Chicago.

Simon Tam (Arts and Entertainment): Founder and bassist of the all-Asian American rock band The Slants, for his successful seven-year battle to defend the right to register the band's trademark after they were denied based on the grounds that the name was deemed disparaging by the government.

Allison Stanger (Education): Russell Leng '60 Professor of International Politics and Economics and founding director of the Rohatyn Center for International Affairs, at Middlebury College, for staunchly defending the free exchange of ideas on college campuses.

218   The Hugh M. Hefner First Amendment Awards, 1980–2020

Joan E. Bertin (Lifetime Achievement): Longtime executive director of the National Coalition against Censorship, for her decades-long commitment to the defense of freedom of thought and expression in all forms.

2018 JUDGES

Michael Bamberger, senior counsel in the New York office of the law firm Dentons and, since 1977, general counsel of the Media Coalition.

Shelby Coffey III, vice chair of the Newseum in Washington, D.C., and senior fellow of the Freedom Forum.

Zephyr Teachout, political activist, former political candidate, and associate professor of law at Fordham University School of Law.

2017 WINNERS

Timothy Garton Ash (Book Publishing): Professor of European Studies at the University of Oxford, Isaiah Berlin Professorial Fellow at St. Antony's College, Oxford, and a senior fellow at the Hoover Institution, Stanford University, for his book *Free Speech: Ten Principles for a Connected World*.

Jenni Monet (Print Journalism): An independent journalist whose on-the-ground reporting of the protests opposing the months-long militarized protection of Standing Rock and the $3.8 billion Dakota Access Pipeline was critical to understanding a volatile, important moment in American history.

Hasan Elahi (Arts and Entertainment): Associate professor, Department of Art at the University of Maryland, for his work as an interdisciplinary artist pushing the boundaries of surveillance, privacy, migration, citizenship, technology, and the challenges of the borders.

Burt Neuborne (Lifetime Achievement): Norman Dorsen Professor of Civil Liberties at NYU Law School, for his lifelong courage and indefatigable defense of the First Amendment as one of the nation's foremost civil liberties lawyers, teachers, and scholars.

2017 JUDGES

Lara Bergthold, a principal partner at RALLY and executive director of the Lear Family Foundation.

Erwin Chemerinsky, dean and professor of law at the University of California, Berkeley School of Law.

Davan Maharaj, editor-in-chief and publisher of the *Los Angeles Times*.

The Hugh M. Hefner First Amendment Awards, 1980–2020 219

2015 WINNERS

Zephyr Teachout (Book Publishing): Associate professor of law, Fordham University School of Law, for her book *Corruption in America: From Benjamin Franklin's Snuff Box to* Citizens United.

James Risen (Print Journalism): Pulitzer Prize–winning *New York Times* correspondent in the Washington bureau who lived for seven years under the threat of imprisonment for vigorously defending journalists' First Amendment right to protect their confidential sources.

Malkia Cyril (Government): Executive director, Center for Media Justice, and cofounder of the Media Action Grassroots Network (MAG-Net) served as the driving force behind a coalition of 175 grassroots community groups that framed net neutrality as a civil rights and free speech principle of the internet.

Steven Listopad (Education): Assistant professor of journalism and media and student media director, Valley City State University in North Dakota, who served as a shining example to teachers everywhere when he helped his students craft the nation's strongest and most comprehensive statutes protecting North Dakota student journalists.

Victor Navasky (Lifetime Achievement): For his unwavering defense of the First Amendment and distinguished career as a journalist, editor, publisher, and author, who, as an independent, truth-telling bellwether in American journalism, asks tough questions, takes principled stances, and offers contextualized commentary that transcends the ephemeral moment.

2015 JUDGES

Ronald Brownstein, editorial director for strategic partnerships, Atlantic Media, and weekly columnist, *National Journal*.

Mike Hiestand, former staff attorney, Student Press Law Center, and 2014 Hugh M. Hefner First Amendment Award winner.

Pamela Samuelson, faculty director, Berkeley Center for Law and Technology, and Richard M. Sherman Distinguished Professor of Law.

2014 WINNERS

Thomas Healy (Book Publishing): For his book *The Great Dissent: How Oliver Wendell Holmes Changed His Mind—and Changed the History of Free Speech in America*, which constructs in vivid detail Holmes's journey from free speech opponent to First Amendment hero.

Glenn Greenwald (Journalism): Who as author, constitutional lawyer, and investigative journalist for *The Intercept* courageously published the first of a series of reports detailing American and British surveillance programs, based on classified documents disclosed by Edward Snowden.

Chris Finan (Law): Who as president of the American Booksellers Foundation for Free Expression presented key issues on the impact of the attacks of 9/11 on First Amendment rights to middle- and high-school students in his book *National Security and Free Speech: The Debate since 9/11*.

Muneer Awad (Government): Who as former executive director of the Oklahoma chapter of the Council on American-Islamic Relations stood up to an unprecedented, discriminatory proposal to amend the Oklahoma Constitution to target the religious practices of Muslims and undercut a central concern of the free exercise clause and establishment clause of the First Amendment.

Michael Hiestand and **Mary Beth Tinker** (Education): For organizing the Tinker Tour, a national free speech and civic education bus tour to promote the First Amendment to schools and communities throughout America.

Norman Dorsen (Lifetime Achievement): Who as Stokes Professor of Law, New York University School of Law, and counselor to the university president for more than a half-century has been at the forefront of the fight to advance fundamental freedoms and protect civil rights and civil liberties.

2014 JUDGES

Joan E. Bertin, executive director of the National Coalition against Censorship, an advocacy organization that promotes freedom of thought, inquiry, and expression, and opposes censorship in all its forms.

Margaret Carlson, journalist at *Bloomberg News*, where she writes a column. She is best known for being the first female columnist at *TIME* magazine. She was a panelist on CNN's *Capital Gang* for fifteen years and covered four presidential elections for *TIME*.

Laura W. Murphy, director of the ACLU's Washington Legislative Office, a position she held from 1993, where she has maintained strong relationships with leaders in the U.S. Congress and the Obama administration to advance the ACLU's public policy priorities including national security, civil rights, and First Amendment issues.

The Hugh M. Hefner First Amendment Awards, 1980–2020

2013 WINNERS

Marjorie Heins (Book Publishing): For her book *Priests of Our Democracy: The Supreme Court, Academic Freedom, and the Anti-Communist Purge*, a chronicle of the history, law, and personal stories behind the struggle to recognize academic freedom as "a special concern of the First Amendment."

John Perry Barlow, Daniel Ellsberg, Rainey Reitman, and Trevor Timm (Journalism): Who as cofounders of the Freedom of the Press Foundation created an organization to promote and fund aggressive public-interest journalism.

Colonel Morris Davis, (Government): Who as assistant director and senior specialist in national security, Congressional Research Service, Library of Congress, and despite great risks expressed his personal views on the Guantanamo Military Commissions, a matter of intense public interest and debate, thus inspiring others to speak out.

Jessica Ahlquist (Education): For her courageous and successful lawsuit over a prayer banner in her Rhode Island high school, a clear violation of the establishment clause of the First Amendment.

Norman Lear (Lifetime Achievement): For his unwavering defense of the fundamental values laid out in the Bill of Rights and his commitment to nurturing a new generation of young leaders fighting for the American Way.

2013 JUDGES

Dr. Charles C. Haynes, director of the Religious Freedom Education Project at the Newseum and senior scholar at the First Amendment Center.

Ramona Ripston, former executive director of the ACLU of Southern California.

Henry Weinstein, founding faculty, with joint appointments in literary journalism and law, at the University of California, Irvine, School of Law.

2012 WINNERS

Rebecca MacKinnon (Book Publishing): For her first book, *Consent of the Networked: The Worldwide Struggle for Internet Freedom*.

Pablo Alvarado (Law): For successfully using the First Amendment to challenge ordinances that prevented day laborers from soliciting work on city sidewalks in Redondo Beach, California.

Thomas Drake (Government): Who shared an award with **Jesselyn Radack**, who represented him in his case for blowing the whistle on his employer, the National Security Agency, for massive waste, contract fraud, government wrongdoing, and violations of the Fourth Amendment rights of U.S. citizens.

Zack Kopplin (Education): Who led the effort to repeal the Louisiana Science Education Act, stealth legislation to promote the teaching of creationism and intelligent design in public school science class.

Stanley Sheinbaum (Lifetime Achievement): For his unmatched vision and courage on important issues including civil rights and civil liberties, economic justice, human rights, police reform, and world peace.

2012 JUDGES

Robert Scheer, editor-in-chief of *Truthdig*.

Patricia Scott Schroeder, former Democratic representative, Colorado, and previous president and chief executive officer of the Association of American Publishers.

Hector Villagra, executive director of the ACLU of Southern California.

2008 WINNERS

Mark Klein (Government): Whistleblower who spoke out against the participation of AT&T in the warrantless electronic surveillance practices of the government.

Heather Gillman (Education): For speaking out on behalf of the rights of gay students at Ponce de Leon High School in Florida and winning an injunction forbidding high school officials from violating their students' First Amendment rights.

Greg Lukianoff (Freedom of Expression): For defending the freedom of speech, legal equality, due process, religious liberty, and sanctity of conscience of students and faculty on the nation's college campuses.

2008 JUDGES

David Rubin, professor and former dean of the S. I. Newhouse School of Public Communications at Syracuse University.

Geoffrey Stone, Edward H. Levi Distinguished Service Professor at University of Chicago Law School.

Nadine Strossen, president, ACLU, and professor of law, New York Law School.

The Hugh M. Hefner First Amendment Awards, 1980–2020

2006 WINNERS

Geoffrey R. Stone (Book Publishing): For *Perilous Times: Free Speech in Wartime from the Sedition Act of 1798 to the War on Terrorism*, which sounds a clarion call for robust protection of First Amendment freedoms, especially in times of national crisis.

Paisley Dodds (Journalism): Who, as an Associated Press reporter, vigorously supported the public's right to know by reporting on the activities at the U.S. military detention facility in Guantanamo Bay, Cuba, and then suing under the Freedom of Information Act for the release of thousands of pages of tribunal transcripts, which revealed numerous complaints about prisoner abuse.

Shelby Knox (Arts and Entertainment): Who, as a student and subject of the film, *The Education of Shelby Knox*, challenged abstinence-only sex education and alarmist misinformation in her Lubbock, Texas, high school to fight for medically accurate sexuality education and lesbian and gay rights.

Marion Lipschutz and Rose Rosenblatt (Arts and Entertainment): Who, as producers/directors of *The Education of Shelby Knox*, exposed the consequences of abridging students' right to learn through abstinence-only education that prohibits teachers from giving comprehensive, medically accurate sexuality education.

Jack Spadaro (Government): Who, as director of the National Mine Safety and Health Academy, put his life on the line when he blew the whistle on irresponsible mining practices, corporate collusion, and government coverup in the wake of an environmental mining disaster.

Patricia Princehouse (Education): Who, as the leader of Ohio Citizens for Science, seeing a profound and rising challenge to the separation of church and state in our schools, organized a successful coalition to preserve science education in Ohio's public schools.

Rhett Jackson (Lifetime Achievement): Who, with indefatigable dedication to the free exchange of ideas and the proposition that the printed word should be available to all, has committed his life to the First Amendment and social justice for more than forty years.

2006 JUDGES

Anthony D. Romero, executive director, ACLU.

Eugenie Scott, Ph.D., executive director, National Center for Science Education.

Katrina Vanden Heuvel, editor and publisher, *The Nation*.

224 The Hugh M. Hefner First Amendment Awards, 1980–2020

2002-2003 WINNERS

David Cole (Book Publishing): Who, as a constitutional law scholar and professor of law at Georgetown University Law Center, and author of *Enemy Aliens: Double Standards and Constitutional Freedoms in the War on Terrorism*, wrote a masterful and compelling book, educated the public about the discriminatory and abusive treatment of noncitizens in the wake of 9/11 and the Patriot Act.

Ronald K. L. Collins (Book Publishing): Who, as legal scholar at the First Amendment Center and coauthor of the book *The Trials of Lenny Bruce: The Fall and Rise of an American Icon*, cofounded the campaign to exonerate Lenny Bruce of the obscenity conviction that hastened his demise.

David Michael Skover (Book Publishing): Who, as a constitutional scholar and professor of law at Seattle University School of Law, and coauthor of the book *The Trials of Lenny Bruce: The Fall and Rise of an American Icon*, laid the groundwork for the posthumous pardon of Lenny Bruce for his obscenity conviction in New York City.

Talia Buford (Print Journalism): Who, as the courageous editor-in-chief of the *Hampton Script*, served as an inspiration to student journalists everywhere when she won the promise of an uncensored student newspaper at Hampton University.

Bill Maher (Arts and Entertainment): Who, as host of *Politically Incorrect*, spoke out at a time when Americans were being encouraged to abandon the Bill of Rights in exchange for the false comfort of "national security."

Nate Blakeslee (Law): Who, as a reporter for the *Texas Observer*, chronicled prosecutorial misconduct in Tulia, Texas; forced the issue of racial and economic disparity in drug sentencing into the national spotlight; and educated the public about much-needed judicial reforms.

Steven Aftergood (Government): Who, as a senior research analyst and editor of *Secrecy News*, a newsletter of the Federation of American Scientists, keeps Americans apprised of the inner workings of government secrecy and promotes reform of its secret processes.

Trina Magi (Education): Who, as president of the Vermont Library Association, organized a grassroots campaign to amend section 215 of the USA Patriot Act, which undermines Americans' right to read and access information without governmental intrusion or interference.

Linda Ramsdell (Education) Who, as owner of Galaxy Bookshop and president of the New England Booksellers Association, organized a grassroots

The Hugh M. Hefner First Amendment Awards, 1980–2020

campaign to amend section 215 of the USA Patriot Act, which threatens the free marketplace of ideas and undercuts democracy.

Molly Ivins (Lifetime Achievement): Who, as an author and syndicated columnist for nearly twenty-five years, keeps the First Amendment alive through her unflagging dedication, energy, and humor while informing the public of erosions to freedom.

2002–2003 JUDGES

Margaret Carlson, CNN's *The Capital Gang* and columnist, *TIME* magazine.

Ann Richards, former governor of Texas and senior advisor, Public Strategies, Inc.

John Seigenthaler, founder, First Amendment Center.

2000–2001 WINNERS

Michael Kent Curtis (Book Publishing): Who, as a constitutional scholar and professor of law at Wake Forest University School of Law and author of the book *Free Speech, the People's Darling Privilege: Struggles for Freedom of Expression in American History*, recounts America's hard-fought battles for freedom of expression.

Dr. William Lawbaugh (Print Journalism): Who for fourteen years has served as associate professor of communications and faculty advisor to the biweekly student newspaper *The Mountain Echo* at Mount Saint Mary's College in Emmitsburg, Maryland, and who serves as a brilliant example for faculty advisors facing attempts by college officials to muzzle student journalists.

Penn and Teller (Arts and Entertainment): Who, as comedians and magicians, have threaded their work with serious messages and have educated nontraditional and often unsuspecting audiences about the value of the First Amendment's protections.

James Wheaton (Law): Who, as senior counsel and cofounder of the Oakland-based First Amendment Project, for nearly a decade has quietly championed the rights of scores of Californians against lawsuits designed to deter citizens from exercising their First Amendment rights.

Mary Dana (Education): Who, as a teacher at Michigan's Creekside Middle School and as cofounder of "Muggles for Harry Potter," undertook a successful campaign to challenge the school superintendent's decision to ban books from the Zeeland Public Schools' curricula.

226 The Hugh M. Hefner First Amendment Awards, 1980–2020

Nancy Zennie (Education): Who, as a parent of two students attending the Zeeland Public Schools and cofounder of "Muggles for Harry Potter," rallied the public to oppose the ban on Harry Potter books in the public schools of Zeeland, Michigan.

John Seigenthaler (Lifetime Achievement): Who, as founder of the First Amendment Center at Vanderbilt University, has for more than four decades educated journalists and the public on the breadth of First Amendment ideals, ensuring the free flow of ideas that strengthen our nation.

2000–2001 JUDGES

Floyd Abrams, partner, Cahill Gordon & Reindel.

Lucy Dalglish, executive director, Reporters Committee for Freedom of the Press.

Paul K. McMasters, First Amendment ombudsman, The Freedom Forum.

Robert M. O'Neil, director, Thomas Jefferson Center for the Protection of Free Expression.

Nadine Strossen, president, ACLU.

1999 WINNERS

Bruce Sanford (Book Publishing): A partner in the law firm of Baker & Hostetler, who, through his book *Don't Shoot the Messenger: How Our Growing Hatred of the Media Threatens Free Speech for All of Us*, sounded a wakeup call about the dangers to democracy from the public's ever-increasing mistrust of those who present the news.

Michael Moore (Arts and Entertainment): Muckraker, author, and documentary filmmaker who, with humor and satire, serves as the voice of the common man while educating the public about issues critical to preserving First Amendment rights.

Jeri McGiverin (Law): Who, as past president and cofounder of Mainstream Loudoun, a nonprofit, grassroots, membership organization whose purpose is to preserve personal and religious freedoms, successfully challenged the policy of requiring internet filtering in public libraries.

Elaine Williamson (Law): Founding member and president of Mainstream Loudoun, who organized a grassroots campaign successfully challenging the policy of requiring internet filters in public libraries, ensuring that libraries adhere to the First Amendment.

Dr. Eugenie C. Scott (Education): Executive director of the National Center for Science Education, who, with very limited resources, tirelessly defends the

The Hugh M. Hefner First Amendment Awards, 1980–2020 227

separation of church and state by ensuring that religious neutrality is maintained in the science curriculum of America's public schools.

Nicholas Becker (Individual Conscience): Sunderland, Maryland, Northern High School graduate who showed great courage in speaking up against prayer at his graduation and for the rights of those who do not share the majority religious belief.

Donald Parker (Lifetime Achievement): Cofounder and co-coordinator of the Long Island Coalition Against Censorship, for his indefatigable dedication to informing the public about free speech for nearly forty years, and for his unflagging energy that keeps the First Amendment alive.

1999 JUDGES

Mark Goodman, executive director, Student Press Law Center.
Molly Ivins, author and nationally syndicated columnist, Creators Syndicate.
Barbara Kopple, Academy Award–winning filmmaker.
Clarence Page, nationally syndicated columnist, *Chicago Tribune*.

1998 WINNERS

Goodloe Sutton and Jean Sutton (Journalism): Who, as the owner, editor, and publisher of the *Democrat-Reporter*, and investigative reporter and managing editor, respectively, showed great courage and persistence in the face of enormous political and personal pressure by informing the citizens of Linden, Alabama, about corruption and malfeasance by county law-enforcement officials.

Lee Brawner (Education): Who, as executive director of the Metropolitan Library System, with energy, clarity, and devotion to the principals of intellectual freedom, educated the citizens of Oklahoma City about the dangers of censoring library materials, despite unrelenting attacks by religious conservatives.

Tisha Byars (Individual Conscience): For, while a high school student in Waterbury, Connecticut, upholding her right to refuse to recite the Pledge of Allegiance and successfully challenging the school district and, by her action, affirming the right of other students to freely express their beliefs without fear of reprisal.

1998 JUDGES

Peter S. Prichard, president, The Freedom Forum.
Nadine Strossen, president, ACLU.
Ann K. Symons, president, American Library Association.

228   The Hugh M. Hefner First Amendment Awards, 1980–2020

1997 WINNERS

Katharine Swan (Journalism): Teacher and advisor to the staff of the *West Wing*, a student publication, who in the face of daunting odds, including opposition from the school administration, understood and enshrined the value of the First Amendment and the pursuit of journalistic truth in her students.

American Civil Liberties Union (ACLU) (Law): For its successful challenge to the Communications Decency Act, the most important free speech case of the decade, which affirmed the vitality of an unfettered marketplace of ideas, thus extending free speech protection to the internet.

American Library Association (Law): As the organizer of the Citizens' Internet Empowerment Coalition, the American Library Association successfully challenged the Communications Decency Act, thus ensuring the importance of libraries in making information in all forms available and accessible to everyone.

Dr. Frederic Whitehurst (Government): Supervisory special agent and forensic chemist for the FBI, for jeopardizing his life's work and, despite retaliation for his efforts, making public his assertions of fraud and scientific misconduct within the FBI crime lab.

Cecile Richards (Education): Who, as the founding executive director and moving spirit behind the Texas Freedom Network and the Texas Faith Network, successfully organized a broad coalition of clergy and community leaders to challenge the extremism of the religious right.

Kelli Peterson (Individual Conscience): Who, in a daring act of conscience, organized the Gay Straight Student Alliance at Salt Lake City's East High School and serves as a role model for youth and adults to work against homophobia in their communities and schools.

1997 JUDGES

Anthony Griffin, attorney, 1994 Hugh M. Hefner First Amendment Award winner.

Bobbie Handman, vice president, People for the American Way.

Burton Joseph, attorney, Barsy, Joseph & Lichtenstein; chairman, The Playboy Foundation.

1995–1996 WINNERS

Seth Rosenfeld (Print Journalism): Legal and investigative reporter, *San Francisco Examiner*, who waged an extraordinary and successful fourteen-year

The Hugh M. Hefner First Amendment Awards, 1980–2020   229

struggle to expose government encroachments on freedom of speech, the right to dissent, and academic autonomy at the University of California, Berkeley.

Mary Morello (Arts and Entertainment): Retired school teacher and founder of Parents for Rock and Rap who tirelessly defends the artistic freedom of musicians.

Tom Hull (Law): Cofounder of the "No Censorship—No On 19" campaign for educating and mobilizing a broad coalition of voters to defeat censorship efforts in Oregon.

Jeffrey DeBonis (Government): Founder, Association of Forest Service Employees for Environmental Ethics, for galvanizing federal employees to speak up about their environmental concerns and become a voice for collective reform.

Jocelyn Chadwick-Joshua (Education): Author and associate director of the Teachers Academy at Dallas Institute for Humanities and Culture, for eloquently and courageously defending the right of teachers and students to study the works of Mark Twain in the classroom.

Morton Mintz (Lifetime Achievement): Author and freelance journalist, for his high-minded and principled dedication to freedom of the press and the freedom of all Americans from corporate and government negligence and malfeasance.

1995–1996 JUDGES

Chris Finan, executive director, The Media Coalition.

Marjorie Heins, director and staff counsel, The American Civil Liberties Union Arts Censorship Project.

Sydney Schanberg, journalist, 1991 Hugh M. Hefner First Amendment Award winner.

1993–1994 WINNERS

Jeff Cohen and **Norman Solomon** (Book Publishing): Media critics, syndicated columnists, and coauthors of *Adventures in Medialand: Behind the News, Beyond the Pundits*, a collection of commentaries in which they boldly and irreverently critique the news media.

Robert Landauer (Print Journalism): Who, as editorial page editor of the *Oregonian*, when faced with an anti-homosexual constitutional amendment, challenged homophobic fears and myths and predicted the consequences of a bigoted policy, thus ensuring continued civil liberties and civil rights for all citizens of Oregon.

230   The Hugh M. Hefner First Amendment Awards, 1980–2020

Anthony Griffin (Law): Attorney and volunteer counsel for the Texas Civil Liberties Union, for his dedication to the principle that the First Amendment protects even those whose ideas are offensive, by defending the rights of the Ku Klux Klan to be free of government intrusion.

Jim Warren (Government): Computer columnist, who, as the first person to use online advocacy and network-assisted citizen action, organized a grassroots campaign to bring access to state government records to citizens throughout California.

Carole Marlowe (Education): Drama teacher, Flowing Wells High School in Tucson, Arizona, who, when her students were denied the right to perform *The Shadow Box,* staged a dramatic reading of the play that provided a far greater opportunity for community discussion of censorship, the First Amendment, and artistic freedom.

Jean Otto (Lifetime Achievement): Guiding force behind the First Amendment Congress and the Education for Freedom curriculum, which educates children in the rights and responsibilities of citizenship, and who has devoted her life to informing the public of its First Amendment freedoms.

1993–1994 JUDGES

Rex Armstrong, attorney and volunteer counsel, ACLU of Oregon, 1988 Hugh M. Hefner First Amendment Award winner.

Carl Jensen, founder, Project Censored, 1992 Hugh M. Hefner First Amendment Award winner.

Jessica Mitford, author and social activist.

1992 WINNERS

Natalie Robins (Book Publishing): Distinguished poet and author of *Alien Ink: The FBI's War on Freedom of Expression*, who, by conducting diligent and exhaustive research, exposed the government's continuing campaign to undermine freedom of expression for American writers and journalists.

Dannie Martin (Journalism): Freelance journalist and essayist who for six years wrote for the *San Francisco Chronicle*, risking his personal freedom to inform the public about life in prison, despite attempts by the Federal Bureau of Prisons to silence him.

Peter Sussman (Journalism): Editor of "Sunday Punch" in the *San Francisco Chronicle*, who waged a four-year battle against the Federal Bureau of Prisons'

The Hugh M. Hefner First Amendment Awards, 1980–2020

attempts to restrict the First Amendment rights of inmate Dannie Martin and the news media.

Bruce Rogow (Law): Professor of law, Nova University Law Center in Florida, and cooperating attorney for the ACLU, who eloquently and successfully challenged the application of obscenity law to a musical composition.

Carl Jensen (Education): Professor of communications studies, Sonoma State University, and founding director of Project Censored, who, through his commitment to the public's right to know, challenges the news media by annually publicizing media censorship, thus stimulating coverage the public needs to make informed decisions about important issues.

Jules Feiffer (Individual Conscience): Cartoonist and social satirist who for nearly forty years has promoted First Amendment values in his weekly strips and his life, giving selflessly of his time and talent to defend the principles of free expression and the First Amendment.

1992 JUDGES

Dennis Barrie, executive director, Contemporary Arts Center of Cincinnati, 1990 Hugh M Hefner First Amendment Award winner.

Norman Dorsen, Stokes Professor of Law, New York University Law School.

Mark Goodman, executive director, Student Press Law Center.

Barbara Kopple, two-time Academy Award–winning documentary filmmaker.

Reginald Stuart, assistant news editor, Knight-Ridder Newspapers.

1991 WINNERS

Allan Adler (Book Publishing): Attorney who for almost ten years served as editor of the annual editions of *Litigation under the Federal Freedom of Information Act and Privacy Act* and as author of *Using the Freedom of Information Act: A Step-by-Step Guide*, played a key role in defending the public's right to obtain and disseminate information.

Debbie Nathan (Journalism): Freelance journalist who through her articles exposed the witch-hunt mentality behind day-care sexual-abuse cases and used the First Amendment to defend those accused of sexual abuse against a lynch mob of social hysteria.

Bella Lewitzky (Arts and Entertainment): Founder and director of the Lewitzky Dance Company, who, despite the risk posed to her dance company and future sources of support, on principle successfully challenged the National Endowment for the Arts anti-obscenity pledge, thus providing a shining and courageous example of dedication to the letter and spirit of the First Amendment.

Traci Bauer (Law): Editor-in-chief of the student paper *The Southwest Standard*, who successfully challenged the refusal by school officials to permit access to campus crime reports, thus enhancing the First Amendment rights of student journalists and the rights of students to make informed decisions about their safety.

Sydney Schanberg (Government): Columnist and associate editor of *New York Newsday*, who, through his boldly written critiques, challenged his readers to examine the Pentagon's control and manipulation of the press during the Gulf War. Serving as an individual plaintiff, he joined others in filing suit to end such censorship.

James Dana (Education): Bookstore owner and president of the Great Lakes Booksellers Association, who, in the face of organized pressure from right-wing zealots, effectively mobilized a broad coalition to oppose Michigan censorship legislation.

Inez Austin (Individual Conscience): Senior engineer at the Westinghouse Hanford Tank Farms, who jeopardized her career when, through an act of conscience, she refused to consent to the hazardous disposal of nuclear and chemical wastes, thus serving as an example and hero to others who blow the whistle on issues of public health and safety.

1991 JUDGES

Arthur Kropp, president, People for the American Way.

Barry Lynn, co-host *Battleline*, news radio talk show, 1986 Hugh M. Hefner First Amendment Award winner.

Eve Pell, investigative journalist, Freedom of Information Project, 1989 Hugh M. Hefner First Amendment Award winner.

Tom Wicker, political columnist, the *New York Times*.

1990 WINNERS

Paul Conrad (Journalism): Editorial cartoonist at the *Los Angeles Times*, who for forty years has used the power of his pen to inform and educate his readers and defend the rights of the powerless.

The Hugh M. Hefner First Amendment Awards, 1980–2020   233

Danny Goldberg (Arts and Entertainment): Record producer and chairman of the ACLU Foundation of Southern California, who, as cofounder of the Musical Majority, has effectively and energetically used his position to galvanize the recording industry and consumers to oppose the muzzling of recording artists and the labeling of records.

Hans A. Linde (Law): Retired justice of the Oregon Supreme Court, who, through his efforts as a teacher, lecturer, and judge, has made outstanding contributions to the development of state constitutional law that secures greater First Amendment protection for the citizens of Oregon than those established by federal courts.

Marilyn Athmann (Education): Teacher and yearbook advisor at Ben Davis High School in Indianapolis, Indiana, who saw a dangerous precedent in allowing the principal to control student publications. Despite being fired from the position as yearbook advisor, she valiantly maintained the First Amendment rights of student journalists.

Dennis Barrie (Individual Conscience): Director of the Contemporary Arts Center of Cincinnati, who, despite organized pressure from right-wing forces and despite having been indicted on criminal charges, upheld the right of the museum to exhibit works it finds worthy.

Studs Terkel (Lifetime Achievement): Whose enduring commitment to First Amendment freedoms has been exhibited consistently throughout his career as oral historian, author, broadcaster, and lecturer.

1990 JUDGES

Herbert N. Foerstel, head of branch libraries, University of Maryland, 1988 Hugh M. Hefner First Amendment Award winner.

Robert Scheer, national correspondent, *Los Angeles Times.*

Maxine Waters, U.S. representative, California.

1989 WINNERS

Eve Pell (Journalism): Investigative journalist, for her commitment to freedom of speech and open government and devotion to exposing threats to the First Amendment through her reporting.

James A. Haught (Journalism): Chief associate editor of the *Charleston Gazette*, who, as a sometimes lonely voice in Appalachia, has waged a consistent battle to educate his readers on the First Amendment principle of separation of church and state.

234 The Hugh M. Hefner First Amendment Awards, 1980–2020

Joann Bell (Law): Who, despite great personal loss, had the courage and steadfast belief in the principle of the separation of church and state to challenge an Oklahoma schoolboard's vote to hold religious meetings on public school property.

Thomas Michael Devine (Government): Who, on behalf of both government and corporate whistleblowers, played a central role in the passage of the Whistleblower Protection Act, which guarantees the free speech rights of federal employees.

Louis E. Ingelhart (Education): Professor emeritus at Ball State University who, as a fountain of information on student press freedoms, has spent a lifetime dedicated to championing the First Amendment rights of student journalists.

John Henry Faulk (Individual Conscience): Humorist, author, and lecturer who successfully ended blacklisting in the television industry and who, for more than four decades, has defended the Bill of Rights with indefatigable humor and dedication of principle.

Anthony Lewis (Lifetime Achievement): Columnist for the *New York Times* who through his column, "Abroad at Home," serves as America's conscience by informing and educating the public on constitutional issues and on the basic values embodied in the First Amendment.

1989 JUDGES

Judith Krug, director, The American Library Association Office for Intellectual Freedom.

Jack C. Landau, attorney at law; nationally syndicated columnist, The Newhouse Newspapers, 1985 Hugh M. Hefner First Amendment Award winner.

Clarence Page, Pulitzer Prize–Winning columnist, *Chicago Tribune.*

Harriet Pilpel, attorney at law, Weil, Gotshal & Manges; general counsel, Planned Parenthood Federation of America

1988 WINNERS

Jamie Kalven (Book Publishing): Journalist and editor, for his singular and outstanding achievement in completing and editing his father's book, *A Worthy Tradition: Freedom of Speech in America*, a critically acclaimed examination of the dialogue between society and the courts.

David Arnett (Journalism): Editor and publisher of the *Independent Student News*, who, despite the uncertainty of looking to the courts for First Amend-

The Hugh M. Hefner First Amendment Awards, 1980–2020   235

ment protection for students, fought for an independent student press for Tulsa's junior colleges.

Rex Armstrong (Law): Attorney and volunteer counsel for the ACLU of Oregon who, in the face of adverse precedents from the U.S. Supreme Court, presented creative and articulate arguments that provide greater protection for freedom of expression under the Oregon state constitution.

Eric Robert Glitzenstein (Government): Attorney for the Public Citizen Litigation Group, for breathing life into the Freedom of Information Act by winning two landmark cases that paved the way for public access to presidential records and mandated that the act provide broad disclosure of government records.

Herbert Foerstel (Education): Head of branch libraries at the University of Maryland, for his vigorous efforts to maintain the basic right of privacy and access to public information by bringing attention to the chilling effect of the Federal Bureau of Investigation's vigilante Library Awareness Program.

Roy Woodruff (Individual Conscience): Director of the Nuclear Weapons Program at the Livermore National Laboratory, who jeopardized his life's work in a daring act of individual conscience that made public his assessment of the Strategic Defense Initiative.

1988 JUDGES

Charlayne Hunter-Gault, New York correspondent, *The MacNeil/Lehrer NewsHour*.

Anthony Lewis, syndicated columnist, *New York Times*.

Steven Pico, First Amendment lecturer and advocate, 1982 Hugh M. Hefner First Amendment Award winner.

Tom Wicker, political columnist, *New York Times*.

1986–1987 WINNERS

Walter Karp (Book Publishing): Author and contributing editor of *Harper's* magazine, for his boldly written critiques and lectures on the government's systematic attempts to suppress information.

Charles Levendosky (Journalism): Editorial-page editor and columnist of the *Casper Star-Tribune*, for maintaining public interest in First Amendment issues at the grassroots level.

William A. Bradford Jr., Ricki Seidman, and Mary Weidler (Law): For providing *pro bono* legal representation, advice, and counsel to parents and

236   The Hugh M. Hefner First Amendment Awards, 1980–2020

teachers who intervened to defend the Alabama State Board of Education against religiously motivated censorship.

Barry Lynn (Government): Ordained minister and legislative counsel to the ACLU, for leading the effort to inform the public about the flaws in the attorney general's Commission on Pornography.

Glenna Nowell (Education): Director, Gardiner Public Library, and past president, Maine Library Association, for her articulate and successful effort to mobilize early opposition to the Maine censorship referendum.

1986–1987 JUDGES

Julius Chambers, president, NAACP Legal Defense and Educational Fund.
Maxwell Lillienstein, general counsel, American Booksellers Association.
Anthony Podesta, founding president, People for the American Way.

1985 WINNERS

Ronnie Dugger (Journalism): For his resoluteness in challenging vested interests as owner and publisher of the *Texas Observer*, the biweekly advocate of the neglected and voiceless.

Clifford McKenzie (Government): Whistleblower who sought redress of grievances after a retaliatory dismissal from the Bureau of Indian Affairs for exposing the misuse of government travel funds and property.

Jack C. Landau (Education): For championing the First Amendment and the free flow of information through the Reporters Committee for Freedom of the Press, and for publishing *The News Media and the Law*.

1985 JUDGES

Burton Joseph, attorney at law, Barsy, Joseph & Lichtenstein; chairman, Media Coalition.

Harriet Pilpel, attorney at law, Weil, Gotshal and Manges; general counsel, Planned Parenthood Federation of America.

Melody Sands, former owner, *Athens News*.

1984 WINNERS

Helen Troy and **Forrest Troy** (Outstanding Community Leadership): For continuing the muckraking tradition of the free press through their biweekly newspaper, the *Oklahoma Observer*, and for their selfless commitment to the rights of the disenfranchised.

The Hugh M. Hefner First Amendment Awards, 1980–2020   237

Angus Mackenzie (Outstanding National Leadership): For exposing illegal espionage and harassment of the dissident press by U.S. governmental agencies.

Frank Wilkinson (Lifetime Achievement): For his continuing commitment to civil liberties as founder of the National Committee to Abolish the House Un-American Activities Committee.

1984 JUDGES

Martin Agronsky, award-winning journalist and television talk-show host, *Agronsky and Company.*

Alan Dershowitz, professor, Harvard Law School.

Liza Pike, program director, Center for Investigative Reporting.

1983 WINNERS

Tom Gish and **Pat Gish** (Outstanding Community Leadership): For their courage and determination in reestablishing freedom of the press in the face of open hostility, through their daily newspaper, the *Mountain Eagle.*

Mark Lynch (Outstanding National Leadership): For refusing to bow to the federal government's efforts, under the guise of national security, to limit First Amendment rights.

Osmond K. Fraenkel (Lifetime Achievement): For pioneering and lifelong dedication to civil liberties as a lawyer, author, teacher, and inspirational leader in the fight for constitutional rights.

1983 JUDGES

Harriet Pilpel, attorney at law, Weil, Gotshal and Manges; general counsel, Planned Parenthood Federation of America.

Studs Terkel, author and nationally syndicated radio show host.

William Worthy, international journalist and civil liberties activist.

1982 WINNERS

Franklyn S. Haiman (Book Publishing): For his book *Speech and Law in a Free Society*, a distinguished, intellectual achievement that advances thought on complex First Amendment issues.

Melody Sands (Journalism): For her exemplary efforts, as the owner of the small and independent newspaper the *Athens News* to give meaning to the public's right to know.

238   The Hugh M. Hefner First Amendment Awards, 1980–2020

Robert Berger, Herbert Brodkin, Ernest Kinoy, and Herbert Wise (Arts and Entertainment): For producing a powerful dramatization of free speech struggles in the television movie *Skokie*.

Steven Pico (Law): For his willingness to serve as the lead plaintiff in the critically important case *Board of Education v. Pico* and to speak out against book censorship.

Billie Pirner Garde (Government): For her courageous persistence in exposing the betrayal of the public trust by a federal executive, despite sexual harassment and other jeopardy to herself.

Gene D. Lanier (Education): For his contributions at the grassroots level to defeat censorship legislation and to support hundreds of librarians threatened by would-be censors.

Frank Snepp (Individual Conscience): For his great personal sacrifice in the cause of the public's right to know, through his book *Decent Interval* and his articulate defense of First Amendment freedoms.

Frank J. Donner (Lifetime Achievement): For a lifetime of dedication to the First Amendment as lawyer, scholar, author, and unremitting foe of government political surveillance.

1982 JUDGES

Yvonne Brathwaite Burke, partner, Kutak, Rock & Huie.

Hamilton Fish III, publisher, *The Nation*.

Florence McMullin, chair, The Washington Library Association Intellectual Freedom Committee.

Aryeh Neier, professor of law, New York University; vice chairman, The U.S. Helsinki Watch Committee; vice chairman, The Fund for Free Expression.

1981 WINNERS

Frank Rowe (Book Publishing): For *The Enemy Among Us: A Story of Witch-Hunting in the McCarthy Era*, which describes the devastating personal effect on his life brought about by his refusal to sign a loyalty oath in 1950.

Todd Crowder, Charles Reineke, and **William Hoffmann Jr.** (Journalism): For their willingness to challenge high school officials and to resist peer pressure in order to defend the freedom of the student press.

Edward Asner, Allan Burns, Seth Freeman, and **Gene Reynolds** (Arts and Entertainment): For their creative contributions to the television program the *Lou Grant Show*.

The Hugh M. Hefner First Amendment Awards, 1980–2020 239

William Schanen III (Law): As the persevering client in the Wisconsin civil suit that established that a commercial printer cannot be held liable for the contents of a publication he has printed unless he knows it to be libelous or defamatory.

Morton Halperin (Government): Director of the Center for National Security Studies, for his work defending public access to government information and protecting the privacy rights of citizens.

Kathy Russell (Education): Director of the Washington County Public Library, for her courage in preserving the independence of the library's collection and her resistance to attempts to censor books and reveal the identities of readers of certain books.

Stanley Fleishman (Lifetime Achievement): For expanding First Amendment rights and for appearing as counsel in some of the most important First Amendment cases of the last twenty-five years.

1981 JUDGES

Edward Brooke, U.S. senator, Massachusetts.

Nat Hentoff, author and columnist, *Village Voice,* and 1980 Hugh M. Hefner First Amendment Award winner.

Fay Kanin, president, The Academy of Motion Picture Arts and Sciences.

Judith Krug, director, American Library Association Office for Intellectual Freedom.

Charles Nesson, associate dean, Harvard Law School.

1980 WINNERS

Nat Hentoff (Book Publishing) for *The First Freedom: The Tumultuous History of Free Speech.*

Erwin Knoll and **Howard Morland** (Journalism): For their fight to publish "The H-Bomb Secret: How We Got It, Why We're Telling It," in *The Progressive* magazine.

Saul Landau and **Jack Willis** (Journalism): For their production of *Paul Jacobs and the Nuclear Gang,* aired on the Public Broadcasting Service.

David Goldberger (Law): For his defense of the right of a neo-Nazi group to march in Skokie, Illinois.

Louis Clark (Government): Director of the Government Accountability Project, for his support of government employees who dissent or blow the whistle on government corruption.

Carey McWilliams (Lifetime Achievement): For his longtime dedication, in the pages of *The Nation* and elsewhere, to defending the rights of migrant farm workers, Japanese Americans, victims of McCarthyism, and other persecuted people.

1980 JUDGES

Tom Bradley, mayor of Los Angeles.

Jules Feiffer, playwright and social cartoonist.

Fay Kanin, president, The Academy of Motion Picture Arts and Sciences.

Victor Navasky, editor, *The Nation*.

Tom Wicker, columnist and associate editor, *New York Times*.

Acknowledgments

I AM GRATEFUL TO SO many people who have influenced my own First Amendment journey, instilling in me a continued passion for free speech and free press values.

This book would not be possible without the cooperation and inspiration of the Hugh M. Hefner Foundation; its chairman, Christie Hefner; and its executive director, Amanda Warren. And, of course, Hef himself, who I never met. I gained deep admiration for his lifelong commitment to free speech and free press values that are embodied in his namesake foundation and in the continuing Hugh M. Hefner First Amendment Awards, which were created to honor this legacy.

The eight giants who are in conversation with me here have my great respect and gratitude for sharing their thoughts about freedom of speech and freedom of the press within the context of their own remarkable First Amendment journeys. Put simply, Geoffrey Stone, Floyd Abrams, Nadine Strossen, Burt Neuborne, David Cole, Lucy Dalglish, Bob Corn-Revere, and Rick Jewell are national treasures.

I also am deeply appreciative for the sensational team at the University of Missouri Press. I enjoyed working with Andrew Davidson, Robin Rennison, Deanna Davis, Drew Griffith, Megan Casey, as well as freelance copyeditor Margaret Hogan—all top-notch professionals.

During my formative educational years—from high school through law school—I had the benefit of an extraordinary group of teachers, professors, and academic advisors: Arza Dean, Elaine Levine, Frederick Crouter, Alexander Bell, William Clifford, Frances Lazarus, Judith Paul, Austin B. Johnson III, Franklyn S. Haiman, John L. McKnight, Irving J. Rein, Lawrence W. Lichty, Don L. LeDuc, Charles Sherman, Joanne Cantor, Ordean Ness, Edwin Black, Stephen Barnett, Paul Mishkin, Jesse Choper, and Herma Hill Kay.

Numerous lawyers have been important to me as well. These include my cherished mentors Henry Geller, Newton N. Minow, Morton I. Hamburg, Geoffrey Cowan, Monroe E. Price, Paul Weiler, Richard E. Wiley, and Bertram Fields.

Daniel L. Brenner, Harry Plotkin, George Shapiro, Mark Goldberg, Howard Nemerovski, David Cantor, Bruce Sunstein, Rikki Klieman, Christopher Fager, Stuart Shorenstein, Tedson Meyers, Charlie Firestone, Michael Fricklas, Ronald Cass, Robert D. Joffe, Maxwell M. Blecher, Bonnie Eskenazi, Bruce Goodman, Christopher Wolf, Howard Liberman, Ann Bobeck, Patrick Campbell, Phillip Spector, Kevin Smith, Gene Korf, Sally Stevens, Fabio Bertoni, Robert Sachs, Carole E. Handler, Robert McDowell, Jules Polonetsky, Randy Tritell, Blair Levin, Howard Homonoff, Michael Whalan, Jerry Papazian, Michael Sanders, Shaun Clark, Jerry Fritz, Ike Williams, Charles B. Ortner, Larry Irving, Erwin G. Krasnow, Cameron Kerry, Patricia Diaz Dennis, David Apatoff, and Ken Basin have offered invaluable sage advice and counsel along the way too.

Judges David L. Bazelon and Douglas H. Ginsburg of the U.S. Court of Appeals for the District of Columbia Circuit have been generous in sharing their insightful legal perspectives. Their wisdom has been beneficial in shaping contemporary jurisprudential thought.

Within academia, I have been blessed with wonderful colleagues: Fred Cate, Marty Linsky, Robert Frieden, Peter Blanck, Harvey Jassem, Barry Umansky, Ron Kovac, Anne Klinefelter, Everette E. Dennis, Ellen Hume, Miriam Berg, John Dale, Norman Marcus, Jay Gillette, David Klatell, Wenhong Chen, Maria Lombard, Patrick Burkart, Bob Pepper, Craig LaMay, Margaret Hu, Dom Caristi, Patricia Phalen, Martha Minow, David Kennedy, Ron Rizzuto, C. Raj Kumar, Arpan Banerjee, John Palfrey, Elena Kagan, Denis Simon, Monica Black, Sandy Ungar, Terry Fisher, Nana Sarian, Mark Wu, Jeannie Suk Gersen, Peter Gross, Michael O. Wirth, Catherine Luther, Joe Mazer, Douglas Blaze, Joan MacLeod Heminway, Marianne Wanamaker, and Donde Plowman.

Professional colleagues representing various disciplines have enriched me in many ways too. They include Fred Friendly, Bill Arthur, Ned Schnurman, Jane Harman, Fred Friendly, Bob Katz, Meg King, Bob Stearns, Walter S. Baer, Ruth Vitale, Bruce DuMont, George de Lama, Susan Kohler Reed, Joyce Tudryn, Larry Patrick, Coleman Bazelon, Roslyn

Layton, Bill Zarakas, Deb Gordon, Marc Ransford, Ryan McKenna, John Milewski, Joyce Kulhawik, Joan Hamburg, Suzie Katz, Richard Kaplar, Margery Kraus, Alan Blaustein, Barry Glassner, Jack Moline, Robin Blatt, Dan Glickman, Brent Crane, Jonathan Adelstein, Sandra Baer, Adrian Basora, Jeff Frazier, Joan Myers, John Della Volpe, Cecile Willems, and Gabriela Oliván.

One of the great joys of teaching is having an extraordinary group of former students around the world. I am immensely proud of Matt Bruck, Mark Seidenfeld, Sandra Bresnick, Marc Kenny, Eric German, Shawn Ambwani, Jeffrey Carlisle, Olaf Groth, Brett Perlman, R. D. Sahl, Jennifer Paul, Ariel Shpiegel, J. Hillyer Jennings, Ruchi Desai, Edward Felsenthal, and Mark Mower.

Cherished friends from kindergarten onward continue to play an important role in my life. Thanks to Andy Cohen, Bob Males, Rick Schultz, Cornell Christianson, Larry Chalfin, Bruce Malashevich, Len Bierman, and Nell Minow.

And at a most personal level, my wife, Gloria Z. Greenfield, and children, Daniel, Rachel, and Gabriel, along with my late parents, William and Edith Brotman, remind me everyday about the importance of deeply held and freely expressed viewpoints. Through them, I have learned that the First Amendment's values help nurture our closest relationships as well as the larger ideals that remain central to America's highest aspirations.

About the Author

STUART N. BROTMAN IS AN American government policymaker, tenured university professor, management consultant, lawyer, author and editorial adviser, and nonprofit organization executive. He has served in four presidential administrations on a bipartisan basis and has taught students from forty-two countries in six separate disciplines—communications, journalism, business, law, international relations, and public policy.

Brotman is the inaugural Howard Distinguished Endowed Professor of Media Management and Law and Beaman Professor of Journalism and Electronic Media at the University of Tennessee, Knoxville. This interdisciplinary tenured position is the only one of its kind in the world.

Brotman is an Eisenhower Fellow. He served as an appointed fellow of the Woodrow Wilson International Center for Scholars, based in its Science and Technology Innovation Program. He also has served as an honorary adjunct professor at the Jindal Global Law School in India, and an affiliated researcher at the Media Management Transformation Centre of the Jönköping International Business School in Sweden.

He served two terms as an appointed member of the U.S. Department of State Advisory Committee on International Communications and Information Policy (ACICIP), serving in an advisory capacity concerning major economic, social, and legal issues and problems in international communications and information policy.

Brotman was the inaugural Professor of Communication in Residence at Northwestern University in Qatar, teaching and conducting research on free speech and free press in a country that has neither of these legal rights. He also is a fellow of the Salzburg Global Seminar, where he was a Visiting Scholar on Free Expression in its Academy on Media and Global Change.

Brotman served as the Fulbright-Nokia Distinguished Chair in Information and Communications Technologies in the Faculty of Social Sciences, Department of Social Research/Media and Communication Studies, at the University of Helsinki. He also served as president and CEO of the Museum of Television and Radio, the premier trust of television's and radio's heritage under his leadership (now the Paley Center for Media). He was a member of the museum's board of trustees; Los Angeles Board of Governors; Media Center Board of Governors; and International Council Advisory Board.

After graduating with a B.S. degree, *summa cum laude*, from Northwestern University, Brotman received his M.A. in communications from the University of Wisconsin–Madison and his J.D. from the University of California, Berkeley, where he served as Note and Comment Editor of the *California Law Review*. He also completed advanced professional training in negotiation and mediation at Harvard Law School.

He held a professorial-level faculty appointment in international telecommunications law and policy at Tufts University's Fletcher School of Law and Diplomacy. He also chaired both the International Communications Committee and International Legal Education Committee of the American Bar Association's International Section.

Brotman was the first Harvard Law School faculty member to teach telecommunications law and its first Visiting Professor of Entertainment and Media Law. He served as a faculty member in Harvard Law School's Institute for Global Law and Policy and in the Harvard Business School Executive Education Program. He held the first concurrent appointment in digital media at Harvard and MIT, respectively, at the Berkman Klein Center for Internet and Society and the Program on Comparative Media Studies, and created the first study group on communications policymaking at the Harvard Kennedy School Institute of Politics. He also served as an annual visiting lecturer in entertainment and media law at Stanford Law School.

Brotman served as Matthew H. Fox–Century Fund Fellow in Law and Journalism at the National News Council and as an annual lecturer at the Columbia Journalism School's Knight-Bagehot Fellowship Program. He was a nonresident senior fellow in the Government Studies Program,

Center for Technology Innovation, at the Brookings Institution; a senior fellow at the Annenberg Washington Program in Communications Policy Studies of Northwestern University; and a senior fellow at the Edward R. Murrow Center for International Communications at the Fletcher School of Law and Diplomacy, Tufts University.

He currently serves as an editorial board member of the *Federal Communications Law Journal*, the *Journal of Information Policy*, and the *Journal of Media Law and Ethics*; as a director of the Telecommunications Policy Research Institute; as an advisory board member of the Future of Privacy Forum; and on the Media Institute's First Amendment Advisory Council.

Brotman is the only two-time recipient of lifetime achievement awards from the Broadcast Education Association—in law and policy (2014) and in scholarship (2016). He has written over three hundred articles and reviews on business, technology, policy, history, negotiation, law, regulation, and international trade that have appeared in scholarly and professional publications. His articles on free speech and free press have appeared in the *American Bar Association Journal, American Journalism Review, Boston Globe, Chicago Tribune, Christian Science Monitor, Communication Law and Policy, Federal Communications Law Journal, Harvard Political Review, The Hill, Journalism History, Journal of Communication, Legal Times, Los Angeles Times, National Law Journal,* the *New York Times,* and the *Washington Post.*

He is the editor or author of over fifty books (in multiple editions), including *Communications Law and Practice,* the leading treatise covering domestic and international telecommunications and electronic mass media regulation.

Brotman is a frequent analyst for leading newspapers and magazines, including *Fortune,* the *Guardian, Los Angeles Times,* the *New York Times, TIME,* and the *Wall Street Journal.* He also has provided expert commentary for ABC's *World News This Morning,* NBC's *Today Show,* NPR's *Morning Edition, Court TV News,* and the Voice of America.